S0-AEM-733

I hope you enjoy my memories.
God's Richest Blessings!

Sarah Bertram
"Sally"

PASTOR HONEY AND ANGEL

by

Sarah Bertram

A Hearthstone Book

Carlton Press, Inc.   **New York, N.Y.**

Copyright © 1993 by Sarah Bertram
ALL RIGHTS RESERVED
Manufactured in the United States of America
ISBN 0-8062-4575-1

To all those who loved him,
recognized who he was,
and love him still.

All Scriptures are quoted from the King James Version of the Bible unless otherwise identified:

TLB or The Living Bible: Paraphrased 1971 by Tyndale House Publishers, Wheaton, Illinois 60187

ACKNOWLEDGMENTS

This is the place in a book where a huge amount of heartfelt gratitude is condensed into the fewest words possible. I owe so much more to my typist, my husband's former secretary and now my encouraging friend, Rita McGinnis, than just monetary rewards.

My daughters, Leslie Boudouris, and Sally Amos, provided the ears that endured listening to preliminary chapters, and the love that encouraged me to continue.

The spiritual encouragement subtly given by Dr. Russell Killman through his letters to me kept my mind and heart focused on the enabling power of the Holy Spirit, without Whose Power I could never have written this book.

The dear Sisters at Lourdes College in Sylvania, Ohio, who lovingly listened to chapters and aided with encouragement, will forever be treasures in my heart.

The insight into my husband's family received through talks with John Vance, family friend, proved invaluable to my understanding of them. For details of information, I am grateful to our former church secretary, Cindy Addison.

For these people and all the friends who shared their letters and stories of my husband with me, I will be forever grateful.

For the tolerance, patience, understanding, and sheer excellence of advice and work from my editors and publishers, I am most grateful.

Forgive my grief for one removed,
Thy creature, whom I found so fair.
I trust he lives in Thee, and there
I find him worthier to be loved.

Alfred, Lord Tennyson
In Memoriam

"Rejoice, and men will seek you,
Grieve, and they turn and go; . . .
Ella Wheeler Wilcox,
"The Way of the World"

Foreword

Listen, if you want to read a book with a lot of new theological ideas expounded and explained, or one that delves deeply into insights about Scripture, put this one down.

But if you're curious about how a life was completely changed by the influence of one man who lived the life of the Man he was influenced by, then read this true love story. My hope is that you will laugh, be thrilled, and perhaps be inspired by it.

My husband was the Pastor, the "spiritual" one, the teacher, the TV and radio personality, the dynamic leader, the personable, yes, the physically attractive force in my life. He not only taught Christ, he lived Him.

I'm the "baby" Christian. I just want to tell you our love story. I just want to share some of the dramatic, humorous, uplifting, sad, inspiring, and I hope, helpful events in our lives that make me know God is, was, and always will be, personally interested in me.

Through one man's life another Man touched me!

You'll see how a minister's wife could be a baby Christian. You'll find out whether a childlike faith, without a backlog of theological insight, can accomplish the overcoming of the ultimate tragedy, the loss of a loved one.

If you are wondering how a minister coped with cancer and imminent death, or whether he continued in faith in the goodness of God during a time of crisis, this story will give you answers.

If you want some hints on how to have a good marriage, you'll find them in this book.

If your interest lies primarily in being entertained by a true love story—read on!

1
I Must Write a Book

"Set not your goal too near at hand,
Lest it be early won,
And you, content with some small aim,
Leave greater tasks undone."
> Frances Crosby Hamlet
> "Far Goals"

I make a feeble start.

Everything seems to try to prevent me—I must empty the dishwasher, telephone calls come, I must get to the bank to deposit my widow's pension.

My goal? To write a book.

Why must I write a book? I have to. That's all there is to it. Too many things have happened for me *not* to know that this is a destined event in my very eventful life. Too many people have said, "Oh, your life has been fascinating—you should write a book," or, "I could listen to you speak for another hour, you give me such encouragement," or, "What a surprise! You are such a beautiful, dignified lady—yet you are so funny to listen to," or, the most flattering compliment I ever received from a stranger just met, a college president and a gracious southerner, who said, "I've been watching you. You are so vibrant, I feel I would get a spark if I touched you." (And that to a widow of only eight months!)

The idea to write a book came about a month before my husband's death. He was sitting in his favorite chair resting from the effects of his latest chemotherapy injection. He said, "Ach, darling," in a way that I knew meant, "Oh, the pity of it all." When I asked, "What does that 'Ach darling' mean?" he answered, "I have so much I want to do yet for the Lord. How can this be happening?" I knew at that moment he had allowed the idea of

9

death to creep into his consciousness, and I felt a great desire come over me to cheer him up.

What came out of my mouth was something that had *never* occurred to me before. I said, "Oh, my darling, don't sound so sad. Your work isn't finished. Even if something should happen, I'll write a book about you, and your words will go on helping people just as they always have." I said it facetiously, with no real intention except to cheer him up, change his thoughts.

From that moment on, it was as though "fate had conspired," as Omar Khayyam wrote. A friend, Dean Picton, brought us one of the five books that were to eventually inspire me to the huge task of putting into words the story of the life of a fascinating human being. The book was *A Severe Mercy* by Sheldon Van Aucken. My husband, Ozzie, and I started to read it together. It was a beautiful story, and we identified with that, as we thought our own love story was special and beautiful. We had only read half-way through the book together when my husband died. The fact that we did not finish the book together seemed meant to be that way. It was in the last half of the book that the author's wife died. He struggled to find meaning in her death, and eventually found it with the aid of some correspondence with C. S. Lewis. Through the musings of Mr. Van Aucken's mind, I derived the beginnings of some answers to my own "whys."

A month after my husband's death, a book came in the mail from Bill and Jeanne Babcock in California. We had met Jeanne and Bill in Washington D.C. at the National Religious Broadcasters' Convention (N.R.B.) five years before, and we saw them only once a year at the conference, but had become good friends. *Funny*, I thought, *this is the only book by Catherine Marshall I haven't read*. It was, *To Live Again*. Those of you familiar with it know it to be the story of Catherine Marshall coping with widowhood after her famous husband, Dr. Peter Marshall, died.

The thought crossed my mind—why is this the only book by Catherine Marshall I have not made an effort to obtain and read? I had long admired her, and felt privileged to actually hear her speak one year at the National Religious Broadcasters' Convention.

When I read the book (every night in bed before attempting to sleep after my husband's death), I knew why I had not read it. I had had no need to read it. It seems as though God had intended this particular book for me to read at this time in my life. Oh, how I identified with the author. I felt wounded, too!

I had to clear out my beloved's large office and desk at our church, too!

I needed to know what kind of a plan of God's would include the demise of such an effective, godly man. I needed to know what God's will for me was!

I mentioned before that five books of all the many, that I have read, really helped me. You must know that I have always been a "bookworm," and continue to be one. I can still hear my mother saying to me at age eight, "Why don't you go out and play? You mustn't have your nose in a book all the time." Reading has always been one of my chief delights and sources of understanding. The third book of the five that helped me most during the most devastating year of my life, was loaned to me by a friend, Sheila Dressler. It was Eugenia Price's, *Make Love Your Aim*. It helped to clarify in my mind what real love is.

The Helper, also by Catherine Marshall, gave me the knowledge of where my ability and strength to write this book were going to come from.

If you're already a Christian, you'll have guessed what the fifth book is. If not, and you are reading this book to find out whether a minister is really as good as he seems, or how it happened that "The" Reverend Bertram chose me for a wife after his first beloved wife was killed in a tragic car accident; or out of curiosity about a TV personality's personal life, or for whatever other reason, know now that the fifth and most important inspiration for my writing came from God's Word, the book called the Bible.

If you are not a Christian and you are reading these words for the first time, "He (God) will wipe away all tears from their eyes, and there shall be no more death, nor sorrow, nor crying, nor pain," (Rev. 21:4) don't you almost wish you were a Christian? Then you could believe that a Diety exists so powerful that He really could change *your* life or personal sorrow?

Whether you are a Christian or not, is your choice. I only know what I know, that I thought I had a dream love come true, and a life filled with adventure, the proverbial storybook romance; and that period of my life was terminated by one of the most insidious of all human ailments, cancer.

Whether I coped with sorrow or not remains to be seen. You

11

can judge for yourself as you read this book, the story that asks the question (in a parody on the words of the old radio days soap opera, "Our Gal Sunday"), "Can this blonde, former model and schoolteacher from a little town in the midwest find happiness as the wife and then the widow of the well-known and fascinating TV clergyman, the Reverend O. H. Bertram?

Tune in your heart and find out!

2
How I Start

"For stormy limits cannot hold love out and what
love can do, that, dares love attempt."
Shakespeare
Romeo and Juliet

The seeming conspiracy to compel me to write continued. Every once in a while in these months of widowhood, episodes of our life together would flash into my mind, and I would think, *That would be fun to include in a book*. I would stop and scold myself and say, "Stop that dreaming—you know you are all talk and no 'do' " (as my father used to say).

As I cleared out my husband's office, I found a journal for every year of his pastorate. *What a rich source of material for a future book!* And then, *Oh, quiet, you know you'll never get to it*.

Boxes of tapes of his lectures, old letters, video tapes of his interviews with senators and other notables on their Christian convictions, began to emerge and arrive at our home; plus, I had all the original "Clergyman's Corner" articles written for nine newspapers. Letters from many states poured in by the hundreds from those whose lives the Reverend O. H. Bertram had touched and inspired, or those who just simply missed his "Worship for Shut-Ins" half-hour program every Sunday morning and considered him to be "their pastor."

A darling friend said out of the blue one day, "Oh, Sarah, you've got to write a book about you and Pastor; if only to show the world you two were the 'beautiful people,' not of St. Tropez, but of Christendom! Everyone thinks Christians are 'little brown bird' types, or should be, and have good but dull lives. You've got to

12

disprove this." Oh, the bias of prejudiced and beloved friend! But this remark, too, seemed to be another prod toward what was to become my goal.

Finally, two more incidents occurred—so powerfully clear in purpose that I said, "Enough, Lord; I get the idea. You really do want me as your 'mouthpiece' to get across something that You will help me say to others." One was the attendance at a seminar called Challenges and Opportunities in Christian Literature Today, given at the National Religious Broadcasters' Convention in Washington D.C., the end of January, 1980. I attended this convention at the request of the Executive Director of the N.R.B., Dr. Ben Armstrong, and Dr. Eugene Bertermann, N.R.B. Secretary and former N.R.B. President, who invited me to come to Washington to accept a posthumous citation for my husband's thirty-seven years of work in broadcasting.

At this workshop I heard three most attractive and knowledgeable men speak on the subject of writing. Two were editors, and one was a published author. Their names were Leonard LeSourd, John Sherrill, and Richard Schneider. They had a question time at the end of their comments. I had dozens of things I wanted to ask. I decided just to listen to the others and profit from the answers to their questions.

One of these men said they had met in prayer before the group gathered and had prayed that someone in attendance would be the author of their next best-seller. "It's me, guys!" I wanted to shout, "Here I am, the fiftyish blonde in the white pant suit in the front row, the one with tears rolling down her cheeks." I realize everyone there must have felt it was he to whom the men were speaking, but I also felt it was the turning point for me in making a firm commitment to really do something with an idea that had started out as a "cheering up device." As if to clinch it all, the only two persons at the conference with whom I shared my aim were strangers, one a dear lady with whom I had a slight acquaintance, and the other a man who sat down at the snack bar on the only seat left, next to me. He turned out to be a public relations person with much experience and good advice. Both wrote encouraging letters, which were waiting for me when I arrived home after spending five days in Connecticut after the convention, visiting with my brother, Dr. Richard Breck, and his wife and daughter.

That did it. Two letters waiting to spur me on. Bernice Flynn wrote, "Your inner beauty plus the evident is a rare combination." Oh, dear Lord, You know me so well, You even provided an appeal to my feminine vanity. David L. Eno, the public relations advisor, wrote, "I think the Lord may be using you in a dynamic new role aimed at ministering to His people through your life experiences and abilities." He then proceeded to list my qualifications as he saw them:

1. "Your exposure in the fashion industry certainly will impress on you the need for writing for NOW audience.
2. "Your knowledge of Scripture, and experience as the wife of a prominent clergyman who ministered to many through the mass media.
3. "Your ability at public speaking.
4. "Your attractive looks and personality, which are key to promoting the book . . ."

When I told my two precious daughters, Leslie and Sally, of my goal, they said, "Mom, you've got to do it. Everyone will want to read your and Papa Oz's story. Others who are alone can be helped by what we know you can write. You can make them laugh, Mom, and hang on every word; and Papa Oz can sock it to 'em with his forceful spiritual and Scripturally-based writings."

There it was; even the format outlined for me; chapters of our life's experiences together with pertinent meditations, letters, and prayers by my husband, included.

I was committed, and I decided I would do it, with the help of God!

3
We Begin

"Do not despise this small beginning, the eyes of the
Lord rejoice to see the work begin, . . ."
Zechariah 4:10
"Fear not that thy life shall come to an end, but
rather fear that it shall never have a beginning."
Cardinal Newman

I sit here at my glass-topped patio table and start to write. What is this table that we bought together doing in a small condominium bedroom, I ask myself. I just couldn't part with it when I moved from the parsonage. *I'll put it out on the balcony when warm weather comes*, I think. Then my bedroom will look like a boudoir again, as Ozzie always liked it to look.

The sun is streaming in on this table (formerly the scene of many a happy patio meal) that I have made my desk, and I am suddenly filled with love for this physically beautiful world of ours. Oh, how grateful I am for this day. Again, I can't wait to begin my work. I see I have fallen into a pattern each writing day. Up, morning prayer, coffee with TV, take care of the day's phone calls, my own tiny exercise routine, and a morning scented bath where I dream, pray, and plan my written thoughts. Do other women writers have such a luxurious feminine routine as this before they work? How lucky I am! God is being so good to me—why do I still find myself thinking like a spoiled child, "But don't try to make it up to me, God; nothing You do for me will ever make up for losing Ozzie."

My bathtub reveries this morning were taking me back to our first meeting. I gazed down into the water and reflected back to me were scene after scene.

I had gone off to school that February day in 1972 in what I thought was my most unattractive "schoolteacher type" dress. It was brown, and looked like I felt that morning, dull, but serviceable.

Of course, after I arrived in school, had a second cup of coffee with my fellow teachers, and interacted with my little darlings in class for a while, I came alive as I usually did. It was lunchtime. I was sitting in the cafeteria with all my first graders. I looked up and saw a tall, slim figure in a black clerical suit with a white clergyman's collar enter and walk toward the custodian. I recognized who it was. I had seen that face on TV just that morning before I left home, giving a thirty-second "spiritual commercial" (as I later grew to call them). I knew it was the Reverend Bertram. My first thought was, *Who died? Someone was in an accident and he's here to break the news to some child.*

The dignified figure turned and began to walk toward our table. Immediately some of my small students began calling out, "Hi,

Pastor, Hi, Pastor Bertram." I later found out they attended his church.

"Are you Mrs. Martin? I'm Pastor Bertram. Harriet Gray, the parent of one of your pupils, has told me many good things about you. Would you consider speaking to my Sunday school teachers sometime on new methods of teaching?" (*What an interesting approach,* I thought. Mrs. Gray had mentioned him to me, too. I wasn't too intrigued with the idea of ever meeting him. Sometimes he seemed too stern on television, too New England "wrath of God" type to suit me.)

As I looked up (remember, I was seated on a cafeteria bench), I looked into deep-set, kindly blue eyes (*So that's what twinkling eyes are,* I thought), and the most attractive and compelling smile I had ever seen. *Well,* I thought, *I see what Mrs. Gray meant. He is much more attractive in person.*

"I'd be happy to speak to your teachers sometime. I hope it won't be in the next two weeks, however, as I am in the middle of hearing testimony afternoons and evenings for a teacher case I am helping to adjudicate," I said.

"No," he said, "we just had our monthly meeting last night, so it would not be for another month. Shall I get the manuals and books they are using to you?"

I gave him my address and phone number, and the Reverend O. H. Bertram departed, after hugging and greeting several of the children who clustered about him. He left the cafeteria and I watched many children from first grade on up go to him and speak, or catch his hand or hug his leg. That was my first experience with reversing the "stern" image I had held in my mind of "the Rev," as he was called by some here in Toledo, Ohio.

I finished my teaching day and drove to the high school where I had several teachers waiting to tape their testimonies for a teacher grievance case on which I was conducting an inquiry. I had been appointed that year to serve as chairman of our Teacher Association's Rights and Responsibilities Committee, and this was proving to be a source of great interest and involvement for me. It filled my nonteaching time in what I thought to be a good, productive, and helpful way.

You must know that at this time in my life I was alone. I had been compelled to divorce the father of my two daughters two years previous to this time. At the time of the divorce I was not a Christian, and great problems in the marriage had made it irreconcilable in my mind. I am not making an excuse for this devastating event in my life, only stating the facts of my past as they related to O. H. Bertram.

Our daughter Leslie, over twenty-one and a teacher, was living with a girlfriend who had also decided to attempt self-sufficiency, and my other daughter Sally was in Elkhart, Indiana, attending an institute for training as a medical laboratory technician.

I had not gone out in a strictly social way with anyone that I really was interested in—until just recently. I had met a most interesting and handsome man to whom I developed an intense attraction. We thought we were in love. He was ideal in every way, but not free in the final, legal way a person should be before involvement. I deluded myself into thinking that things like this only happen in the soap operas; that no one would tell another they were getting a divorce if they were not. Besides, I needed to love someone, and I'm sure you know how easy it is to love if the need, the timing, and the person seem just right.

About this time my oldest daughter Leslie, twenty-three years old, was experiencing a dramatic change. Her life outside of teaching had deteriorated in many ways, and while staying with a dear Christian couple, Barbara and Dan Cain, she accepted Christ and miraculously had become, almost overnight, the dear, precious girl she had been before leaving home to be on her own. I saw unbelievable changes happening before my very eyes. Leslie stopped smoking overnight. She gave up friends whom I considered a bad influence, and most marvelous of all, she asked if she could come back to live at home. Of course I was overjoyed, and I must confess, impressed by the the evidence of what this "being a Christian" was doing to her.

As the weeks progressed, and I saw her change from the daughter I had not known or admired for several years, into the most glowingly alive and happy girl I had ever met, I began to be curious about what brought about such a fabulous metamorphosis.

One Sunday as she prepared to go to church, as she did every Sunday now, I asked if I might go along. I truly wanted to see what she was finding that made her so happy and had converted her to her old, sweet self. I had not been to a church for a half-dozen years or more, and had become disenchanted with my own

17

religion, Christian Science. I did not seem to derive any inner satisfaction or mental growth by attempting to apply it in my life. In other words, it did not seem to work for me. I felt that this was partially my fault, and had lost interest in attempting to work out my "own salvation," had been unsuccessful in getting the girls to go with me as they reached their teen years; and I had become just plain lazy about going to church after teaching first graders all week.

Leslie said that of course I could go to church with her that Sunday. It was then that I began to experience what Christianity was all about. I was met with love, concern, and interest by the minister and the congregation. I began to hear who Jesus Christ really was. Of course, I had always loved Him as the most perfect Man to have ever trod the globe, but I didn't know who He really was!

I remember crying brokenheartedly when I was about nineteen years old while reading one of the best sellers at that time, *The Day Christ Died*, by Jim Bishop. What that dear, precious Man endured I thought, and oh, how I loved Him! But I still didn't know who He was.

As the weeks continued and I found I was receiving more knowledge about Jesus Christ and what being a real Christian meant, I began to realize what I had been missing in my life. I began to see what I needed and wanted. I longed for what my new church friends and minister called "a relationship with Christ." And so, at a lay meeting for evangelism, conducted by Gladys and Harry Dickleman, who were visiting my very Christ-centered First Congregational Church in Toledo, Ohio, I took the first concrete step in becoming a committed Christian.

I remember clearly what I did. Mrs. Dickleman had just finished telling us to write down all the things we had ever done that we were ashamed of, or felt were sinful, or unforgivable, or wrong. I was still writing my list when I heard her say, "Time's up." I was so hoping we didn't have to read them aloud, or that we didn't have to turn them in. Oh, how dreadful our big and little transgressions look when written! Then Mrs. Dickleman said, "Tear your list into little pieces." My first reaction was, "Oh no! I worked so hard at these sins." Then I got the impact of what this device was to dramatize—how a belief in Christ obliterates the past. As He forgives our sins, they are wiped away as the small torn bits of paper in my hands were being completely annihilated.

I am chuckling now as I recall that first reaction of "Oh no." Isn't the truth that we all somehow want to cling to past sins, rehash them, can't quite believe they are wiped away, and even though we know *God* has forgiven us by a trusting faith in Jesus Christ and His promises, we find it the hardest to forgive *ourselves*. Just as I really didn't want to tear up my carefully written wrongs, we don't always want to turn over our lives to Christ. After all, we worked hard and devoted a lot of time to those sinful thoughts and actions. It is hard to give up the known (as wrong as we come to see it), for the unknown (as right and blessed as we know it will be).

I have never forgotten this night when I first invited Jesus Christ to come into my being and heart. I really didn't fully understand what I was doing. I just did it trustingly, lovingly, because these Christians told me this was the way to eternal life. I believed them and the words of Jesus Christ.

I started attending a weekly women's Bible study, and then joined the church after several enlightening conferences with the then-minister, Dr. Robert Croskery. Every phase of life immediately began to improve and fall into place for me. I know that some new Christians note no immediate or noticeable change in the quality of their lives because it is so gradual, but I was one of the lucky ones. I seemed to myself to be the prodigal daughter who saw the light and was being rejoiced over by all the angels in heaven.

As the light of our Lord's truths began to infiltrate my mind and heart, my eyes began to be opened to what the relationship with my friend really was. I began to see him now through new eyes, loving still, but seeing his weaknesses and his own self-deception as clearly as I saw my own faults. It was as though a veil had been torn away from my eyes. I realized that loving someone who was attempting to get a divorce, even though his unhappiness and disillusionment with marriage had occurred before he met me, was wrong. But I could not end the love, and so my will, not God's prevailed for the time being.

But I had started to pray every night for God to help me in my predicament, and I continued going to my Bible study and was receiving much encouragement by attending church on Sundays.

This was the status quo at the time of the momentous first meeting of "Pastor Honey and Angel." The same evening as that first encounter of a special kind at my school, I received a phone call: "Hello, this is Pastor Bertram. I have had a cancellation of one of my pastoral calls this evening, and wonder if I might stop by with the Sunday school materials you wanted."

Of course, my response was, "Of course."

I remember my thoughts as I dressed for his arrival. "I'll show you, Pastor Bertram. I don't always look like the little brown bird type schoolmarm you saw this morning." I selected a long plum wool skirt (these were "the" fashions in 1972), slit up the front to show off plum suede boots, and a deep plum turtle neck sweater designed to show off me. Grandmother Sarah's gold filigree watch pin and chain and gold watch, earrings, and my mother's chunky gold bracelet completed what I thought was a smashing outfit.

As I ushered Rev. Bertram into my living room, I could see that he was properly impressed. Later on he was to tell me that he had been properly impressed that morning at school!

Oh, how clearly I remember his answer as I invited him to sit on the couch with me where, I thought, we could look at the teacher manuals together more easily. "I'll sit over here, thank you," he said, placing his tall frame down in a chair *across* the room from me. I must confess that this was the first time anyone had ever refused to sit next to me, and I was somewhat disconcerted by his not wanting to do so.

Sometime later he explained that ministers and doctors need to be especially careful about any type of closeness that could be construed to be personal when they called on women. There are many lonely, troubled people in this world, and doctors, ministers, and other consulting persons such as lawyers, social workers, and psychologists, must be careful that relationships stay strictly businesslike.

As I grew to know more about my darling's personality and character through the next seven years, I found this courteous caution to be a definite trait. Every step of life was so well planned, thought out, and expedited with the utmost care and loving tact.

We planned the next Sunday school teachers' meeting at which I was to speak, and the call was over, I thought. Then the Reverend Bertram said, "You know, I had no dessert tonight. How

20

would you like to go out and get some Indian pudding with me?" The Indian pudding, something about which I had heard of as a typically New England dish, intrigued me; and yes, the unusualness of this man was beginning to penetrate my consciousness; and I said that I'd love to have dessert with him. We went to a Howard Johnson's Restaurant, Westgate, Toledo, Ohio, which was near both our homes.

This was our first "date." As we ate the warm cornmeal and molasses dish which had a scoop of vanilla ice cream on top (Pastor's version), we discovered many interesting things about one another. We found out we both had twenty-four-year-old daughters, we both had eighty-four-year-old mothers and were going through the throes of the "elderly parent" syndrome. Further discussion brought out the fact that Pastor Bertram was born in Iowa, but was not overly fond of that part of the country; and I was born in Nebraska and also was not at all fond of that part of the U.S.A.

He told me briefly of the circumstances of his wife's death in an automobile accident a year and a half earlier. Then, in my most dignified "out with a minister in his clerical garb" manner, I asked, "And where was your first church, Reverend Bertram?" He answered, "Oh, it was in a small town in Connecticut you probably never heard of." (Earlier talk had brought out the fact that I had seldom been out of Toledo for over twenty years.) At this, I said, "Oh, where in Connecticut?" and his answer was, "Wallingford."

Upon hearing this, my attempt at poised dignity flew out the window and I squealed with joy at the coincidence. "That is where my brother lives, and I have been there!" I said. We both took delight in comparing our most favorable impressions of Connecticut, even to the extent of Pastor knowing some of the people I had heard my brother speak of, although my brother and Pastor's paths had never crossed. We discovered we both loved New England.

Later, after my husband's death, I was to find his journal for the year of our first meeting. This was the entry for that day: Thursday, February 17, 1972:

"As I reflect upon this day, it was certainly a gift from God. I met Sally Breck Martin, a first-grade teacher at Monac

21

School. Visited her at school to arrange for her to speak at our Sunday School teachers' meeting on methods. Saw her in the evening. Friendly, kind, and outgoing."

Huh! Not a word about the smashing plum outfit, or the fact that he asked me to have dinner with him the following Saturday. I was to learn that other things were more important to Pastor Bertram than looks!

4
The Dating Game

"... Memories that bless and burn!"
Robert Cameron Rogers
"The Rosary"
"Suddenly you come with love in your hands and eyes and lips,
that I thought I didn't want."
Sarah Breck Bertram
"Is It Because?"

Dinner that next Saturday was lovely. I could dress up and appear proudly before the people of the city of Toledo. I was escorted by a well-thought of, courteous, and interesting widower. What a difference in feelings from when I met my secret friend—the one who was not legally free, to take me out; although he did, many times, for which I am still grateful. This friend's love and concern for me at this time I appreciated greatly, however wrong they might have appeared to others, had they known. Remember, God was not finished with teaching me lessons about self will, and I had just become a "baby Christian."

The Reverend Bertram was that rare combination of a good man with a soupçon of real sex appeal that expressed itself in his eyes, obviously admiring me with every look. He had the marvelous quality of being a wonderful listener and an even better conversationalist. From the moment I stepped into his car to go out for that Indian pudding, I experienced, for the first time in my life, the truly interesting discussions that I had always desired in a relationship. There was never a time when there was not that give and take in sharing our experiences, our thoughts, and our hearts. Being with him produced a new and different reaction in me than I had ever experienced before. I felt safe, relaxed, unworried, at ease; and did not have to act in any way, but be myself. No flirting, no pretense at having a good time, no attempting light conversation, no compulsion to make the other person feel at ease was ever necessary when I was with this man.

I did not realize it at the time, but I came to know later that God was working out His plan for me and on me, during this time of what became one month of once-a-week dinner dates. The contrast of the two men in my life became more obvious as time went on, and with a sudden realization one evening, I knew one of the friendships was becoming lessened in importance to me.

But loyalty and honesty have always been part of my personal characteristics, and I decided I could not handle the difficult emotional pulls I was experiencing. I had told my friend that I was seeing the Reverend Bertram. He did not like this, even though I assured him it was only a dear friendship. And so, out of loyalty and seeming love, I agreed not to see the Reverend Bertram again, after one more meeting to explain my decision to him.

When I did this explaining, and announced my decision to Pastor Bertram, he looked at me with sincere, kindly, and loving concern, and he made me promise to do these things: Set a time limit for some legal evidence of progress toward my friend's freedom, continue my Bible studies, and increase my prayers for guidance in knowing God's will in the matter. I knew of his many years of experience with counseling; and there was something about the man that inspired the utmost confidence. You knew instinctively that here was a person who truly had good motives and only your ultimate good at heart.

I promised I would do this, after we discussed at length, spiritual passages in the Bible that would be helpful; and many subtle (on his part) relating of experiences in personal counseling that were intended to show me the certainty of God's help in cases of troubled personal relationships. We parted, and I can still hear that deep, delicious voice saying he would continue to hold me in his prayers.

In my mind I set Easter vacation as the deadline for the evidence of progress and informed my other dear friend of this. Time passed, and I noticed that a certain uneasiness in feelings had crept into our relationship. I now know that this friendship was not "of God," that it was to be a learning experience that God had allowed to happen to instruct me that my own will was not to be depended upon.

Easter vacation arrived; the morning of Good Friday came, together with a breakfast meeting with my friend. With tears in his eyes he told me of his decision to return to his wife and try to make a "go" of it.

At the time, I did not know whether this was his will out of love for me (which I still chose to believe was real), knowing he realistically had no grounds for a divorce that was not wanted by his wife, or whether he was truly a weak person who had no ability to make overt moves toward a goal. I now know it was the next step in God's plan for me, and my friend was powerless to do otherwise than what he did.

You see, I was still holding onto this sinful part of my life, not really wanting to let go, just as I had not wanted to tear up the list of sins I had so carefully written down the night that I invited and accepted Jesus Christ into my heart.

We parted—I had to accept his decision, and I learned what the expression "a broken heart" meant. I went home to weep uncontrollably over my lost love, over remorse over the whole friendship, over guilt, over worries of what we had done to each other's emotions and lives. This was as close to a breakdown as I had ever experienced. My daughters realized this and called on our dear friend, Barbara Cain, who called our minister. Barbara and Dr. Croskery came to me and prayed with and for me. I don't remember the words of those beautiful prayers in my behalf, I only remember the calming love I felt pervading my whole consciousness. How beautifully God works through our caring friends!

I then went to bed to rest those crying eyes, after a cup of tea made by my precious daughters, and brought to me with so much love and concern that I found myself thanking God again for our beautiful mother-daughter relationships.

Now, people, get ready for a thrill up your spine. I got in bed, only to feel a strong compulsion to get out of bed and get down on my knees and pray, to again ask God's forgiveness, and to ask Him again to come into my heart. I did so, throwing my arms out on the bed in an utter expression of surrender. I had never prayed on my knees before! I had always felt God heard me just as well lying comfortably under the covers before I went to sleep at night.

I remember clearly just what I said. You see, this was *the* turning point in my life, and God had allowed me the great privilege of remembering every word of that prayer. I said, "I give up, God. I turn my will over to You completely. If You want me to have someone in my life, You pick him, because I don't know how. I have been a failure at this two times now. If Your will is for me to be alone the rest of my life, give me the strength to bear it. Thank you. With love, in Jesus' Name. Amen." I wept more contrite (look up that word in the dictionary right now for my meaning to the fullest) tears for forgiveness, and then lay down to rest. I had scarcely closed my weepy eyes when the telephone on the bedside table rang.

It was the Reverend Oswald H. Bertram! I gasped, remembering I had sent him out of my life; the thought of my sending such a wonderful person away was also part of my great sorrow.

He said, "I know you told me not to call, but it is Easter time, the happiest part of my year, and I just wanted to see how you were, and to wish you a Happy Easter."

With tears in my voice, I told him the other relationship had come to an end; and that I did not feel the happiness or joy of Easter time—on the contrary, I was experiencing my own Good Friday crucifixion of a sort. He said, "I am taping (his television half-hour program) tonight, but I will see you after that."

"Oh no, Reverend Bertram, I am in no shape to see anyone—my face and eyes are swollen from crying." (Oh, vanity was still alive and functioning, all right.) "I shall pick you up at ten o'clock," he said. And the phone call ended with his hanging up the receiver.

"Oh Lord," I murmured, "Is this what You have in mind for me? Is this the strength that I need in a man in my life?" I experienced a strange exhilaration as a reaction to those firm, authoritative words, "I *will* pick you up."

And then I was half afraid of what I felt was God's immediate reaction to my prayer. My next feeling was doubt that this could be, that perhaps my daughters had phoned him. But no, they had not.

As I looked back with wonder and understanding, I can see how beautifully God worked out ways that truly were "wondrous to behold." Ozzie told me in the months that followed, that the night before, he had stood at his window and had prayed, "Oh God, how much longer must I endure this loneliness," and the next day he had an irresistible urge to phone me to see how my life was coming along. He revealed to me that *he* had known I was the one for him, and was just marking time until God revealed this fact to *me*.

He did arrive to pick me up at ten, and we had a beautiful time talking together while having dessert again. I was to eventually learn that my darling had a definite sweet tooth.

It was really a counseling session. His wisdom and understanding of this period in my life astounded me. If anyone expressed Christ's teachings, it was this man. It was as though he were saying, "neither do I condemn you."

We began to see each other several times a week, and I experienced a spurt of spiritual growth at this time that seemed to "cinch" all that I had been learning in my weekly Bible study and church experiences.

Oh, I began to see this Ozzie, as I called him now, in a new light all right. It was as though the "scales were peeled from my eyes." He began to look handsome to me—whereas before I had not thought him to be, although others had commented to me on his striking appearance. I began to appreciate the brilliant mind of the man, his wisdom, his outgoing manner, and his extreme kindness and courtesy toward me. I discovered he had a delightful wit. That was a quality I had always longed for in a man. And oh, the wonderful feeling of this being a "right and honorable" friendship continued to grow.

But I was fearful of falling in love again. I had an "out of the frying pan into the fire" sort of feeling. So much so, that I was most distant when it came to any type of physical contact besides just holding hands.

I remember one evening's drive to Detroit, Michigan's Metro Airport to look at the planes and then have dinner at a beautiful dining place near by. During dinner he had looked into the smokey mirrored tile wall that our table adjoined, and gave utterance to the most extravagantly beautiful compliment I had ever received. "You have the profile of a lovely Marie Antoinette," he said. One has to admit that we women love this type of compliment, and this was certainly the most original one I'd ever heard.

As the years went by, I discovered sincere compliments were a part of this dear man's personality. They were not lightly given—and were not only given to me, but freely given to all, both men and women, whom he felt deserved an admiring or grateful comment. This definitely was part of the O. H. Bertram personality.

He drove back to Toledo that night with one hand holding mine so tightly that it actually hurt. I was getting messages through that hand that said, "Oh, how I need you," and, "I'll never let you go," and, "This is right and good," and, "This love is of God," and he did not have to say a word aloud.

I was still afraid of my feelings, afraid to trust completely in what I now know was God's choice of mates for us; and so I never showed in the subtle ways we women have that I would be ready for such a giant step in our relationship as a kiss. You see, I somehow knew that this was a man not to be trifled with, that a kiss would not be "just a kiss" to him, but a real commitment, and so I continued to be somewhat standoffish, although growing in fondness and admiration for this unusual man. Our friendship was my first experience with what love should be—a growing process over a period of time.

My past experiences even as a girl with those "puppy loves" we all go through, were all based on physical attraction. You know, the intense feelings, the heart poundings, the dreamy dreams that make up this type of attraction, and then the diminishing of love as the person becomes more familiar.

This was not what I was feeling with Pastor Bertram at all! This was different, somehow. I was caring for someone for all the right reasons for the first time in my life. Such wonderful discussions we had! Every question I had about Christianity was being answered in a way that was understandable and valid to me. What fun we had just taking walks or rides in the country. How beautiful those twinkly blue eyes were becoming to me, and how wonderful the feeling of being cared about by such an understanding, and yes, godly man.

The hurt from the other friendship was diminishing. I had already asked and received God's forgiveness for my past, and was being blessed on top of this undeserved grace by an association with the most influential force in my spiritual growth I had ever come up against. The wonder of it all was slowly dawning on me.

My whole life was falling into place, as the cliché goes. My daughters' lives were progressing nicely, my teaching days were satisfying. Committee work with my Professional Rights and Responsibilities group was continuing well, and several cases were coming to a conclusion. God *was* in His heaven and all was coming right with the world. I was beginning to experience the "abundant life" that Christ promises in John 10:10.

And then that night in April came that was to put my whole life into focus as the "new creature" Christ promised I would become when I accepted Him as my Lord and Savior.

Ozzie and I had returned to my home from having dinner together. It was Saturday night, and I knew from experience that even our joy in being together would not keep him from getting in early, as Sunday was his "big day," and I knew he let nothing interfere with rest and mental preparation for his sermon the next morning at Good Shepherd Lutheran Church.

He pulled his car into my driveway, shut off the ignition, and turned to me. He looked deeply into my eyes for a moment and then said, "When you get ready to let me kiss you goodnight, I guess you can put it in writing!" With that he got out of the car, came around to help me out and escort me to my door.

I was flabbergasted! That was the suavest, "coolest," most charming and witty remark I had ever heard. And did it ever have an effect! As he declined my invitation to come in for a cup of chocolate (because it was getting late), and stood in my doorway, his black snap brim hat in hand, fur collar turned up to frame that aristocratic and smiling face, it dawned on me fully as does the warmth of a rising sun that I loved the man, and I leaned over (he was on the lower step) and kissed him!

Heaven shone out of those blue eyes as he realized my love for him had finally been realized by me, and of course he took me in his arms for a real kiss before he left. He told me later that he knew I would love him; he was just patiently waiting until *I* would realize God's plans for us. As he walked to the car, I looked after him in wonderment. I had truly fallen in love with a wonderful man, and the relationship seemed planned by God.

The following week, on April 11, we announced our engagement to our daughters at a family dinner. Their happy reaction made our joy complete, and the wedding plans began for our "happily ever after" life together.

5
Trouble in River City

"Has God deserted heaven,
And left it up to you,
To judge if this or that is right,
And what each one should do?"
                              Unknown Author

Ozzie used to say, "One of the reasons I like Toledo is that it is on the Maumee River, which leads to Lake Erie. Being on the St. Lawrence Seaway, a connection to the ocean, I don't feel land-bound here." Every seagull we saw triggered a happy reaction, usually some remark referring to past sightings of the birds in New England, together with an analogy of how a seagull compared with the ideal Christian. "You know, pure, free, beautiful, cared for, industrious, and admirably vocal about his beliefs," Ozzie would say.

Therefore, it was not quite a surprise to me to learn that my quite vocal fiancée had already talked about me to his friends in the congregation. Friends were telling me that he literally glowed, and they were happy that he was happy. He had been devastatingly lonely. His sermons reflected his sadness in their sometimes tragic tone. Although always sound in principle, up-lifting to others, and delivered in Ozzie's own special attention-holding way, those sermons were not the ones that the congregation began to be treated to hearing from April 1972, on. Friends have since said that the change in the Reverend Bertram was immediately noticeable, that a feeling of "all's well, God's in His heaven," permeated every aspect of the church's functioning.

But, as the title of this chapter indicates, all was not completely well. Some people who did not personally know me were not over-joyed at the prospect of their beloved Pastor falling prey to the "wiles of the blonde, merry, grass-widow," as they saw me. In fact, a few were so nonjoyous that they started a campaign to prevent our marriage. It seems as though one woman in particular was crying out, "Pharisees of the world, unite, to oppose and find evil in these wedding plans."

It came as quite a shock to me. You must know this about my

personality: I have always seen the world through rose-colored glasses. Whether this is due to my optimistic Christian Science upbringing where I was sheltered—perhaps a bit too much—from any unpleasant realities; or whether it was the natural reaction to quite a lovely life up to the several years preceding the divorce, I do not know. I only know I have always seen the good in things and people.

I remember one incident in my teaching days when I was reviewing taped testimony my Progressional Rights and Responsibilities Committee was hearing in order to adjudicate a case we were working on. Steve Kerlin, one of the committee members, and a fiery friend and teacher, had listened patiently as I led the committee to try to see the person's motives from another viewpoint. "Oh, Sally," he said in exasperation, "You make me so mad! If Adolph Hitler walked in here, you'd find something good to say about him." In defense, I suppose this quality was the very thing that made for any success I might have had in this committee work.

Consequently, I expected the congregation of the church my husband was serving to welcome this baby Christian of two years with open loving hearts and arms. If I had thought otherwise, I'm sure I would not have agreed to marry Ozzie, as the thought of doing him any harm would have been abhorrent.

As I look back and attempt to see things from their viewpoint, I realize that they felt it unscriptural and against church teachings to divorce and then remarry.

I had acknowledged to God and my Pastor my guilt over having to obtain a divorce. I realized it was an act against God's laws for our good, as expressed in the Bible, God's Word. I ask forgiveness from all who were offended.

The success and joy of my second marriage to Ozzie, after I had become a Christian, was not God's sanction of what I had done before I accepted Christ as my Lord and Savior; but rather, I feel, an example of His mercy on my repentant spirit.

As Paul said in 1 Timothy 1:12-17, in the Revised Standard Version Bible, ". . . But I received mercy because I had acted ignorantly in unbelief, and the grace of our Lord overflowed for me with the faith and love that are in Christ Jesus."

But how unbelievably cruel were the circulated letters to members of our church, the sign, "Adulterer" at the church office, left anonymously, the phone calls of a distressful nature, and believe it or not, even an attempt at a petition of protest. Several letters that I found in my husband's files were written to him personally, and were especially judgmental, as they assumed from hearsay the reason for my divorce. They seemed to feel they had a right to judge what to us was a personal matter.

Perhaps it would be sufficient to say that the most insidious effect of all this turmoil was the planting of a seed of doubt in many dear people's minds; doubts of their beloved Pastor, yes, even of their church.

You see, what they did not know or care to find out, was that the Lutheran Church-Missouri Synod recognized two reasons for divorce as acceptable. What people thought was the reason for my being compelled to get a divorce was not the real reason! Only Ozzie and his Synod superiors and my family knew just how scriptural the divorce really was. I did not feel it was the business of others as long as the Synod upper echelons and my husband understood.

I can smile now as I look back on this trying time. There I was, a Christian of less than two years, fresh from my beautiful conversion, filled with love and joy and the amazing grace of God's forgiveness, going every week to church and to a great women's Bible study, and finding that what I had been learning about Christianity was not occurring. I had been hearing and reading how all the angels in heaven would rejoice over me as was the prodigal son, how Christians were kind, tender-hearted, forgiving of one another, even as "God for Christ's sake has forgiven you" (Ephesians 4:32).

I had been learning that Jesus said, "It is finished" as He hung dying on the cross; His task of saving us from our sins being accomplished. I was learning that His resurrection proved that we no longer are in our sins when we adopt and adore Him as our Lord; I was learning that Jesus Christ made it possible for me to be forgiven. I had been learning that his assurance of being at peace with God was what makes a Christian willing and able to be compassionate, tender-hearted and forgiving toward those who offend us. And I was learning especially from Second Corinthians 5:12 that *all* who accept Christ as their Savior are righteous in God's sight.

Yes, I was learning and believing and trusting, but it wasn't

31

what I was experiencing. What a shock to this well-thought-of in the community teacher, to this admittedly self-assured, yes, even almost spoiled by loving attention, woman. It was an awakening to the reality that I know the Lord intended for me to have, and to learn from. To this day, however, I sometimes have a problem understanding how, if they knew him at all, some could think Ozzie could have ever done anything to harm his church, or that would be offensive to God. Christ came first in his life. He informed me of this before we were engaged. But oh, he made second place so wonderful!

While all this was going on, my future husband went on about his work, never doubting that "God and I always make a majority," one of his favorite quotes from Dwight L. Moody. And he was right. The trouble in River City (Toledo) died down, the trouble makers left the church, and the rest of the congregation made up for the distressing time by their overwhelming love and joy at the prospect of the marriage of one of the community's favorite teachers (who had become a reborn Christian just two years before) and their beloved Pastor.

A humorous incident occurred about this time. One evening my beloved came to pick me up for dinner, and as he walked into my living room, he frowned and said, "You didn't tell me something!" "What do you mean?" I said.

"You didn't tell me what you were!" he continued in the serious almost stern way he was able to affect at times.

I frantically tried to think what I had ever done that I had not told him about. *Oh, dear Lord,* I thought, *What have I done that would cause him to be upset with me.* The teasing time ended with the flashing of that special and beautiful smile that all who knew him loved.

"You didn't tell me that you were voted the 'Outstanding Teacher of the Year' in 1970 and almost 550 teachers in your township!" he said.

I then explained that I didn't feel it was something I wanted to say to him casually. Can't you just hear a person trying to impress their date by saying in an offhand way, "Oh, guess what—I was teacher of the year in 1970. It just wasn't in me to divulge this fact out of a clear blue sky. And anyway, if I had thought about it at all, I would have felt that he would eventually find it out anyway. I must confess that this award was one of the highest

32

points of my life, and I was secretly pleased that someone had told Ozzie about it. He was always so proud of me, and he let me know that he was. One of his outstanding qualities was that he always informed a person, whether a man or woman, of his feelings of admiration for their special qualities or talents.

Several incidents happened that I now consider humorous, although at the time they seemed rather upsetting. One evening after our engagement was announced, I received a phone call. "Is this Mrs. Sally ?" "Yes," I said. "You big hunk of baloney," the woman, obviously motivated by jealousy, commented. Then she hung up. At first Ozzie and I laughed over this; then we felt pity for such an obviously sick woman.

Another time, the July after we were married in 1972, a postcard arrived, printed in an obviously disguised hand, "I saw you and your wife at the Bob Evans Restaurant. She don't look like no pastor's wife to me." I had been wearing a sundress and the top part of my back was bare. Ozzie loved it since it was red, white, and blue, one of his favorite color combinations, for obvious reasons.

In September, 1973, Ozzie received this letter anonymously, written in somewhat the same printing, disguised as an illiterate person:

"Dear Mr. Bertram: I owe apology. Sorry I tell you your
wife not perfect. May God Forgiv me. She is now very nice
lady. May God bless all. Please forgiv.
　　　Love,
　　　Mistaked person"

Shortly after we were married, I received a phone call from a woman asking if I could tell her where the listing of the lineage of Christ was in the Bible. It's in two places, she said. I told her the one I knew in Matthew, and I said, "Just a minute, I'll ask my husband. He is the Bible scholar in this family." She said, "No, I wanted to know if *you* knew," and then she hung up the phone.

Everyone was so lovingly concerned about whether one of Toledo's favorite pastors had chosen the right wife.

In the meantime, dear friends and family and my new church

family-to-be were lovingly supportive and complimentary. It seemed to be true that "All the world loves a lover." Everywhere we went, people took joy in our being together. Many said just to see us walk down the aisle together after Sunday morning second service to greet our congregation as it left, gave them a thrill of happiness.

You see, I had already started to attend my fiancé's church every Sunday, and was also attending his adult membership class every Thursday evening so that I might be confirmed in the Lutheran faith of my clergyman husband-to-be. I noted that after I started to attend this class and was introduced as Pastor Bertram's bride-to-be, two unmarried women never returned to the membership class. I guess their hopes of catching Ozzie's eye were dashed when I appeared on the scene.

And so, having never been baptized, I was baptized by my darling April 27, confirmed by him May 11, and then married to him June 21. The year 1972 was an eventful one for me. Ozzie used to say, "What a privilege! I baptized her, confirmed her, and then married her. I bet not many pastors can say that."

6
The Wedding

"Were he not to marry again, it might be concluded that his first wife had given him a disgust to marriage; but by taking a second wife, he pays the highest compliment to the first, by showing that she made him so happy as a married man, that he wishes to be so a second time."
James Boswell
Life of Samuel Johnson

When the Reverend O. H. Bertram asked me to marry him, I remember teasing him by saying, "You can't marry me, I don't look like a minister's wife. I wear green eye shadow!" He laughingly told me, "So did my first wife." Then I seriously queried him about what he expected from me in the role of a pastor's wife.

His answer surprised me, for I had pictured that all kinds of church-related duties and work would be expected of me. He said, "I don't want a ministerial assistant, I want a wife!" Delightedly

I told him of the penciled-in remark in my teaching records, "Left education field to become a church wife," and how some felt that I would be wasting my "exceptional talent for teaching children" by marrying a minister and giving up my career.

Little did they know that I had reached a point after almost thirteen years of teaching, where I was ready to push on toward a higher calling. I felt strongly that God's will was being done, and that He wished me to make this particular man happy so he could continue his productive work of "winning souls for Christ," as Ozzie stated it.

Ozzie's attitude about marriage for himself reminded me of Woodrow Wilson's, who, as you remember, fell very much in love with the charming Edith Galt after the death of his first wife. In one of President Wilson's letters to Mrs. Galt, he stated,

> *"Our happiness is not an ordinary matter of young lovers;
> it is for me, a matter of efficiency.
>
> I am absolutely dependent on intimate love for the right and free and most effective use of my powers . . ."

I was made to know in very certain ways that I was very necessary to my future husband, not only for his personal happiness, but for the continued success of his work as a Pastor.

In very subtle ways, he had led me to the knowledge that he wanted a full-time wife. It was I who felt he would want me to continue teaching, for I had presumed a pastor's salary was not monetarily much "to write home about." It never occurred to me to ask about his income. I guess I assumed he could use the contribution of my salary. It was only after a month of remarks by him such as, "We will be traveling every few months. Will it be fair for your students to have a substitute teacher so often, dear?" Or, "There was a young woman in my office today who can't get a teaching job. Isn't it a shame some of the older teachers don't retire and let the new ones have a chance," that I finally caught on to his true desires in this matter. "You don't really want me to continue teaching," I said. "I thought you'd never

---

*From Woodrow Wilson's letters, edited by Tribble in *A President In Love*.

catch on," was his retort. "I just didn't want you to feel deprived of your career," he continued. I made sure he knew that I'd gladly sacrifice my career in teaching to become his full-time wife. What woman in love would not be thrilled at being made to feel so needed and necessary by her future mate.

I want to include three of the many love notes and letters I received from Pastor Honey (my nickname for O. H. Bertram) before our marriage. I think they show a romantic side to his flair for writing. This one dated June 8, 1972, contains very certain, although artful and subtle, instructions as to what he expected from me as his wife.

My dearest Darling,

As the day approaches when you and I shall become husband and wife, I am almost carried away with impatience. I truly am aware what this bond of life-long union means. I shall do all within my power to make you thoroughly happy and to make your life a foretaste of heaven. So grateful am I that the Lord has brought us together that I find myself expressing my thanks to Him many times during the day.

Furthermore do I realize that much of my success will depend on you. The peace of mind that I will have through your loving concern over my welfare, the composure and tranquility I will enjoy through you serving as a stabilizing force, will add to the degree of my serving the Church of Jesus Christ. Whatever is accomplished will be done through our hands clasped tightly in the hand of God. Our achievements will serve to His glory but a knowledge of mutual accomplishments.

Darling, my Angel, I love you and will always love you as long as we live. Under no conditions will I ever bring you heartache or a moment of unhappiness. I am resolved that you will be the most esteemed wife in the world, and that I will always enfold you in my innermost heart as a gift that could never be replaced. To you I give my heart and will always love you next to God, whom I have pledged to serve.

With my deepest affections,
(signed) Your Oz

36

My darling Angel:

On this, your last day of school, I again witnessed how everyone loves you. As one of your friends said to me, "Sally should have been a minister's wife all this while, since she shows such love for all." Your beauty shines in so many ways, it is you.

I feel so certain that God has united us that the joy within me finds itself inadequate to express its emotion. My love for you will never be expressed fully since I have neither the words nor the power to do so. Darling, thanks for loving me as you do, I feel it. Truly, love is the selfishness of two persons.

Love is something so divine,
Description would but make it less;
'Tis what I feel, but can't define,
'Tis what I know, but can't express,
God bless you.

Your lover, Oz

My wonderful Angel,

Now we are coming ever closer to that eventful day on which we will pledge our love to one another publicly. Certainly many people know how much we love one another, but Darling, it is for you to know and feel my love for you. My love for you cannot be hid. There is no remedy for love but to love more.

Perhaps my ever-growing love is well expressed in the words,

The love of my life came not
As love unto others is cast;
For mine was a secret wound—
But the wound grew a pearl, at last.

My life has grown richer because of you, and may the good Lord make us ever richer in this love from day to day. With Him by our side, we shall set for others an example of perfect love.

My deepest affections,
Your Oz

I'm sure one of the reasons I fell so much in love with this special man was this beautiful strain of romanticism that was so much a part of him. He used to recite German poetry to me. What an irresistible combination! Beautiful words set to the tune of that beautiful deep voice.

"Du bist wie eine blume,
So hald, so schoen und rein
Ick schaudich und wehmut
Sehlecsht mei in herz herin."

"You are like a flower,
So sweet, so fair and pure,
I gaze on you and yearning
comes stealing over my heart."

No wonder people seemed to love to be in our company. I believe there is an electric current that flows between true lovers. Others feel it when they are in the same room; they sense that male-female current that shouts out that two people are deeply involved with each other on all levels—mental, spiritual, emotional, and physical. Many friends entertained us as the newly engaged couple, and we made many calls together on members of my future congregation.

The day for the wedding arrived and it was a beauty! June put all her charms on view that Wednesday the twenty-first in 1972 as I drove my little convertible to Bob Evans, our favorite breakfast meeting restaurant, after a call from Ozzie. "Never mind the old adage that you shouldn't see your bride on the day of your wedding until the ceremony. I can't ever get enough of seeing you!" he said, as he invited me to breakfast with him. It was a lovely way to start our wedding day, and the wedding that evening couldn't have been more perfect.

My brother, Richard Breck, together with my sister-in-law Verne, flew from Connecticut to give me away; he still in his white doctor-making-rounds shoes, but wearing an especially gorgeous tie he had purchased just for the occasion. My two daughters, Leslie and Sally, and Ozzie's daughter, Lorna, who were to attend me, were lovely in their white long gowns, each trimmed

38

an individual way, with a touch of lavender to match my lavender gown.

The church was filled by seven o'clock that evening. The people were practically hanging from the rafters, as the saying goes. Almost the whole congregation, plus all my friends, wanted to be there. My girls, now three, hovered about, fussing over me like little mother hens. My dearest mother and Ozzie's beloved mother and sisters were ensconced in the front pews, and the ceremony began.

As I walked down the aisle, I was somewhat conscious of the loving smiles as I passed by, but more fully aware of that beaming face and form wearing a beautiful white suit with black clerical shirt and white collar awaiting me at the altar.

Our vows were exchanged before the Reverend Victor F. Halboth of Grace Lutheran Church in Detroit, Michigan. He was, besides being the head (similar to a bishop) of Ozzie's district, my husband's dear friend. Attending Ozzie as his best man was Vincent Healy from Wilmette, Illinois, another close friend of many years.

My knees were literally shaking, but that beautiful, confident smile and the strong hand that grasped my arm when my brother gave me to Ozzie, gave me courage. I needed it, for although young at heart, I knew in reality that I was approaching middle-age, and this was to be a big change in my life.

We said our vows. Ozzie had written them just for us, and we had them memorized so we could say them facing each other and looking into one another's eyes. What a showman Ozzie was. He knew what would be thrilling to our relatives and friends, and he was not above giving them a wedding to remember. Here are those vows:

"I love you, Sarah, as I love no other. In the presence of God, I promise that all I am, I share with you. I take you to be my wife through sickness and health, through poverty and plenty, through joy and sorrow, now and forever."

"I love you, Ozzie, as I love no other. In the presence of God, I promise that all I am, I share with you. I take you to be my husband through

39

sickness and health, through poverty and plenty, through joy and sorrow, now and forever."

"I, Ozzie, in the presence of God and these witnesses, take you, Sarah, to be my wife, and pledge you my love in every respect, not to part from you until death separates us."

"I, Sarah, in the presence of God and these witnesses, take you, Ozzie, to be my husband, and pledge you my love in every respect, not to part from you until death separates us."

After the ceremony we both "floated" down the aisle together. I have a photograph to prove this. It shows us with our feet giving the illusion of being a few inches above the floor!

At the reception in our church's fellowship hall afterwards, we opened the two large presents our congregation gave us: a truly gorgeous silver tea set and tray, and a magnificent silver punch bowl with tray, ladle and twelve punch cups.

As Ozzie pulled out the punch bowl from its box he said, "What is this, a trophy for winning my beautiful bride? I replied, "No darling, I think it is a christening font for our first-born." The people gathered around us burst into laughter. I'm fortunate to have a picture of this very moment. My new husband and I are smiling with joy, and our friends and relatives and their children, (some my former students) are surrounding us.

After cutting our huge wedding cake, and accepting the good wishes of all, we scurried to the parsonage in the next block, my future home, to change clothes for our wedding trip. We were driving to Cleveland, Ohio, that night, and then on to Washington, D.C. the next morning for our honeymoon trip.

7
Washington, D.C.—Here We Come

"Of 'Americanism' of the right sort we cannot have too much. Mere vaporing and boasting become a nation as little as a man. But honest, outspoken pride and faith in our country are infinitely better and more to be respected than the bad taste ever to refer to our country except by way of deprecation, criticism, or general negation."
Henry Cabot Lodge

What a patriot I soon discovered I had married! This was assuredly my first experience with a person who so unabashedly loved his country. Traveling to our capital, I was regaled with stories of what we were to see during our four-day honeymoon in Washington. My new husband took great delight in being the first to show me around our nation's "first city." It delighted me too.

One of the personality traits Ozzie always told me he greatly appreciated was that I never could be blasé about anything. Those who know me know that I do "bubble over" with enthusiasm for things, and it is genuine. I don't know why I get so excited about events, or take such delight in things that are perhaps mundane to others. Perhaps it was because I was brought up in the Depression of the 1930s, or perhaps it was a quality cultivated by my parents, who themselves were most expressive of the emotions of love, gratitude, joy, and delight. Whether this was due to their natural personalities or to the Christian Science they practiced, I do not know. I do know that this trait of sublime appreciation expressed, was highly enjoyed by my Pastor Honey.

We arrived at the Key Bridge Holiday Inn in Arlington, Virginia, toward evening in time to change for dinner, which we planned to have at the inn. They had given us the bridal suite, and in our room was a huge, lovely bouquet of flowers from Congressman and Mrs. Walter Moeller, friends of my husband. Also, a dozen roses from Ozzie were on the dressing table.

The room was lit up with beauty and love, and I felt that no other bride in the world had such a lovely, welcoming beginning for her honeymoon. We had traveled through the continuous rain and the rising floods around us of what was to be the notorious flooding of June, 1972. But the warmth and sunlight of love, and the beauty and scent of flowers surrounded us now, and we were so happy being together.

How can I tell you more explicitly of Ozzie's special ability at organization and planning than to quote from the small journal I kept of our wedding trip. It shows how much he planned ahead, and how much we accomplished in four days:

Friday, June 23, 1982:
  6:30 –Breakfast at Holiday Inn
  8:15 –White House Tour
11:30 –Mrs. Moeller's Tour of the Capitol Building
12:30 –Lunch with Ohio Congressman Delbert Latta in the Congressional Dining Room
  2:00 –Visited Congressman Taft, Latta, and Donahue's Offices
  3:30 –Went through the Washington, D.C. Wax Museum
  5:00 –Watched the Flood Waters of the Potomac Rising!
  7:00 –Dinner at the Key Bridge Marriott Hotel's Andalusian Room. Marvelous gazpacho, and broiled salmon with little cheesecloth bonnets on the lemon halves

Saturday, June 24:
–After breakfast, visited Peter Marshall's New York Street Presbyterian Church. Shopped in some lovely department stores.
–Toured Ford's Theatre and Museum.
–Lunched at the National Art Gallery after looking around for a while.
–Toured the Smithsonian Institute, especially the Space and Aeronautics Museum. On the way back, saw the famous Iwo Jima Memorial Statue and the Pentagon Building.
–Dinner at the Memorial Bridge Marriott Hotel. A completely Chinese cuisine buffet. Excellent!
–Went to the Kennedy Center French Restaurant for an after-dinner glass of wine.

Sunday, June 25:
–Church service at Pilgrim Lutheran Church with Congressman Walt Moeller and Mrs. Moeller.
–Lunch at fabulous Mrs. K.'s Toll House in Silver Springs, Maryland with the Moellers.

–Drove to Holy Cross Hospital to call on Governor George Wallace.
–Visited the Tomb of the Unknown Soldier at Arlington National Cemetery; saw the changing of the guard, and also John F. Kennedy's grave with its eternal light.
–Drove to Lincoln Memorial, and I walked up to the huge statue of the seated Abraham Lincoln.
–Viewed the Washington Monument and the reflecting pool.
–Drove around the Tidal Basin, saw the cherry trees (not in bloom), and the Jefferson Memorial.

Monday, June 26:
–Toured Mount Vernon, George Washington's home on the Potomac River.
–Lunch with Congressman Latta in the Congressional Dining Room again.
–Toured FBI Building and the Mint.
–Dinner at our Holiday Inn.
–Went to see the play, "1776," at the National Theatre, the oldest theater in Washington.

Tuesday, June 27:
–Homeward bound!

I must add a few footnotes to these Washington notes. Ozzie got the idea to have a small sign made for a reserved "Pastor's Family" pew from Peter Marshall's church. He also was involved in making plans for some future interviews with men in politics for his "Religion in the News" telecasts.

The Alabama Governor George Wallace visit was unplanned. We were passing the hospital in Maryland where the Governor was recuperating from the attempt on his life May 15, 1972. Ozzie said, "Shall we pay him a call?" I said, "Why not!" We both started to giggle. Ozzie turned the car around and soon we were walking up to the front door of the hospital. Two men in Alabama State Trooper uniforms with "Smokey the Bear" hats looked us over, and then let us pass by with pleasant greetings. I must add that we were probably quite a sight. The tall slim clergyman was dressed in a dazzling white suit and a black clerical shirt with the white collar. The tall blonde was in a long white crocheted dress with a high neck, long sleeves, and violets at her waist. We must have looked like visiting dignitaries.

We asked to see Governor Wallace. Ozzie had once held an interview for television with him in Toledo. The nurse telephoned his room, and then told us he had just fallen asleep after strenuous therapy. She said if we cared to wait we could visit him when he awoke.

As we had much to do and see, we left, laughing at our boldness. I discovered another clue to my husband's success in life. What he wanted to do or accomplish, he went after with what I came to call his "holy boldness." He truly believed he could do all things through the strength of his convictions and the guidance and power of Christ, his Lord. I was to see many instances of his tenacity in going after what he believed in, in our years ahead.

One of the honors that had come to my husband that he seemed most proud of was the awarding of The Freedom Foundation's Gold Medal. A news release from the Storer Broadcasting System explains the event:

"Rev. O.H. Bertram, Pastor of Good Shepherd Lutheran Church, Toledo, and the Religious News Editor for WSPD-TV, Toledo, Ohio (Channel 13) was the producer and narrator of the telecast, 'LEST WE FORGET' which won the George Washington Gold Medal of Honor Award from the Freedoms Foundation of Valley Forge, Pennsylvania. The format of this patriotic program included an address by former Congressman Walter Moeller of Lancaster, and the presentation of an editorial entitled, 'The Flag', by Mr. David Drury, Editorial Director for the television station. Patriotic songs were sung by the Archbold (Ohio) High School Choir, under the direction of Mr. Walter Treadway. William Wallace, Jr., a student at Concordia College, Ann Arbor, Michigan, read the poem 'On Flanders Field'. James Watt, a Whitmer High School (Toledo) student, sounded taps with a background of cross-marked graves.

"WSPD-TV was the only television station in the nation to receive three George Washington Gold Medal Awards in 1968."

Because America meant so much to Ozzie, he treasured this award. He believed in not only the promotion of God's plan of salvation, but the promotion of respectful love for our nation.

I discovered another aspect of Ozzie's personality on our honeymoon. Profanity, especially taking the Lord's name in vain, greatly disturbed him. He squirmed with discomfort and audibly expressed his disapproval when the actors in "1776" swore time after time. There were moments when I felt he was ready to walk out. It really killed his pleasure in this otherwise brilliant play. Looking back, I think had we been married longer than five days, his very strong feeling about this would have prevailed and he would have left the National Theatre.

The luncheons in the Congressmen's Dining Room, which you could not enter unless accompanied by a congressman, were a real thrill to me. The first time we were there, Del Latta, the Ohio Congressman and our host, passed a menu around among the congressmen and they autographed it for the "bride." I still have it, framed.

The second time, Ernie, the famous Maitre d', recognized us and pulled a flower out of a basket to hand to me. My cup ran over with happiness at all this charming fuss made over the middleaged bride and groom. Later on, Congressman Latta had our picture taken with him on the steps of the Capitol Building and sent it to us, together with a great congressional cookbook, as a wedding present.

A personal note that might be of interest to lady readers, is that Ozzie enjoyed immensely the variety of lovely night dresses in my trousseau—a different one for each night. I'm a hat and lingerie *aficionado*, loving the best and most beautiful in each category. My new husband also loved the little wrapped gifts I had brought along for him—one for each evening. The last one was a pair of lavender sleep shorts to match that night's lavender nightgown. He laughed delightedly and said, "I'm glad no one else, especially my colleagues, will ever see these on me."

Each morning of our marriage was started with reading some type of spiritual material, together with the Bible. Usually it was a devotion contained in *Portals of Prayer*, a daily devotional guide. This grew to be a part of my life that I continue to this day. During my marriage it proved to be the source of much learning and growth in Christianity for me. It became the basis

45

for many questions on my part that were patiently answered by my Pastor Honey. This is why I have often said that I had seven years of private tutoring in the Christian life by my own private Pastor husband.

All in all, we had a beautiful beginning to our beautiful years together. Our lives and selves merged thrillingly into the "becoming as one" that a real marriage is all about. You can see why I looked out our back bedroom window on our first night home, in the direction of the home of a church member who opposed our marriage and said, somewhat vituperatively, "Eat your heart out, Betsy Potts!" (fictional name, of course).

No, I'm not really an angel, even though my darling called me one. This nickname gave me great joy—and also gave me a lovely goal to live up to as we began our years together.

8
Pastor Honey

"Speech cannot contain our love. There was, there is, no
gentler, stronger, manlier man."
Robert G. Ingersoll
"Eulogy at His Brother's Funeral"

"He was a gentleman from sole to crown, clean favored,
and imperially slim."
Edward Arlington Robinson
"Richard Cory"

Ah, yes—he was a man! The Reverend Oswald Henry Bertram. He was born August 18, 1917, in Reinbeck, Iowa, a part of the United States of which he was not especially fond. His parents were of German descent, and the German language was spoken in the home. With two grandfathers who were Lutheran pastors, you can see he was a "natural" and encouraged candidate for becoming a pastor. His father, Henry Bertram, born in Australia in 1885, was the principal of the Lutheran Elementary School in Reinbeck. His mother, Hulda Castens Bertram, born in Illinois in 1888, must have been a very devoted and spiritual-minded woman. Ozzie reiterated many times stories of their devotions every morning, together with his two sisters, Clara and Irma. He still could recite many prayers in German that he learned as a little boy, and of course, Ozzie spoke fluent German. This served him in good stead in later years when he produced and broadcast special programs for the well-known "Voice of America" on radio. His ability to preach in German qualified him for many invitations as guest minister for German-speaking congregations in New England, and once in a kirche (church) in Germany on one of our trips there.

As I write this, I am chuckling to myself as I think of my own "famous last words." "I'll *never* marry a German," I said in my younger days. "They are stubborn, unromantic, domineering, and completely without any esthetic sense." Oh, how wrong I was to be proven in later years! From the moment Ozzie walked into my life, (this tall, slim, elegantly aristocratic looking man with the handsome features of a German count whom I teasingly came to call "Count Von Hoenzollern," one of my many nicknames for him), he unconsciously reversed all my preconceived notions about traits I thought were indigenous to Germans.

Ozzie told me many little stories of his boyhood in Iowa. One I found in a small notation in German written by his mother. Ozzie was around six years old, and was leaving his family for a brief trip with his beloved grandfather. When asked why he had tears, he explained, "The sun shone in my eyes, Mama!" Such a manly response from such a little boy who was sad at parting, but did not want to sadden his mother.

Other anecdotes and stories of childhood memories were included from time to time in his newspaper articles, sermons and talks. It would not be possible to include them all, but this one appeared in the West Toledo Herald as a response to the editor's request to several prominent pastors for brief Christmas messages for publication in issues near the holiday.

I feel it was important not only in its mention of childhood memories, but because it subtly answered a personal letter received criticizing Ozzie's "promotion of a pagan holiday" by celebrating Christ's birthday in December, when it "couldn't possibly have been then," as the letter writer said. I remember Ozzie laughing when he showed me the letter, and saying, "This person sure is missing the point. It's not the correct exact day (of Christ's

birth) that's important, but the fact that He *was* born for us."
Here is the message as it appeared in the newspaper.

Natural Settings Help us Appreciate Blessings

As a boy I will never forget a Christmas Eve scene
following the evening church service. The fluffy snow was
falling as we were coming out of church.

I asked my father if I could go with him to sing the
Christmas carols for the shut-ins. The setting was perfect!

The white snow seemed to represent the purity of God's
love, sent to us in the person of Jesus Christ.

The message of happiness of the Angel's choir, "For
unto you is born this day in the City of David, a Savior,
which is Christ the Lord," seemed to be more real than
ever.

Natural settings help us appreciate spiritual blessings.
Even though the date of Christ's birth has never been
established, it is proper that it be observed as suggested
by early church custom.

The blanket of snow covering the ground reminds us of
the words of the Prophet Isaiah, "Come now, and let us
reason together, saith the Lord: Though your sins be as
scarlet, they shall be as white as snow; though they be
red like crimson, they shall be as wool." (Isaiah 1, 18)

A sin-cursed world witnesses a sin-forgiving God. God's
gift of love, the Babe of Bethlehem, is the sacrifice for
man's sin, assuring of pardon before a righteous God.

Elementary school days must have been interesting for Ozzie—especially with his father as the Principal. Ozzie's father,
from what I have heard, was an especially dear, fair, and loving
man. Ozzie strove to do well, as the report cards I found showed.
How proud his father and mother and sisters must have been as
he left for high school.

There was no high school in Reinbeck, so O.H.'s parents sent
him to a preparatory school (Fort Wayne Concordia Preparatory
College) in Fort Wayne, Indiana.

Military training was provided with uniforms and all the strict
discipline that goes with a school of this type. The educational

standards were high, as they were preparing the young men for their seminary years.

He entered Concordia Theological Seminary at Springfield, Illinois after graduation with an excellent academic background. This seminary was one of two affiliated with the Lutheran Church-Missouri Synod.

I know about some of the behavior patterns set in these early high school years because of some incidents that occurred that had bearing on our life together.

One evening after returning home from our honeymoon, I entered the bathroom after he had taken a bath, to find him on his knees, bare as a babe. He was stringently wiping out the tub with a towel. As I expressed shocked pleasure, he explained, "I've done this ever since military school. We had to, and it became a habit."

Oh boy, my own private Mr Clean, I thought. *It should happen to every bride.* As I look back over every phase of this very special man's life, I see a pattern emerge of discipline in every area of life, the key to his ability to accomplish so much.

The seminary years were typical ones, I'm sure, difficult Greek language lessons and a regular schedule of theology classes. But they had their lighter moments too. Ozzie used to tell me many stories of those days that showed the seminary students were sometimes all too human.

One of those stories was how he and his fellow student and close friend, Ernie Laabs (who later married Ozzie's sister, Irma), had to flee the porch of their girlfriends one night when they lingered too long after a date, because of the appearance of one of the young ladies' father with a shotgun! Of course, as they looked back they realized it was intended as a joke, hinting at the lateness of the hour, but at the time they were terrified.

Other tales of boyish escapades included hitchhiking home, fun at boy-girl parties, typical dorm experiences and classroom shenanigans, proved that, contrary to public opinion, boys at seminaries behave, enjoy, suffer, study, and evolve just as other college students do.

Ozzie's vicarage was served in Sumner, Iowa, and after graduation and ordination in 1940, he accepted a call to Immanuel Lutheran Church in Bristol, Conn. His family wished so much for him to accept a call nearer the family in Iowa, but he had a wish to experience New England and really felt a divine pulling in that direction. In one of Ozzie's newspaper articles he wrote of this time:

From "Guided by Thee"
"Upon graduating from the seminary, I received an assignment more than one thousand miles from home. I also had the opportunity of serving my home parish, but declined it. Guided by the Lord, through prayer, I took the assignment in New England. It patterned my future life to serve the Lord in a capacity far beyond my expectations."

Along with serving individual parishes, Ozzie was also given the opportunity to use the communications media of radio, television, and the newspaper, for the first time. No wonder his decision to go East brought him great satisfaction as time went on. As Ozzie used to say, "It is always so when we say to the Lord, Thy will be done, and are truly willing to be guided."

He became the assistant to Pastor Bernard W. Janssen at Zion Lutheran Church, in Wallingford, Conn. from 1940–1944, and also taught in the church day school. Pastor Janssen was to become a great influence in Ozzie's life and ministry. He idolized him, and incorporated many of the Rev. Janssen's organizational ideas into his own future church work. Ozzie's businesslike ways of running this side of the church were always attributed by him to this man he so revered. He was an exemplary spiritual mentor to my husband.

He served as Pastor at Zion Church in Wallingford, Connecticut, from 1941–1946, and was also serving as Pastor to St. Paul's in Naugatuck, Connecticut from 1942 to 1955, delivering sermons and ministering to two flocks.

In 1945 he married Lorna Kern, daughter of Dr. and Mrs. Herbert Kern of Bristol, Conn., a lovely, high spirited girl he had met at a church-related function. It is difficult for me to write about a marriage of which I had no firsthand knowledge; but I do know this—my husband had nothing but praise for his first wife. The evidence of happy family photographs and entries in his journals of those early years bears this out.

His wife built her life around him, and in September 1947 they had a baby daughter, Lorna Lee. I'm sure that great love was

50

lavished on her, and as the years progressed all indications were of a super-happy threesome. So my husband knew all about a happy home environment. He knew from experience how to make a happy marriage, and to top it off, Christ really was at the center of *our* marriage and at the head of *our* marriage and at the head of *our* life together also.

How fortunate I was to reap the benefits of his experience with marital joy later on, as I became Reverend Bertram's second wife. His two years alone after a tragic car accident that deprived him of his wife of twenty-three years, was another factor in his intense appreciation of a good wife, which I'm proud to say, he thought I was.

In 1949, under what he strongly felt was God's directive, and after much "pounding the pavement," he became the person responsible for starting a new congregation and mission church in Madison, Connecticut. I can just see this tall young man with the attractive smile and charisma "tramping for the Lord" from one household to the next, canvasing for information as to the need for a church. I'm sure many an unsuspecting housewife and husband were charmed into the realization that they had spiritual needs, and if this young man had something to do with fulfilling those needs, they wanted to be part of it! And so a new church for the glory of God ensued.

During his time at the seminary, Ozzie had his first experience with the broadcasting media. He liked to tell how the class assignment of doing a real radio broadcast had affected him. "I felt a real surge of enthusiasm for this field and the thought of being able to reach so many people," he said. "As I finished my broadcast, I prayed that God would utilize me in this area."

His first attempt along the path toward what would eventually turn out to be a career in radio and television, began in 1941 on Radio Station WELI, New Haven, Connecticut. The program lasted until 1943. On September 28, 1946, Ozzie began to produce his own radio program, "Moments of Comfort," over WATR, Waterbury, Conn., through the kindness of the late Samuel Elman. From that date until May, 1979 not a single week passed without the rich voice of Pastor Bertram bringing the comfort of God's Word to his radio audience.

The television counterpart of "Moments of Comfort" began in

1952 on WNHC-TV, New Haven, Connecticut. In 1953 Ozzie suggested that the sign language for the deaf became a feature of the program. Through the ingenuity of the director, a type of split-screen was devised by taping one-half of the camera lens, and it is thought that this was the first use of the split-screen. This fact received an extensive writeup in television engineering publications.

While serving as pastor at Redeemer Lutheran Church in the Mayfair area of Philadelphia, Pennsylvania, from 1956 to 1964, Ozzie conducted television devotions for several stations. Special productions for national holidays and ecclesiastical holy days were done for WRCV-TV and WFIL-TV in Philadelphia. For several years the "Voice of America" and the powerful shortwave station HGJB, Quito, Ecuador, carried his message in both the English and German languages.

This information is necessarily brief, as I had no personal knowledge of these years except by hearsay. I do know, however, that these experiences in television work, plus the real success he had in reaching and touching peoples' hearts through these productions—which were born out of real life problems, trials, and triumphs,—served him well in polishing him as an effective speaker and producer in both radio and television. Many close friends were made in Connecticut and Philadelphia by the first Mrs. Bertram and Ozzie. After our marriage we visited these people, and they became dear to me also.

The move to Toledo, Ohio in 1964 to Good Shepherd, must have been a difficult one for the first Mrs. Bertram and her daughter, Lorna. The family lived in a lovely manse. Lorna was in the middle of her senior year in high school. They had made many friends for nine years, and it probably seemed hard to leave a familiar area that was also near relatives in Connecticut. But move they did, because Reverend Bertram felt a strong call from his Lord to go to this church that seemed to need him.

A beautiful church, contemporary in style of architecture, had been completed in 1958 in Toledo. The congregation numbered 120 or thereabouts, and needed to grow. And grow it did under the dynamic leadership, guidance, and physical efforts of personal visits by my husband; together with a great group of people who spread the word that a real live wire New England "preacher man" had come to Toledo. The congregation began to grow in number and enthusiasm, and also spiritually. In November 1967, a new educational wing was dedicated, which provided room for eleven classes.

In August 1974, ground was broken for an expansion program of the sanctuary and Fellowship Hall, and in 1975 the expanded facilities were dedicated to the glory of God. This building effort provided over 150 more seats in the sanctuary, a much enlarged Fellowship Hall, and expanded kitchen facilities. A little over a year later, the total debt of $125,000 had been paid. In 1974 the congregation had grown to 859 baptized and 627 confirmed members in the ten years Ozzie had been there.

In one of his messages Ozzie wrote:

> Dear Members:
> Perhaps the best words to express the spirit at Good Shepherd Lutheran Church are the Words of Christ, "By this shall all men know that you are my disciples, if you love one another." (John 13:35) Truly, a spirit of unity exists in our parish through the bond of Christian love and understanding. This is one of the powerful forces that draws members together, and draws new members into the congregation, the fold of Jesus Christ.
> Let us pray daily that all of our members will grow in their faith and knowledge of the Word and become steadfast and unmovable in the Christian faith they hold. Together we shall then receive the crown of glory in heaven, where we will need no pictured church directory, but will be able to say, "I remember you personally from our life together on earth."
> Yours on the upward trail in Christ,
> O. H. Bertram

All who ever received a letter from my husband will recognize this closure to his correspondence. It was his own special ending and is found at the end of every letter.

I guess it is obvious that the church was flourishing. I'm sure many new members were attracted to it by a thirty-minute television production, "A Worship for Shut-ins," begun in 1965 on WSPD-TV through the perceptive ability of its general manager at that time, Keith McKenney, to recognize a real talent plus a true "man of God." This was a formal church-type service taped at the station every two weeks. Two half-hour programs were produced at a time. The Reverend Earl Key of Luckey, Ohio, eventually served as my husband's regular liturgist. His faithful service was appreciated by audiences; and Ozzie especially loved this quiet, dependable man who gave so unstintingly of his time to help make the program the success it was.

In public, my husband was dignified in appearance and bearing. He always wore his clerical collar in public, unless we were on vacation. Somehow the black suit—and it was always the most elegantly cut and "up to the minute in style" he could buy—suited his tall, lean, and handsome looks. In the summer he wore white suits with the black rabat or vest. Striking!

Remember, he knew he was working for his Lord, and he was not above using every advantage to get across the idea that loving and serving Christ was an attractive profession.

He was the type of man who drew immediate attention when he walked into a room. Was it his height, or the beautiful smile and blue eyes that seemed to pierce your inner being? Was it his aura of sincerity, conviction, strength, dignity, dependability, intelligence, wrapped up in an attractive physical package that you sensed was real, here, now, and POW! I guess it's called charisma. Oh, he had it all right, and it wasn't just I, an understandably prejudiced wife, who felt it. Men loved, trusted, and looked up to him. And women had always found him attractive. Many people have told me, "The room came alive when Reverend Bertram walked in!"

As an example of O.H.'s belief that he should maintain a degree of dignity in his profession, I recall this incident.

I had noticed that our congregation always addressed my husband as "Pastor" or Reverend Bertram—contrary to the trend in some churches toward a more casual form of calling their minister "Pastor Bill" or just plain Bill. I soon found out that this formality was deliberately encouraged by my husband; as any attempt by members to "first name" him was met with a cold reception. He later told me that he had found through many years of observation and experience that to allow a first name (on the part of the pastor) relationship, seemed to hinder a respectful trust in the position of counselor, teacher, and especially his divine calling as a Christian minister or shepherd of a flock of God's people.

One evening at a vacation Bible school meeting in his study—it was early in our marriage—I wanted to contribute an idea. Not being able to catch his eye, and not wanting to raise my hand as a schoolchild would, I called out "Pastor Honey!" (Pastor would sound too formal a way to address a husband, and I knew that to call him Ozzie in front of the church would go over like the proverbial lead balloon. What came out was "Pastor, honey.")

This title remained with many when they thought of my husband and me together, and many times afterward I was lovingly teased with questions such as "How's Pastor Honey, Mrs. Bertram?" and "When are you and Pastor Honey going to the Holy Land?" Thus "Pastor Honey" became one of my several nicknames for my beloved husband, together with "P.B." (standing for Pastor Bertram) and of course, Ozzie, for Oswald Henry Bertram.

Searching for facts and incidents that occurred before I came into my husband's life occupied many hours in the writing of this book. I did a lot of article reading to glean anecdotes from Ozzie's life. It proved fascinating, and there were many enjoyable times in the preparation for the writing. What a delight to read all the old newspaper clippings I had found in a desk drawer. I learned things that my Pastor Honey had never thought to mention to me; for example, a sport page article from the Danbury News-Times informed me that my husband must have been a good basketball player in his younger days. It said, "The Reverend Oswald Bertram played a bang-up game. It was his fine off-the-backboard playing and good shooting that was largely responsible for keeping the Lutheran Big Five on even terms with the Sokol Energetics."

A picture of Ozzie with a team called "The Merry Morticians," organized after World War II, also told about the benefit basketball games played to help worthwhile causes. What fun to see a picture of my husband in skimpy basketball shorts, and a shirt with a big N for Naugatuck, Connecticut on it.

Later on in his career, one of Ozzie's big thrills was to be asked to be a guest speaker for the International Lutheran Hour on Sunday, July 31, 1977. This radio program has the distinction of utilizing the most radio stations of any program on the air throughout the world. It is heard in forty-six nations, with over 1,300 stations carrying the program in the United States and Canada.

It is wonderful to hear Ozzie's voice, as I do via a tape, speaking for the Lutheran Hour on the theme, "Conquering All." When I first listened to the tape after his death, I felt he was speaking to me personally, as he spoke on coping with the death of a loved one. At times when I listen to his taped sermons or speeches, remarks I never noticed before seem to be spoken to help me understand, cope with, and assuage my sorrow. How privileged I feel at being able to hear that loved voice again. I have included the complete Lutheran Hour talk in the Appendix, together with the prayers given before Congress, and a biographical outline of my husband's background, so that the "Bertramanians" (my word for the devout admirers of Ozzie's career) may savour each word and some facts of his life.

One of the greatest joys that came out of writing this book to honor not only my husband, but my Lord, Jesus Christ, was the two day visit in July of 1983 of Ozzie's ninety-one-year-old uncle, William Bertram, and his daughter, Gertrude Hoppe. They were traveling from Arlington Heights, Illinois to Detroit, Michigan to visit Uncle Bill's son Paul.

Vital, alert physically and mentally, still conducting choirs, bands, and services, Uncle Bill is himself a composer and the author of the book "Vibrant Health is Yours." In the letter he wrote to me after being my guest, I was thrilled to read:

But, of course, the climax and the high point of our entire visit was listening to your reading of your manuscript of your masterpiece, *Pastor Honey and Angel*. From it I now realize more than ever that Ozzie really was a great man, in man's eyes as well as in God's eyes; that he accomplished more in the Lord's Kingdom, in a brief life span than did other pastors in a life period twice that length. Thousands of people were reached and were touched effectively by his messages over the radio and the TV. His pastoral work with prisoners and their reaction to his counseling proves that there, too, the Lord has blessed his activities. His most dynamic sermon was his own personal Christian life as he lived it from day to day. Ozzie Bertram will long live in the hearts and memories of those that knew him well, members of his family, friends, and listeners to his many sermons and messages. Thank you again, my dear Sally, for those precious days in your company. I love you!

Affectionately,
Uncle Bill

I thank God that He has allowed me the privilege of recognition and approval from the senior member of the Bertram family. This meant so much to me in my efforts to write this book; especially as sought after help from the other members of Ozzie's family was never forthcoming. I feel now more than ever that God intended for me and me alone to write about Ozzie. He and the Holy Spirit He has sent—the Enabler, the Helper, have enabled me to accomplish a goal I could never have achieved on my own.

Ozzie was unique, and many recognized this fact. How I enjoyed being his "Angel," as he called me. How pleased he would be at my writing about him, not so much for himself, but for my accomplishing a goal.

9
Angel

"And Sarah said, God hath made me to laugh, so that all that hear will laugh with me."
Genesis 21:6 K.J.V.

"Oh wad some power the giftie gie us
To see oursels as others see us!"
Robert Burns

One of the current expressions says that in order to really know and understand someone, you must know where they are coming from. To trace a family tree is interesting only to the families involved. Some facts from the past are interesting parts of American history, and I will include these only to form a backdrop for the "before Ozzie" days of Sarah Breck Bertram.

One set of my grandparents were from the Alsace-Lorraine Provinces of that beautiful part of France that lies next to Germany. Great-grandfather was a burgermeister (mayor) of one of the towns there. Consequently, these grandparents spoke both

French and German. They met, married, and came to America. My father was one of their eight children, and was born in the tiny Ohio town of Loudenville where they eventually settled. It was a most handsome family. Pictures show all were tall and beautifully featured; I thought my father the handsomest man I'd ever seen. Religious freedom was one of the reasons the Breckiesen family came to America, and the religion they chose was Christian Science. My grandfather became a practitioner, one of the class-trained Christian Scientists whose work lies in helping others through prayer and the writings of Mary Baker Eddy. Most of his eight children were devout Christian Scientists all their lives. The whole family shortened their name to Breck during the First World War when anything that sounded German was considered to be less than an asset.

My mother's grandmother was a Huguenot whose family had left France in the early 1800s. As you know, a Huguenot was a French Protestant of Reformed or Calvinistic beliefs. She met one John Hamler of German and English descent and they were married. One of their three children was my grandmother, Sarah Hamler, for whom I was named.

Great-grandfather John Hamler moved to Ohio from the East and settled in a small German community near Lima, Ohio. He was a staunch Methodist, a very large and portly man, as his tintypes show. He became much beloved in the community for his good works and kindnesses. Any child without shoes had only to make this fact known to Great-grandfather Hamler, to be taken to the store for a pair, one of the family stories states. The town that grew was named for him, and even today his large portrait, which was given to the town by Grandmother Sarah, hangs in the town hall of Hamler, Ohio.

An amusing incident happened to me in 1976 when Hamler, Ohio was having its centennial celebration. I received a phone call from a lady with a lovely voice who said she was Mrs. William Bradford, the Hamler, Ohio historian. "Is it true," she said, "that you are the great-granddaughter of the founder of our town?" I said yes, and she invited me to come and be in their parade in July.

I was thrilled! She then said that if he wanted to, my husband would be welcome to ride with me in the special open touring car that they had obtained. This car was reputed to have been owned by Franklin Delano Roosevelt and used by him and Eleanor, his wife, in parades in the 1930s. The owner told us that Wallace Simpson, the Duchess of Windsor, had also sat where I would be sitting in the car.

The day came. I dressed in a long skirt, high-necked blouse and large hat in keeping with the 1800s theme. Ozzie and I were ensconced in the beautiful old car owned by a prominent doctor and loaned for the occasion. Off we were driven. The streets were lined with people three or four deep. *Oh*, I thought, *My moment has come. What a thrill!* They had a sign on the side of the car that said, "The Great-granddaughter of John Hamler, Founder of our Town, Sarah Bertram." In small letters at the bottom of the sign it said, "And the Reverend O. H. Bertram."

As we rode slowly past the crowds, I saw a group of women pointing at the car and talking with much animation. As we passed them, this is what I heard: "Oh, there's Reverend Bertram." Not so much as a glance toward the great-granddaughter. Such was my humbling but oh so funny experience of being in a parade. Ozzie could have teased me about it, but being the tender-hearted man he was, he never did.

Grandmother Sarah had a great influence on my life, and so a few lines about her seem pertinent. She was blessed with a beautiful singing voice, well-trained and of operatic quality. She sang at the Lakeside, Ohio, and New York music chatauquas, and also was much in demand for concerts in the East, and the Midwest. I still treasure her book of press clippings, reviews, and photographs in her concert gowns and operatic costumes. The fact that Sarah Hamler Ebersole taught me the stories of the opera when I was a child influenced my life even until this day. I greatly enjoyed opera and am active in the Toledo Opera Guild as an executive board member.

She lived to be 101. Though elderly and in a wheelchair from the effects of a broken hip that occurred in her 80s, she still was a very elegant lady. I can still hear her say, very dramatically, as she did once when I was visiting in her Lima, Ohio home, "Wheel me into the kitchen, please. I'm in the mood to bake a pie!" I'm sure her artistic talents of music, oil painting, drama, sewing, and cooking are responsible for the same tendencies I see in myself.

My mother, Yvonne, was the middle child of three. Her photos

59

show her to be an exceptionally lovely gay nineties beauty, well trained in music. The piano and pipe organ were her forte, to accompany Grandmother Sarah, of course. She also did some touring with a small concert group in the early 1900's. My older brother and I loved to hear her stories of being queen of the Amherst College prom one year, going places by horse and carriage, riding her own gelding, "Teddy," and of course, the part I liked best, descriptions of her ball gowns.

Even though pillars of the Methodist Church, (as I gather my grandparents were) Richard and Sarah Hamler Ebersole had an extremely social life in their community. Grandmother Sarah was the first person I knew who talked to me about Jesus Christ. I was brought up as a Christian Scientist in a devout Christian Scientist family, as my mother wholeheartedly took to this form of religion when she married my father. "Nano," as my brother Richard and I called our grandmother, sang nothing but beautiful hymns in her later days. I remember being impressed with her feeling for Jesus. She and my grandfather, Richard Ebersole, sang many a lovely duet describing a love of Christ that was new to me.

I was born in Omaha, Nebraska in the twenties, that decade of contrast between great affluence and great financial disaster. Mother and Father had first lived in New York, Atlanta, and then Boston before moving West to seek my father's fortune as the owner of the then elegant Walk-Over Shoe Stores in downtown Omaha, Nebraska.

My blue-eyed brother was born six years previous to my birth and was not, I'm sure, cognizant of what changes would occur in his life when this minute brown-eyed, honey blonde female entered it. I have been told that he wanted to have our parents take me back and "get another one that doesn't cry so much." I also know that from the moment I was old enough to really be aware of anyone besides parents, I idolized Richard. What a pain I must have been, toddling after him every chance I had. How thwarting to his freedom to have a four year old sticking to him like a burr when he wanted to play World War I soldier in the trenches he and his friends had dug in the empty lot next door to our lovely Spanish style bungalow on Mason Street.

But he was as patient with me as any eleven year old could be, and although he teased me as brothers do, our parents had instilled in us a love and appreciation for each other. What pride I had as he escorted me across the street near our school. In his white Sam Browne belt as a school guard, there was no one handsomer in my eyes.

My childhood memories are typically wrapped around my immediate family. My mother, beautiful, accomplished at the piano, socially active in Omaha events, always had time to play with me, read to me, and dress me in the latest fashions. One of my earliest memories is of hiding my pair of very chic tattersol checked galoshes in the bushes on the way to school and retrieving them after school. My excuse was that everyone else had red rubber ones. At that early age of six I had not yet learned the fashion joy of being different from the rest. Mother Yvonne's reaction was a mild scolding and a lecture on the value of these particular (high fashion for little girls) galoshes.

Other memories involve seeing her dressed in her sequined or beaded "Roaring Twenties" ball gowns for the AKSARBEN Ball (Nebraska spelled backwards) or Kiwanis Club dances. In my brother's and my opinion there was no movie star more beautiful, and her personality exuded the sweetness and loving charm of a real lady. She emphasized training in good manners and instilled a love for learning in both my brother and me.

My father was tall, dark, and handsome. He and my mother expressed not only a lot of love for each other, but for us, their two offspring. My father's name was Harry Thomas Breck, and I remember hearing my mother play a lot of "I'm Just Wild About Harry" among the other McDowell, Chopin, and current Broadway show music she loved. My middle name, Jeannine, was taken from a New York show that was called "Lilac Time," which featured a song titled "Jeannine, I Dream of Lilac Time."

The interest in Broadway show music was partially inspired by Mother's brother, my uncle Kent Ebersole. He possessed a beautiful tenor voice, and sang small parts in many musicals back in the early 1900s. He was the first one to sing "Sunbonnet Sue" in the George M. Cohan musical comedy of the same name.

Uncle was medium tall, handsome, a little plump, and I was going to marry him when I grew up. The mysteries of age difference and family marriage taboos were unknown to my six-year-old-heart. I just knew I loved my Uncle Kent. He was in "show biz," and I was properly impressed.

My mother's sister, Ida, who never married, visited us often. She was a pal to me all the days of her life—possessed of a wonderful sense of humor and a childlike manner until her dying days in her eighties. We giggled through the years together, and she taught me how to embroider. Her special talent was beautiful needlework of all kinds. To this day I use linens that she embroidered with B for my mother. What a lovely coincidence, the B for Breck and then Bertram.

The Omaha years held financial tragedy for my father. He lost the shoe stores. Not many were buying expensive shoes during the Depression—and being burdened with heavy ownership taxes, and some delinquent income taxes inherited from the former owner, my father was wiped out financially.

We moved to Evanston, Illinois, when I was six years old. The job offer to my father to manage Lord's shoe department took us to this lovely suburb of Chicago. I have many happy memories of those years; swimming in Lake Michigan, shopping in the Loop at the famous Marshall Field department store, entertaining every relative we had during the summer of the Chicago World's Fair, touring the Field Museum, the Shedd Aquarium, and attending sports events at Northwestern University in Evanston. How could I possibly forget my first movie—a Tarzan one, at the Valencia Theater, mostly seen through my fingers while clutching my big brother's arm in fright.

The loss of our lovely Omaha home saddened my mother immensely, but she had adopted my father's religion, Christian Science, and she chose to "rise above" this material loss. She seemed, as I now look back, to have conquered this loss by doubling her efforts of raising her two children in the positive, happy, and optimistic environment of a family who put their emphasis on love, church attendance, and gratitude to God for what we did have—health and a lot of love and togetherness.

I never remember seeing my mother or father ill. My brother and I never missed a day of school. Any childhood diseases were never named, and occurred during summer months. We were not vaccinated, nor were we ever given any type of medication. All problems were met with study in *Christian Science with Key to the Scriptures*, by Mary Baker Eddy, and prayers. I remember my first prayer, learned when I was three years old, and taught to

62

my own two little girls years later. It went, "Father-Mother-God; loving me. Guide my little feet up to Thee."

The optimistic "see no evil, hear no evil, speak no evil" qualities learned as a child by the example of my exceptionally loving and idealistic parents, are part of my personality today, I feel sure. The years in Sunday school and attending Wednesday evening church services gave me a wonderful basic study of the Bible, and it was not until years later that I gave up the study of Christian Science, when I experienced a very real feeling of something missing in my spiritual life.

Our family moved to Toledo, Ohio, just before my teen years. Both my parents had relatives in Ohio, and a new business opportunity opened up for my father at Lamson's Department Store. It was an exciting moment when Father announced we were moving to Toledo, right on Lake Erie. We imagined we would be living a few blocks away from the lake, as we did in Evanston, which is on Lake Michigan. We were surprised after our move, to find it to be entirely different from lovely Evanston.

My high school years at Scott High School in the old West End of Toledo are vivid in memory. It was during these years that I changed from the "big eyed, shy girl into today's Sally!" as my favorite teacher wrote in my yearbook. I blossomed from shy and skinny, to popular and pretty. No one had as many wonderful dates as I during my junior and senior years in high school. I managed to be in the top third of the class while being extremely active socially. I was elected secretary of my senior class, and this together with other club activities, and always the wonderful dating weekends of dances, parties, movies, and club activities, filled my life.

Only the event of World War II marred my active years at the University of Toledo. But even with the lack of football, other sports, and the young men connected with a normal college life, I managed to have a great four years acquiring my Bachelor of Arts Degree. I majored in English literature.

Being elected Vice-president of my freshman class started me on a four-year stint of activities that made college life very rewarding for me. I was on Student Council for three years. I held a long list of offices in many organizations, was involved with numerous committees, was "tapped" for the women's honorary society, Peppers, (later to become national Mortar Board) which

63

was comprised of only thirteen women at any one time. All this plus continued scholarship ability helped me to win the "Gold Medal Activities Award" at graduation.

I did not join a sorority until I was a junior at the University of Toledo, choosing to be an "independent" until that time. When I joined the national Pi Beta Phi, I became acquainted with the joys of sorority life. Becoming the group's scholarship chairman was an experience in speaking and interacting with a group that was invaluable in later years.

I met the father of my two, beautiful-in-every-way daughters at the University. He was handsome, older than I by seven years, previously married, and the captain of the T.U. basketball team. Men were scarce during these war years, and I was overwhelmed by the determined wooing of this handsome and talented man.

I married the September after my June graduation from the University, against the wishes of my parents and friends, who felt the influence of this older, sophisticated charmer was not right for me. The artistic and creative talents in the field of architecture of the man who was to become the father of my daughters, was the source of a great deal of pride. Many buildings and homes in Toledo today were designed by, or supervised in construction by this man, now deceased.

A beautifully planned home in the Frank Lloyd Wright style was designed just for me, and I lived in it for seven years. Counters were higher, (I'm five feet seven inches tall) and claristory windows on four sides of the living area, fourteen glass doors that opened out a large terrace, a cantilevered fireplace, a seven-foot sky light in the kitchen area, interiors of cypress and natural brick, radiant heating, and many built-in furnishings, were features of this special home designed by my husband.

Being a disciple of the great architect, Frank Lloyd Wright, my husband and I and our daughters were invited to visit the F.L.W. fellowship in Spring Green, Wisconsin, one year. All of us spent an interesting week involved with the group there. It was an unforgettable experience, culminating with a private discussion with Mrs. Frank Lloyd Wright.

The humanistic philosophy promoted there, plus the experience of an almost communal type of living gave me an experience with which to contrast my later spiritual and Christ-centered life.

When Leslie Diane and Sally Yvonne, four years apart in age, were old enough to be in school all day, I returned to Toledo University to obtain a teaching degree. My practice teaching was done at Ottawa Hills Elementary School, and I decided to accept a position as a first grade teacher at Monac Elementary School in the Washington Local School district in Toledo. I taught there twelve and one-half years, again becoming very active in the teaching association and a member or chairman of many committees to further the cause of the education of children, my primary interest during these years.

Instead of telling you that I was intrigued, wrapped up in, and fulfilled by my teaching career, I want to include this letter that I had written to the Superintendent of the Washington Local School System in Toledo, Mr. Homer Nightingale.

Mr. Nightingale reprinted it in a special newsletter, "From the Superintendent's Desk," and it went out to the more than 500 teachers in the school system.

My youngest daughter Sally, then in a high school in the system, had the paper with this comment written by her English teacher, placed on her desk the day after the paper came out.

"Sally, this letter of your mother's is a tremendous example of expression and good writing! And I'm convinced that you, her daughter, have the same ability. Work hard to meet the challenge of your potential! (signed) J. Rice."

"Dear Colleague:

"The following is a report submitted by Mrs. Sally _____, first grade teacher at our Monac Elementary School, upon attending the Ohio Education Association's Annual Conference on Instruction:

"My first attendance at an O.E.A. conference, the Fourteenth Annual Conference on Instruction, to be exact, was an exciting and truly inspiring occurrence in that part of my life dedicated to education.

"Although Akron, Ohio, and the Sheraton Hotel put on the best facade they could, it was not the physical aspect of this city or hotel that created the excitement I felt as my four colleagues and I arrived at the conference, which started one Thursday morning, last November.

"Just what made this such a worthwhile adventure for

me? I've since questioned myself. Was it the speeches by men and women who, by intellect and experience, were my superiors in the field of education? Was it the fact that I gained all kinds of little 'goodies' (six pages of notes) in the way of actual usable classroom ideas, via the school visitation on Friday, where I saw a primary reading clinic in action, a science class enthralled under an outstanding teacher, and reading groups in progress? Was it the new focus on actual learning that was the theme of this conference, that encouraged me to believe that educators all over *are* working on the one angle of teaching that most interests me personally—that of actual classroom instruction?

"Was it the hearing, in one of the special assemblies headed by the administrative assistant of the Cleveland City Schools, James Tanner, that 'traditional approaches' aren't working anymore in the classroom—and that when we speak of the unmotivated student, we should really say 'de-motivated' because somewhere along the way in his school career, this is what happened to him—usually by one or more of us, his teachers? Was it hearing statements like 'Schools should be *human-centered* rather than *lesson-centered*, made by Professor Evelyn Davidson, from Kent State University; and 'Let's stimulate rather than dominate' and 'New modifications (buildings mediae, techniques, textbooks) are not the answer to better teaching—it lies in each teacher's approach,' as said by Dr. Donald Emery, Superintendent of the Scarsdale, New York Schools? Was it the fact that the very good luncheons, dinners and the hotel bill were being paid for by my own Washington Local Association that made this a memorable event? Or was it just the small things—such as learning to say 'Read in big eyefuls', from a new friend and fellow first grade teacher met at the conference?

"I'll never be able to pinpoint it to one reason. I only know that if you ever have the chance to experience a marvelously well-organized conference such as this one was, you, too, will be impressed, as I was, with the feeling that permeates the very air—a pride in your profession, and a conviction that forces are at work, bettering,

66

searching, and aiming at the truth, in the furthering of education for us as teachers, and for the children of America, our primary concern."

H.S.N.

Ozzie told me after we were married that he had mentioned me to Mr. Nightingale on the occasion of their meeting one day before our engagement. According to my husband, Mr. Nightingale had said that not only was I an outstanding teacher, but had an above-reproach reputation in the community and was much beloved. I was thrilled at these kind words.

The career of teaching was extremely rewarding to me, culminating in the "Outstanding Teacher of the Year" award in 1970, chosen from over 500 teachers. I had thrown myself wholeheartedly into the joy of teaching, and it made up somehow for the problems I was having in my personal life. Through being awarded this honor, I was invited into and became a member of the National Educational Honorary Society, Delta Kappa Gamma.

Little did I ever dream that "the twain shall meet." The Lutheran, Missouri Synod Pastor, and the woman with a Christian Science background must assuredly be an unlikely combination for a successful romance and marriage. And yet my Pastor Honey thought of and called me his ministering "Angel." "Are they not all ministering spirits sent forth to serve, for the sake of those who are to obtain salvation?" (Hebrews 1:14) he used to quote. I am so proud God chose me to minister to the lonely widower and become his beloved wife. There are messenger angels, there are guardian angels, there are serving angels. I see myself now as a rejoicing angel, applauding God not only for the salvation he accomplished through Christ, but for the beautiful life I had as Ozzie's "Angel."

10
The Television and Radio Ministry

"Work is love made visible. And if you cannot work with love, but only distaste, it is better that you should leave your work and sit at the gate of the temple and take alms of those who work with joy."
Kahlil Gibran
The Prophet

"The finest eloquence is that which gets things done; the worst is that which delays them."
David Lloyd-George

One of the traits I seem to have and am not proud of, is putting off things until tomorrow that I should do today. As I begin my writing this morning, I feel thoughts sift down within me as did the sand in the egg timer I used as I fixed breakfast this morning. Perhaps I should get those two letters written before I work on the book. Oh, I must call Mrs. DeWallace at Hudson's about that modeling stint tomorrow. Heavens! There is another moth flying around; where are they coming from? I'll look in that drawer with my sweaters right now. Maybe I should work on filing these anecdotes and other snatches of writing today. On and on my thoughts go, keeping me from the task of writing.

As I flip through the file of "Thoughts For Today," the thirty-second "spots" that Ozzie called his spiritual commercials and had televised two at a time for the stations that carried his television "Worship for Shut-Ins" one-half hour program, my eye lands on one titled "Procrastination" taped May 7, 1978. I can see him now standing in front of the then call lettered WSPD television cameras, with a lovely New England fall scene chromokeyed behind him. This is the TV process whereby his image was superimposed over a picture or a slide.

Speaking quickly in that deep cultured voice of his, he said, "One of humanity's greatest failings is to put off living by dreaming of some magical rose garden just over the horizon instead of cultivating now the roses that can bloom outside our window today. The only way to obtain the fullness of each day is to place our trust in God and let Him guide our lives, saying with confidence, 'This is the day which the Lord hath made; we will rejoice and be glad in it' " (Psalm 118:24).

You are speaking to me through your written word again, Pastor Honey, I think. I am reminded of where I must place my priorities, and prayer comes first. I get down on my knees by the side of the bed where Ozzie prayed every night of his life. I ask for God's guidance as I begin to write of Ozzie's television work.

The TV taping sessions that occurred every other Friday evening were the source of great delight and relaxation for Ozzie. He made them almost festive occasions for me and others connected with the taping. Sometimes we would have dinner in downtown Toledo, at the Golden Lily—Chinese food was one of his favorites—or at the Commodore Perry Hotel's Captain's Table Restaurant. On occasion we would have as our guests, Ozzie's liturgist, the Reverend Earl Key of Luckey, Ohio, and his dear wife, Donna. Sometimes the soloist for the taping was invited to dine with us, or guests who had asked to see how the program was taped.

Sometime Ozzie would stop and pick up the doughnuts or an ice cream pie to share with the men and women who were working the cameras that evening, the floor director and the men in the recording room. Even the news anchormen who were good friends were included in the treat time.

I'm giggling to myself as I remember one such occasion when Ozzie stopped at a drugstore to pick up some small napkins to go with the ice cream for the TV studio people. As I served Gordon Ward, WSPD Toledo's popular anchor newsman, he looked up at me and said, "Sally, are you and Pastor trying to tell us something?" He held up the small napkin that Ozzie had purchased hastily, liking the springlike colors. On it was a design of a blue baby carriage on a deep lavender-pink background. We had been married less than a year, still bride and groom, and the whole studio was cracking up at the thought of what this middle-aged couple so obviously in love was perhaps trying to tell them. We hastily explained that we were not expecting. Years later, on occasions, we were still teased about our "baby" napkins. I've often wondered if this was an accidental occurrence, or a deliberate expression of my husband's sense of humor to tease me. I must ask Ozzie about that when we are together again.

Ozzie's flair for television work, plus his natural poise and beautiful voice, made him a professional in the eyes of the studio. A timed resumé of the evening's television was always in the hands of the director, with appropriate notes for the special slides to be used that evening, together with the actual script.

Danny Kasprzak, who worked at WSPD-TV, Toledo, Ohio, tells how he used to tease Pastor before the televised taping of the "Religion In The News" segment that Ozzie used to do before the formal worship service was to be taped. He would say jokingly, "Remember Pastor, if the Catholics aren't mentioned in the first three minutes of your news, I'll cut you off the air." Ozzie enjoyed the comraderie of the television and radio men and women he worked with almost as much as he enjoyed the opportunity to proclaim the Gospel each week.

He was always especially fond of and grateful to Keith McKenney and Buddy Ray, the general managers of WSPD-TV Storer Broadcasting Company, for their kindness in allowing him the facilities to tape his broadcast each week on a regular basis, as one of their public service programs.

Although he loved to joke with the camera people and the floor director between "takes," the moment he was signaled "on," he was all business. This was his life, his work, his joy, his chance to tell thousands of the hope and salvation in Jesus Christ. And the love of the work showed in the finished production. Thousands of letters came in throughout the years from viewers who were grateful for the special sincerity and meaning that Ozzie projected. People wrote and confided in him as they would in their own private minister. They told him their troubles, sometimes in detail, confident that here was a man who would understand. "There is just something about you, Reverend Bertram, that makes me know you are a real Man of God," was echoed over and over again in letters from many different states. Oh people of the television audiences, if you felt this over the television and radio waves, you should have experienced Ozzie in the flesh! The hundreds of people who had known the man called O.H. Bertram over the years felt it; and they honored and loved him. "There was just something about the man," as stated the death-row prisoner in a letter to his sister that I have included in this book.

It was so obvious that here was one of those rare breeds: a truly strong, dedicated man, living the life Christ wanted us all to live; a real live-wire type minister and a man one could look up to

70

and have confidence in. Not your meek, mild, ineffectual pastor stereotyped in television and movies today. I think of the Casper Milquetoast type priest portrayed in the television show M.A.S.H., Father Mulcahey. He is charming and intelligent, your heart goes out to him, but he is hardly the strong leader type you'd want to emulate or seek counsel from. Think of the movies you've seen. Ministers are shown briefly at a wedding or funeral service, intoning in what Ozzie used to call "pulpit tones," pious-sounding clichés. They are invariably either mousey or unmemorable looking, or white-haired and pompously forgettable.

This always annoyed me. I don't know Ozzie's thoughts on these stereotyped portrayals. We never discussed it. Somehow I suspect he would never have expressed an opinion on this subject, as it would have been an implied criticism—something he never liked to do. He never scolded satirically or naggingly, and one instinctively knew any necessary reprimands would be made in the most lovingly, subtle, and constructive way possible. As far as discipline in his confirmation classes with children, usually a look or brief comment in a stern but kindly voice was all that was necessary. Such was the respect commanded by the bearing and personality of the man. He was loved not only by those adults who knew him, but also by the children. Men were especially drawn to his forceful, manly approach to life. It goes without saying that women were drawn to him for many reasons. He was handsome in his own distinguished-looking, tall, slim way. But it was that inner beauty that shone out and attracted.

One member of our congregation, Bob Liest, told me how he felt the first time he came to church. Pastor and I stood at the door after the service greeting people as they left, as was our practice. It was this gentleman's first experience with the famous O.H. smile and firm handshake. The man said, "I felt a thrill go up my spine, as if I were hearing the Star Spangled Banner played, as Pastor grasped my hand strongly and looked directly into my eyes and smiled his greeting to me."

This strong, manly magnetism, together with the beautiful message of salvation, based on a firm belief in Christ was, I'm convinced, why people were always drawn to Ozzie. Not only did he have something to say that people seemed to be longing to hear, but he had the God given ability to say it strongly, beautifully, and with Bible-based convictions that could be felt over the

71

airwaves. This, I feel, was the reason his television and radio programs were so well received.

In the spring of 1979, thirteen television stations and nine radio stations were carrying Ozzie's programs from Vermont to California; and the prospect of adding two new television stations was imminent. Ozzie was thrilled at the success and the prospect of the task he felt the Lord was calling him to do. Every trip we took, either for vacation, pleasure or for speaking engagements, always included a trip to the local TV station to see if Ozzie could interest them in using his program. Whenever a station was added and he would be congratulated, he would always say, "Yes, thanks, by the grace of God they took the program."

As I look through the file folder on the various TV stations' area coverage maps, it dawns on me just how many hundred thousands must have been exposed to "A Worship for Shut-ins" program. It was no wonder so many sympathy cards arrived after Ozzie's death. There were piles of loving notes and letters telling me how much the television program meant to the writer; how much the people were missing him! One letter from Connecticut asked if I had any of Ozzie's writings, as the person wanted so much to hear more of his spiritual encouragement.

It is for the many who loved the Reverend Bertram through his radio and TV work and considered him to be their pastor, that I write this book. I feel they would like to know more about the man they had grown to love. It was their support and prayers that kept my husband's programs on the air waves.

At the time his illness began, he was negotiating with KCIK-TV, Channel 14 in El Paso (Sun City), Texas. El Paso is the fourth largest city in Texas with its coverage extending into New Mexico and Mexico. KCIK claimed a viewing audience of over 1,200,000 people. I knew and Pastor hoped that a nice percentage would become new devotees of his special worship for shut-in messages.

I'll never forget the pleasure my husband and I derived from the welcomes extended to us on our public relations calls to the various television stations. "Welcome Reverend and Mrs. Bertram" on a menu board in the lobby of a Milwaukee station gave us a thrill. The courtesy shown at lunches for us with station managers showed clearly their high regard for Ozzie and his television program.

11
The Clergyman's Corner

"Every man's work shall be made manifest."
I Corinthians 3:13

It is hard to choose a representative sampling of "The Clergyman's Corner" articles that appeared in nine different newspapers every week. One has almost 500 to choose from. Each article was pertinent to the times, simply written and to the point, and was meant to edify, comfort, or give encouragement to its reader. Each takes three to five minutes to read, and always included quotes from God's Word, the Bible.

Many, many people have told me how they had cut out the articles each week and saved them to re-read. Ozzie intended to publish a collection of the articles some day. Perhaps it will yet be, for so many loved these weekly writings. I can never forget the woman who wrote me after Ozzie's death, asking if I had any extra articles to send her, as she "longed to hear him speak to her, even if it was through his writings."

On every trip we took, Pastor Honey had his eyes opened for every town's newspaper office we might chance to see. He kept an envelope of his "Clergyman's Corner" articles, which we had cut out of many different town's newspapers, in the glove compartment of the car.

I can see him now, pulling up in front of the Podunk Daily News office in some town we were passing through on our travels, slinging his long legs out of the car and striding in to charm the local editor into taking his articles on a weekly basis. He never asked for, nor did he ever receive any payment for these writings, choosing to think of them as another way to proclaim God's truths to as many as possible.

An incident happened one January when we were in Del Ray Beach, Florida, after my husband's very busy Advent and Christmas season church duties were accomplished. A dear friend, Alvin Walker invited us to stay at his condominium for a few days of rest. Ozzie always threw his whole being into everything he did pertaining to his beloved Lutheran Church work, and this season had proved to be extra tiring.

We went to a lovely cafeteria where the choices of food were dazzling to these two Northern food appreciators. As we traveled down the line, one of the ladies behind the counter spoke to my husband. "I know you," she said, "You're that Reverend Bertram who writes the articles my sister in Toledo cuts out of the paper and sends to me!" She recognized him from the tiny newspaper picture that was always printed with the column. I'm sure she will never know how she delighted Ozzie by not only recognizing him, but by her expressed gratitude for the help she obtained by reading the articles her sister sent to her.

The syndicated meditations that had appeared on a weekly basis for over fifteen years in various towns across the country, had some interesting reactions. One reader who wrote to the Toledo Herald, told them she clipped the columns and sent them to her sister who is a missionary in Honduras, Central America, who in turn translated them and mimeographed them for general distribution.

The Herald wrote, "Industries and colleges use them in their publications in order to encourage better relations between management and labor. Church periodicals use some of the meditations to share with their parishioners."

I have chosen excerpts from some of my favorite columns. As you will see, the Reverend O. H. Bertram wrote on many subjects applicable to people's lives. I think it will be most interesting to my husband's many fans among his TV and radio audiences, and devotees of his written articles, to see how Ozzie utilized his travel experiences. The following are some excerpts from "The Clergyman's Corner" articles.

On attending a meeting of the National Lutheran Church–Missouri Synod Board of Evangelism, Ozzie wrote:

"While flying from Chicago to St. Louis recently, I sat beside a young man who was reading the book, *Life After Death*. In the fifties, we passed through a period of many books written and much being said about 'peace of mind'. In the sixties, the main topic of many writers was the family circle and how to have a happy marriage. In the seventies, we are passing through a period in which many authors are emphasizing life after death and similar topics. This is a topic with which we cannot toy or speculate, because the Gallup Poll will never go wrong by saying that every one out of one people will die, and there is no second chance for an earthly life after this death. One cannot speculate, for there is no such thing as reincarnation.

"Let us seek an authority on the subject of life after death. Christ, by His own Godly power, raised His physical body from the grave. He predicted that He would raise Himself from the dead in final payment for man's sins and reconcile us to the Holy God. He gave us the assurance, 'I am the resurrection and the life. Whoever believes in me will live, even though he dies; and whoever lives and believes in me will never die. Do you believe this?' (John 11:25,26). He gives the promise, 'I go to prepare a place for you' " (John 14:2).

Lincoln country in Illinois, Gettysburg, the Pennsylvania Dutch area, Valley Forge, and Philadelphia, PA, historical sights were favorite places for Ozzie and me to visit. Upon our return from one such trip, Ozzie included this in one of his weekly articles.

"On the battlefield of Gettysburg, Pennsylvania, where more than 51,000 Americans lost their lives during the Civil War in the three-day battle of July 1, 2, and 3 in 1863, stands the Peace Light. Upon its pedestal are inscribed the words, 'Peace, eternal in a nation united.' Thank God that a peace does exist between the states of our nation, but the phrase 'Peace, eternal' can only hold true of the peace with God through Jesus Christ, which alone establishes peace among men. In writing to the Ephesians, St. Paul says, 'Let all bitterness, and wrath, and anger, and clamor, and evil speaking, be put away from you, with all malice: And be ye kind to one another, tender hearted, forgiving one another, even as God for Christ's sake hath forgiven you' " (Ephesians 4:31,32).

When we returned from a trip to Atlantic City where we took Ozzie's daughter, Lorna, and my oldest daughter, Leslie, both unmarried at the time, for a vacation, Ozzie wrote:

"Stand at the seashore or on a mountain top, and in studying the vastness of God's creation you will ask yourself, 'Who am I in all this greatness?' To our fellow man, we are very insignificant. If we were to die, how many people would even identify us by name and consider our death any more than just another name in the obituary column?

"To God, you and I are everything through Jesus Christ. Christ's death on the cross makes us VIPs. His birth, death, and resurrection have paid the ransom for rescuing us from the jaws of hell and opened unto us the gates of heaven. 'Christ bore our sins in his own body on the tree, that we, being dead to sins, should live unto righteousness: By whose stripes ye were healed' " (1 Peter 2:24).

Washington, D.C. inspired him to write:
"When I visit Washington, D.C., I enjoy arising early to walk around and view the spectacular scenes of that city. Under the shadow of the Capitol dome, one feels a spirit of exhilaration, of pride in being an American. This is truly the greatest country in the world, endowed by God with untold blessings, among them many excellent leaders.

"I have been privileged to attend several national prayer breakfasts in Washington."

A brief vacation in New York after the busy and tiring time for a clergyman's church work connected with Christmas brought forth this observation:

"In visiting Radio City Music Hall with the express purpose of seeing the Christmas pageant, one is also given the benefit of a motion picture. Recently I viewed a picture in which God's name was profaned repeatedly, and suggestive remarks were made. What a contrast it was to the Christmas pageant that glorified Christ as the gift to the world and the Savior of humanity. From the same stage there sounded forth the irreverence and the reverence of Christ. It is humanly illogical to demonstrate the dual standards we have in America. In one way, we say as Americans, 'God, we don't need you', and in the other, 'In God we trust.'

"The Bible says, 'Blessed is the nation whose God is the Lord; and the people whom He hath chosen for His own inheritance' (Psalm 33:12). The citizens of the nations that have worshipped God and sought His guidance have always profited, even as it has been in America since her founding. Today a different spirit takes hold of the majority of citizens. We are a lustful and corrupted nation because we seek not God, but gold, not Christ, but cash.' "

One of the places that was Ozzie's favorite to visit was Holy Hill in Wisconsin. It seems as though he wanted me to experience all his favorite sights; and I was always ready and willing to go. This is part of what he wrote when we returned:

"While standing on Holy Hill, a Roman Catholic shrine near West Bend, Wisconsin, one observes the panorama of God's beauty stretching out before one for many miles. One cannot help but reflect on the turmoil of life in the affairs of nations, homes, and the lives of individuals, and by contrast, see how the peace that God projects in nature could be easily applied in our lives if we would submit to the will of God. While standing at the entrance to the majestic church built on a high hill, your eyes look heavenward and follow the towers to their peaks on which are mounted two golden crosses. One reacts automatically to the words of the author, John Bowring, 'In the cross of Christ I glory, towering o'er the wrecks of time.' Standing there on Holy Hill, you hesitate to come down to the reality of the hustle and bustle of life and the confusion that our every day activities involve."

Another favorite spot Ozzie took me to is mentioned in another article:

"One of our favorite spots of historical interest is the home of George Washington at Mt. Vernon, Virginia. Walking down the footpath toward the Potomac River, one stands before the tomb of the 'Father of our Country.' His testimony of Christian faith is found on the plaque that reads, 'I am the Resurrection and the Life. He that believeth in Me, though he were dead, yet shall he live' (John 11:25). George Washington had made his statement

77

of faith in Jesus Christ as his personal Savior repeatedly from boyhood until the day of his death."

Another year, Ozzie wrote about our trip to Nova Scotia:

"While driving through Nova Scotia, my wife and I saw a beautiful white church in a village with a slender steeple. It was in contrast to the many dark blue pines in the area. That steeple was symbolic of the direction that the Church's message directs the individual, but what made it even more significant was a hand with a pointed finger heavenward. Could anyone misinterpret this symbol? The crucial moment in the life of each and every person is today. Guilty of sin as we all are, Jesus urges us to repent. Today He offers pardon for our sin, peace with God, and victory over death and hell. To accept His offer and acclaim Him as our Lord and Savior is to become acceptable in God's sight. Then we are numbered in the company of saints for whom the promise holds, 'I will come again and receive you unto Myself, that where I am, there ye may be also.' His reentry, then, will be a day of boundless joy, for which we wait expectantly."

Ozzie loved our travels to New England, especially loving to drive through Vermont. The obtaining of the Burlington, Vermont television outlet was a source of great joy for him, and it gave him a good reason to travel once a year to this city for a few days' vacation, besides the good public relations he wanted to keep with the station officials. He wrote this paragraph on one such trip:

"As you wend your way through the mountains of Vermont, you come to a setting overlooking a village. The traditional freshly painted white homes and buildings in the village are a beauty to behold, surrounded by the green foliage. The eyes of the traveler are suddenly directed to a church spire on the top of which is not the traditional cross or rooster, but a carved hand with a finger pointing heavenward. This dominates the entire setting of the village. How typical this is of our lives, since

78

it directs us to the source of strengthening help and reminds us of preparing for the life to come. We must be directed heavenward in order that we might understand God's motives in our lives."

Another time in a Clergyman's Corner he said, "My wife and I had a favorite place in Vermont called 'Hog Back Mountain,' where a person can stand on a clear day and see the panorama of God's beauty for 100 miles. While you sit in a fine restaurant on the mountain top and eat Indian pudding, you have the closest concept of God's presence. While breathing in the pine-scented air, you exclaim, 'This is the next thing to heaven. You feel the spirit of God in His created beauty.' "

Ozzie seemed to want to experience the places that had been inspirational to others. He wrote, "Standing on the entrenchments of Fort McHenry in Baltimore, Maryland, one is reminded of the expectation and consternation confronting Frances Scott Key on the night he was held prisoner in a British ship while Fort McHenry was being bombarded by the British . . . In our lives we have many such moments and days of waiting, wondering what the outcome of our present problems will be, or what the purpose of this trial may be. Directing our thinking to a power that overcomes our problems and fears, the Apostle Paul writes to the young preacher Timothy, 'For God hath not given us the spirit of fear, but of power, and of love, and of a sound mind' " (2 Timothy 1:7).

Twice Ozzie took me to Bardstown, Kentucky. The countryside was beautiful, and it was lovely touring the home that was Stephen Foster's inspiration for the song, "My Old Kentucky Home." Ozzie wrote this for an article he called "Reborn Free":

"In Bardstown, Kentucky, on the courthouse circle there is a flat stone inscribed with the words 'slave block.' Before the Emancipation Proclamation, slaves were auctioned off to the highest bidder on the spot. I have stood there several times, and could not help but reflect upon the course of human lives that were changed at this spot. Either they would be sold to a lenient and kind master or a harsh and cruel taskmaster. Yet, there was one declaration that made this slave block obsolete; it was the signing of the Emancipation Proclamation by Abraham Lincoln on January 1, 1863. To enforce this proclamation took the shedding of much blood on the battlefields of the Civil War. The freedom of the slaves was purchased at the cost of human life.

"How similar our lives are in relationship to God. By nature we are born into sin, slaves of Satan, and enemies of God. Although God could have declared the human race free from such slavery, it cost the life of One who died on the cross, namely Jesus Christ. Although the individual may think that he will prescribe his own form of righteousness, he is subject to God's judgment, 'There is none righteous, no, not one; There is none that understandeth, there is none that seeketh after God. They are all gone out of the way, they are together become unprofitable; There is none that doeth good, no, not one' (Romans 3:10-12). Man, by his own ingenuity, wisdom, or planning, cannot escape the punishment of his sin and is destined for hell, since he is under the curse of God.

"Because God is love, He offers to every human being an escape from His wrath.

"We may remain in our slavery of sin and chains of Satan, but we may also have the burden of every sin lifted and the assurance of eternal life in heaven through rebirth in Christ. What is your choice?"

One time while driving through New England, Ozzie saw a billboard, which from a distance read, "God Bless Me". When he drove closer, he saw the period after the phrase. It was meant to read, "God Bless Maine." The personal pronoun had become an abbreviation. This experience became the basis for a Clergyman's Corner column called, "Rejected or Accepted." Its theme centered on the idea that people are inclined to think of themselves instead of others, seeking their own good and blessings and forgetting their fellowman. Again, a simple billboard had given him an idea to expand and proclaim the Word of God.

In another Clergyman's Corner article, Ozzie mentions Williamsburg, Virginia. We traveled there almost every April after

his busy Easter season was completed. I grew to love this recon-
structed Revolutionary War era town not only for the pleasures
it afforded at the time, but for the wealth of golden memories it
still brings forth.

In "What Can We Expect From God?" Ozzie said, "The
health of our nation depends upon the health of the individual citizen. The Bible was the guide in establishing
our nation. Go to Williamsburg, Virginia where the eighteenth century capitol building of the Old Dominion has
been restored. On the counsel table in the assembly room
lies the Bible, which was consulted frequently by our forefathers as they drew up their documents. Clergymen
came in regularly to pray for divine guidance. Although
the U.S. Congress begins each session with prayer, and
currency still bears the motto, 'In God We Trust,' our
spiritual faith is slipping. The time has come for our trust
in Jesus Christ as the ruler of man's affairs to be publicly
confessed. If we truly want security in our nation, we
must first find it as individuals in the pardon that Christ
offers us for our sins and the security that He gives us
through His promises."

I was always impressed at my husband's ability to see connec-
tions to God's teachings in our travel experiences. It was his gift
of verbalizing and writing so that others could see a practical
application of Bible truths to their own lives that made him so
"down to earth," and consequently understood by his many readers and listeners. This, together with his inordinate sympathy
for his fellow humans, his supreme kindness, wrapped up in the
attractive package God made him come in, were, I feel, the reasons for his successes in reaching people's hearts.

There were many references to our European, Greece and Holy
Land trips in the Clergyman's Corner articles. Here are a few.

"While writing this meditation I am lying on a bed in
the Swiss Alps and am looking up to lofty mountain peaks
covered with snow. God has put these majestic mountains
here to make us have a two-fold reaction: first, one feels
very insignificant in God's creation, and second, to realize

that the Creator of these immense stone mountains has promised to care for us. I gazed upon this phenomenon of creation and was reminded of Psalm 121, which reads, 'I will lift mine eyes unto the hills, from whence cometh my help.' "

"While traveling through the Alps of Switzerland last summer, I could not help but be reminded of this Psalm as the jagged mountains pointed heavenward like a directional arrow to the source of their creation from whence our help comes. Life is much like traveling through the valley, surrounded by high mountains. Our vision is always upward. They serve as road markers for our lives, directing us to God, our refuge and strength."

"How strong is America? This question was asked of me by the secretary of a West German bishop a few weeks ago in Hanover, Germany. He had just returned from a visit to churches in East Germany. He showed slides of crumbling church buildings and told of the physical and material hardships of pastors and their people. No repairs can be made with local materials or state money spent on repairs. The war on the Church continues by atheistic Communism. Seeing this struggle and enslavement of the Church in East Germany, with the Iron Curtain between them, the clergyman was looking for the assurance of their American allies that they were physically strong enough to meet this cruel and satanic enemy.

How strong is America? This question must be answered by every American on the basis of his relationship to God."

"Standing in the crumbling ruins of the great stadium in Nuremberg, Germany last July, I could visualize the thousands upon thousands of Germans raising their arms in salute to Adolph Hitler as he entered the arena. The echo of the 'Sieg, Heil!' (Victory, hail) still seems to ring through the vastness of the space now in disarray and a witness of past glory.

"The hopes of a good economy and employment rested upon one man, the 'Fuhrer.' How disappointing when millions saw their hopes shattered through the bombings of allied airplanes and then the suicide of Adolph Hitler.

"How different are we from these disappointed Germans? We look to our government for an easier and more abundant life. During election year we hear all kinds of promises by candidates running for office. Yet we know that many of these promises are hollow. Many people are gullible and fail to see that man has his limitations."

"In July I visited the concentration camps at Belsen and Dachau in West Germany. I saw the crematorium where thousands were burned. I tried to envision how I would have felt living behind barbed wire walls, treated worse than an animal, and knowing that death by starvation or gas would be my fate. Only the sky above seemed to offer freedom.

"How true are the words of the Psalmist, 'Oh, that I had wings like a dove; for then would I fly and be at rest' (Psalms 55:6). Millions of people, both Gentiles and Jews, suffered execution at the hands of these Nazi fanatics.

"At Dachau the monument reads, 'Never Again,' and yet I thought, 'Just a few miles from here, behind the Iron Curtain, there are thousands who are suffering and dying at the hands of atheistic Communism just as those who died at the hands of fanatics in West Germany prior to the end of World War II.' "

"In a larger sense, the world is a concentration camp to most people who are enslaved by sin."

"While visiting in Vienna, Austria, I attended an evening concert at the Stadtgarten (city garden), and heard many of Johann Strauss' masterpieces, including the famous 'Blue Danube.' The waltz never sounded more meaningful and more beautiful than in that setting, graced by his statue. The music was a reflection of its composer. "The Apostle Paul describes God's people as the work of art of the heavenly Author. 'We are His workmanship, created in Jesus Christ unto good works, which God hath before ordained that we should walk in them" (Ephesians 2:10).

"As creatures of God, we should show holy works because we have been called out of the darkness unto the marvelous light of our adoption as God's children.

"Our every word and act should bear witness that we are God's people.

"We cannot boast of our own good deeds and righteousness, but only that we are able to work through God's will."

Every experience in the Holy Land called for an article, from sailing across the Sea of Galilee to experiencing the traditional place of Christ's ascension. The references are too numerous to include, but they enriched his life to the point that his writings became even more inspired. If I heard him say it once, I heard him say a dozen times, "I want to go back there. I want to see the Holy Land where Christ walked again!" I'm sure he has his wish fulfilled now in the living *with* his Lord in heaven.

Three of the Clergyman's Corner articles are included in the Appendix of this book for those who wish to read a typical article in its entirety.

12
A Few Views Expressed

"As to Jesus of Nazareth . . . , I think the systems of morals and His religion, as He left them to us, is the best the world ever saw, or is likely to see."
Benjamin Franklin

Although convinced that the Lutherans came pretty close to being the balance between the strict traditionalism of the Catholic faith and the far-out radicalism of some of the fundamentalists, Ozzie often struck out at the organized church. Who in the congregations he served had not at one time or another heard him say, as he wrote in the Clergyman's Corner titled, "Lost and Found."

"Too often the organized church is a 'country club for saints instead of a hospital for sinners.' During His earthly ministry, Christ was found associating with the individuals who recognized that they were sinners, and chided the Pharisees because of their self-righteousness. . . The true Christian is vitally interested in the unsaved and estranged sinner, and rejoices when repentance of sins is made and Christ is accepted as Lord and Savior. The prime purpose of the Christian Church is to tell all men of Christ as a personal Savior who offers forgiveness of sins and eternal life to all."

With this strong belief, I can see why he was thrilled about my conversion a year and a half before we met. He'd tell people, "I baptized her, I confirmed her, and I married her!" He seemed to be the embodiment of all the Christian beliefs I had been taught. Not only did he realize the importance of the emphasis Christ put on the "lost sheep," "the lost coin," "the prodigal son," as told in Luke Chapter 15, he fell in love with one and married her!

Ozzie was so truly ecumenical that he saw the good parts in all religions that called Jesus Christ Lord and Savior. There are in his writings, and understandably so, many quotations from Martin Luther. But there are also excerpts from the good old Methodist hymns, and quotes from John Wesley, founder of the Methodist church, and references to saints and places revered by Catholics. He thought the Christopher Movement was great, and admired the zeal of the Seventh Day Adventists. There is even this quote from a Clergyman's Corner entitled, "Faith, Forgiveness and Healing," written long before I entered his life.

"Mary Baker Eddy, in her book of *Science and Health* stated, 'The sick are never really healed except by means of the Divine Power. Only the action of truth, life, and love can give harmony.' We must be in harmony with Christ Who says, 'I am the Way, the Truth, and the Life,' (John 14:6) before we can experience a healing of mind or body."

Ozzie went on to quote Dr. Charles Mayo of the Rochester, Minnesota, Clinic, who was known to have adopted the ancient physician Galen's motto, "I bound his wounds, but God healed him."

Ozzie ended the article with this: "A true Christian possesses faith, forgiveness, and healing. The cures for many ills is trust in Christ and His power to forgive sins. The hidden treasures of healing can only be uncovered when you find Christ as your personal Savior. When sin is removed, we have peace with God and peace of mind. When the fear of death is destroyed, we know that God's miracle has become effective in our lives, and that we have eternal life through Christ."

Ozzie was open to the best efforts of all denominations. He mentions in one writing his favorable impression upon walking

85

into the Mormon exhibit at the New York World's Fair and seeing a beautiful marble statue of Jesus Christ "with the outstretched arms of invitation, which symbolize His words, 'Come unto me, all ye that labor and are heavy laden, and I will give you rest' (Mathew 11:28). This is not a vain promise, this is a guarantee to those who place their trust in Him. With faith in Christ, life has a purpose and eternal life has a design."

He was esteemed in the Jewish community of Toledo for his knowledge of and reference to the Jewish leaders of the Old Testament times, his fair and equal time with news, and interviews with rabbis televised for his Religion In The News program. He wrote:

> "One of the great blessings of our day has been the ecumenical movement approached in Christian love, not only between Protestants, but also between Protestants and Catholics, and Christians and Jews. In His high priestly prayer directed to His heavenly Father, Christ said, "Neither pray I for these (disciples) alone, but for them also which shall believe on Me through their word, that they all may be one: As Thou, Father, art in Me, and I in thee, that they also may be one in Us: That the world may believe that Thou hast sent Me" (John 17:20,21).
>
> Our discussions on ecumenism must be based on the Word of God as is revealed to us in Holy Scripture. It is then that we shall understand that the will of God is truly in both the Ten Commandments and the Beatitudes, the Law and the Gospel. This message of life-giving spiritual food is what the world about us needs for its confusion, frustration and turmoil."

In another article he wrote:

> "Belonging to the saving Church of Christ does not necessarily mean that I must belong to a certain denomination. However, the denomination must adhere to the truths of God's Holy Word, the Bible, in order to strengthen the faith of its members through its message. This places a tremendous responsibility upon the pastor of the parish. For this reason, the clergyman must heed

well the command of Christ, 'Teaching them to observe all things whatsoever I have commanded you.' "

Ozzie truly thought that to be a disciple of Christ was one of life's most satisfying blessings. He was proud of his black friends in the clergy, the community, and in his parishes. He included black musicians, singers, interesting people in the news of the religious community of our city, and made numerous mention of his sympathy of the plight of the blacks in America. It was obvious that to instruct a person in a saving knowledge of Christ was a thrill for him. In one article he said, "I will never forget the comment of a black woman in my parish in Connecticut whom God permitted me to lead to Christ. She recently wrote to me, 'I pray for you every day, and thank God that I was led to my Savior through your invitation.' "

In another Clergyman's Corner my Pastor Honey wrote, "When our heart is in tune with God, Who demands, 'Love one another,' it is impossible for us to be racists or 'classists.' All the laws that are passed by man will not change the attitude of mankind toward one another. It is only where love is found in the soul of mankind that there will be an understanding and consideration of our fellowman . . . As Americans we had better learn to be considerate of one another, less civil strife erupt . . . We must bear in mind that those who resort to force and violence are stimulated by the seeds of hatred and antagonism sown by the devil. Satan wants us to live in conflict and fear; God wants us to live in love and harmony. What will be your choice?"

". . . Since with God there is no variance of people in race or class, all have an equal stand and respect in the Church."

Another time Ozzie wrote, "The Church of Jesus Christ has always practiced segregation. Not the kind of segregation that seems to have but one meaning in our day, namely the segregation between white and colored, but the segregation between the righteous and the unrighteous . . . he Church of Jesus Christ has the longest history of integration between the peoples of various colors. The command of Christ, 'Go ye and teach all nations,' . . . makes it obligatory that the Gospel of Jesus Christ is designed for all people."

He continued, "In a parish that I served for twelve years in Naugatuck, Connecticut, we were a happy family of white and

87

colored members. There was no question in the worship service or at the communion rail who was going to attend at certain times, but rather, all were one in Christ. The words of the hymn, 'we are not divided, all one body we,' was applied in the congregation."

In an article entitled "The Church and Prejudice," written in 1968, Ozzie wrote, "The Apostle Paul sets the pattern for the clergy and expresses the purpose of their activities in these words, 'I determined not to know anything among you, save Jesus Christ, and Him crucified' (Corinthians 2:2). If the clergyman exercises this policy from the pulpits and in administration, then he will soon lead his people to love all persons regardless of their creed, color, or nationality."

Ozzie felt that the words Carl Boberg wrote for the hymn, "How Great Thou Art" seems to "say it all" for believers. It was his favorite, and not a month of Sundays went by without it being included in a service. In the article entitled, "Forgiveness Brings Happiness," Ozzie quoted the hymn,

"And when I think that God, His Son not sparing,
Sent Him to die, I scarce can take it in;
That on the cross, my burden gladly bearing,
He bled and died to take away my sin."

and then wrote, "No wonder that the author could then so eloquently formulate his faith in the refrain,

"Then sings my soul, my Savior God to thee;
How great Thou art!"

He finishes the Clergyman's Corner article by writing, "we are all very much like Christian of *Pilgrim's Progress*, for when we reach the hill on which stands the cross, we cling to Christ for our redemption and find peace of mind through the forgiveness of sins. Let us show our appreciation by obeying Him and by showing love to our fellow man."

Ozzie was probably the most joyous person I ever knew. Even with tragedy in his life, when I see him in my mind he is always smiling, looking kindly at someone, or expressing a firm interest in someone or something. He conveyed this when he wrote in

"Healing Through Forgiveness," "Because of God's pardon for us through Christ, we are filled with joy. No other religion offers happiness such as St. Paul expresses in the words, 'Rejoice in the Lord always, and again I say to you, rejoice.' Christianity is not a drab religion, running around with folded hands, but a beautiful experience with no fear for today and no anxiety for the tomorrow. I cannot conceive of Jesus not smiling and laughing and exchanging a bit of humor with His disciples. Happiness comes of being reconciled with God and being at peace with Him. This reconciliation is attained by a trusting faith in Christ."

I feel that my Pastor Honey exuded what I called "holy boldness." There was nothing he wouldn't dare to say or do if he were convinced it was God directed. He seemed to feel like Paul, "If the trumpet give an uncertain sound, who shall prepare himself . . ." (I Cor. 14:8). Who else that you or I know would send a Christmas card like this, which told about a "Peace at Christmas."

"Several years ago I sent the late Mr. Nikita Khrushchev, then premier of Russia, a Christmas card. It read as follows: 'All over the world it is Christ in Christmas. He came to earth to remove our sins and to open the door of Heaven. ('Poxogecmbou Zpucmobsceu!' which means, 'A Blessed Christmas To You!'). May God be your Guide in the New Year."

"How sorely we need to share the one cure for the world's ills. Only where Christ lives in the heart is there perfect peace."

Just as enthusiastically as Ozzie seized every opportunity that a newly visited town or city offered as an outlet for either the weekly newspaper article or for the television program, just so his "holy boldness" caused him to be the confident, outgoing person he was. He loved visiting the local restaurants and sitting up at the counter with strangers. They were never strangers for long, for his warm smile and cheerful conversation was personal, definitely not the "Are you saved?" type that one might expect from a man wearing the collar. But many, sensing his true interest in them, would confide worries or problems to him, and he never failed to give them some remark or passage from the Bible that was helpful. Strangers have, since his death, come up to me in the coffee shop he went to frequently, to tell me of the outstanding impression he had made on them.

The "holy boldness" trait came out humorously at times. He would say in mock seriousness upon receiving the bill for our after-Sunday church brunch, "Well, I guess I can pay this, the collection was very good this morning." I was always afraid a waitress would believe him and spread the word that the Reverend O. H. Bertram dipped into the collection plate to take his wife out to lunch. Ozzie always laughed at my fears—and he was right. Who would ever have believed that!

For all this "holy boldness" he never wanted to take any credit for his successes in life. Many times I heard him say, after receiving an honor or a compliment, "Thanks, by the grace of God." In his Clergyman's Corner called "Humility—A Virtue", he said, "Let people speak well of you behind your back because of your deeds of kindness. Let the public praise you for your loving actions beyond the call of duty, but give God the credit for placing into your heart the virtues of charity and love . . . To be humble, one must be loving. Vainglory is a characteristic of a person filled with pride and conceit. To be humble is one of life's greatest virtues, which cannot be achieved by oneself, but must be instilled in us by God."

Ozzie was human enough to be hurt at times, discouraged, and have self-doubt; and for years he carried a little poem, writer unknown, in his wallet. He would read it when he needed to be "reminded of God's great care and love for me," as he stated in the article entitled, "Jesus The Bread of Life."

When he had new business cards printed after his move to Toledo, that same little poem was printed on the back, together with one of Ozzie's favorite Bible passages from Philippeans 4:13 which says, "I can do all things through Christ Who strengthens me." The poem says:

Doubt sees the obstacles;
  Faith sees the way!
Doubt sees the darkest night;
  Faith sees the day!
Doubt dreads to take a step;
  Faith soars on high!

90

Doubt questions, "Who believes?"
Faith answers, "I."

Many article followers and television listeners would write and ask advice for their problems, or request some literature that would show someone the error of his or her ways. Ozzie was always sure the writer was made aware of two things: the power of prayer, and that only God could change a heart from sin to holiness.

When the Reverend O. H. Bertram wrote or spoke he used every cliché known to man. Someone was "on a bed of pain," people fell "to a watery grave," one could be "driven to distraction," or experiencing "the storms of life," "a brighter day," or "reverses in life." Yet, when he said them or wrote them, these phrases were somehow helpful and consoling to his listeners or readers. They were familiar phrases perhaps connected with their parents' or grandparents' way of speaking. They gave him the "common touch", made him homey and easily understood. And always there was that strength in his convictions, that "holy boldness" that shone out like beams from the lighthouses be loved, confident, sure, dependable, and always helpful. As he said on occasions, "Christ was not neutral when He died on the cross."

He wrote on all the topics most would avoid. He was not afraid to discuss racism, politics, the creation theory, sex, sin, lust, athiests, death, immoral movies or television, alcoholism, homosexuals, strikes, and the lottery. In a day when Christianity is being weakened by "middle-of-the roaders," Ozzie's manner of speaking and writing was refreshingly strong. It was so simple to him. "Jesus Christ died and rose again, and through His resurrection He has assured us, "Because I live, ye shall live also." "No man cometh unto the Father (God) but by me." And because Ozzie was so sure of this, others believed.

I love this quote from "Your Future Begins Today," in which Ozzie said, "Nothing perishes; it only changes form. Just as a golden wedding ring recovered after a fire as a tiny lump of gold was changed; yet even dearer after being lost, then found again. It still embodied its purest elements. It may be as Christians, we human beings, tempered by the fires of life's experiences, emerge in a new spiritual form; more acceptable to God for His divine purposes."

I think Ozzie's own words in the preface he wrote to a small mimeographed collection of his newspaper articles he titled, "Blueprints For Living," best express why he wrote the weekly articles regularly for ten years:

Preface

Dear Friend:

"Prayer is the language of dependence." It is because of this total dependence on prayer that I have found full satisfaction in serving the Lord. My work is my delight and my service to His church brings complete joy.

Most of these meditations are born out of personal experience. As God would lead and direct, I have written them attempting to find the solution to many problems and finding the secret of a true meaning in life through Christ. It is my intention in these meditations to help the individual find his way through life in a closer walk with God. These "Blueprints For Living," are based upon Holy Scripture and should help lead the individual to a greater concept of God's love.

I have dedicated these meditations to the glory of God, through Christ my Savior, to my family, which through the years have proven to be a source of inspiration to me and to the many people who comprise our unseen congregation through mass communication.

As I reflect upon the early years of my ministry, I am convinced that the zeal that Christ placed into my heart spurred me on. It was my family that encouraged me to use the greater outreach of sharing the saving Gospel of Jesus Christ in as many ways as possible.

My payment for the efforts put forth in the endeavor of sharing Jesus Christ as man's only Savior are the many letters and comments of appreciation. I pray that God's continued blessings will rest upon those who read these meditations. To you I say, "God bless you."

Yours on the upward trail in Christ,
(Signed) O. H. Bertram

January 5, 1984, a woman came up to me as I worked at Toledo

92

University for winter registration. "Are you related to that Bertram who used to write The Clergyman's Corner?" she asked. When I said yes, she told me of her collection of cut out articles by Ozzie that she rereads on many occasions. How wonderful to know that after almost five years, my husband's written insights to life were still being appreciated.

13
Day by Day

"We may live without friends; we may
live without books;
But civilized man can not live without cooks."
Owen Meredith
Lucile

"Where did you get that hat?
Where *did* you get that hat?
from the song by Joseph J. Sullivan

It is with complete pleasure that I think back on my life with Ozzie. He influenced so many areas of my life. Among them were food and dress. Because he took such intense pleasure in day to day living, it was doubly enjoyable for me to please him by cooking certain favorite foods. Everyone who knew him was aware of his love for a good meatloaf. He would say he actually preferred my meatloaf to a steak. Lorna Lee, his daughter, would tease him and say, "Oh Dad, you are a lazy chewer."

One day while reminiscing about his boyhood, he told me of a family dish that was a favorite. It was hot cherry soup made with dumplings, spice and sweetened cherries. I couldn't imagine a soup with fruit, although I had heard fruit soups were a favorite of Scandinavians. That afternoon I concocted a soup as close as possible to what he had described, and was dropping in the dumplings as he came home from the office that evening. He stopped at the door, closed his eyes in ecstasy and said, "I smell cherry soup!" I was enfolded in a bear hug and treated to such praise and happy smiles that my joy just floated up like a helium balloon until it touched the kitchen ceiling.

Just before Easter in the first year of our marriage Ozzie explained the German custom of Fast Nacht to me. This was the last night before the Lenten Season and Fast Nacht doughnuts were a tradition his family had observed. These special doughnuts were made with a little handle; so nothing would do but that I plan to secretly make some to surprise him. I looked for a simple doughnut recipe, stuck the cut-out doughnut hole on the side of the doughnut before I dropped it in to fry, and voilá, a Fast Nacht doughnut.

The delight and gratitude Ozzie expressed to me was something that I had become addicted to. He possessed and showed a delightful, boyish appreciation at times. It was an irresistible trait and surprising in a man of his stature and dignity.

Olga Jomantis, now a member of our church, told me that she and her mother were deciding where to move in Toledo when the following incident occurred: They were familiar with Ozzie's television work, and being impressed with my husband's spiritual expressions, had decided to visit our church. My husband called on them, as was his habit after someone visited our church who was not a member of another congregation. As Ozzie left Olga's home, she tells me, she pointed out a dove's nest in a branch above the car. He stood on tiptoe to peer at the baby birds and was so "boyishly excited" about the sight, that Olga and her elderly mother were charmed. The ensuing plan to move to the vicinity of our church was strictly based on their decision to make Good Shepherd their church home. Not only had "the Reverend Bertram satisfied their quest for a truly scripturally based pastor," Olga said, "but we loved the man's personality."

This quality of taking extreme pleasure in all facets of life was indigenous in Ozzie and made him a pleasure to be around. He seemed to particularly enjoy my cooking for the family dinners we regularly had, and especially liked roast turkey with the special oyster dressing I made, as did my mother before me. A dish called "pan haus," a recipe from my Alsace Lorraine ancestored father became a favorite. This is similar to corn meal mush, only made with the broth of cooked beef stew meat. The beef is put through a meat grinder and added to the mush. It is then packed in a loaf pan, cooled, and sliced to fry crisp and tasty for breakfast with syrup or eggs. Ozzie adored it, as did my father and brother.

Another day when Lorna dropped by for dinner, she and Ozzie

requested sautéed green peppers, something I had never made before. Luckily, they turned out to be delicious, and another item was added to my collection of dishes to please Pastor Honey. Chocolate cake, a former favorite of Ozzie's, was a "no-no" on the diet he was following, but angel food was acceptable. I never made or ate so many different angel food cakes as I did during our marriage.

Friends were also aware of his particular fondness for strawberries; and when he made calls, or when we were invited to their homes, strawberry shortcake was usually the dessert served. I think he could have enjoyed strawberries every day of his life, and I served them often.

Meals at home were special chances for extra closeness through sharing communication for Ozzie and me. Breakfast always started with Ozzie holding out my chair for me to sit down. This puzzled me when we were first married. How could I prepare breakfast and sit at the same time? I finally caught on to the routine. I would start our breakfast, let my elegantly mannered husband seat me, and then after prayer, I could continue to finish the eggs or cereal and serve them.

Ozzie came home for lunch several times a week, sometimes every day. Some of my friends would say, "How can you stand fixing lunch all the time? I couldn't get a thing done if my husband came home for lunch!" I would just smile and say, "I like it because we have a chance to talk more."

Those who know us know that neither of us were ever at a loss for words; and the precious gift of being able to always enjoy each other's conversation was one of our greatest joys. Besides, after lunch Ozzie always lay down, fully dressed and on his back, for twenty minutes or so, on the advice of his physician. He always wanted me to join him. Who wouldn't love a twenty-minute respite in the middle of a busy day, especially if you were always held in the arms of your beloved husband?

As we often had dinner out, either at places where Ozzie was speaking, at banquets where he had been asked to give the blessing, or at a restaurant with friends, dinner at home was especially enjoyable. I really love to cook, and Ozzie and I took pleasure in this form of combined action—my creating and he audibly enjoying. I planned our dinners to be in different places in our home. One night the dining room, one night on TV trays in the family room, one night at the kitchen table, or on the coffee table in front of the living room fireplace.

In 1978 I worked on the Toledo Opera Guild's special Toledo cookbook. I had been, and am presently on the Executive Board of this hard-working group, and spent many hours with Shirley Joseph, the dynamic chairman of this effort. Ozzie never complained about the time I spent on this project, nor did he ever begrudge me participation in my special interest activities. Another year, I was chairman of a study group connected with the American Association of University Women.

He encouraged me in whatever committee work or social activities I was involved, saying, "A person can't just be with Christians all the time. How will your light shine out enough to others so that they might be attracted to your way of life?" I always felt his pride in me. He made it clear that part of my charm for him was that I was not completely dependent upon him for my only outlet for companionship, friendship, and activity. I think he felt that this freed him for his main work, that of working for his Lord.

My choice of clothes changed immediately after I became Ozzie's wife. I had always been a "hat lady" (one who enjoys and wears hats a lot), and now I had a man who not only appreciated my looks in a hat, but was traditional enough to feel it was doubly nice for a lady to wear one in church. As I have worn my medium long, medium blonde hair pinned up in what is known as a French twist for years, hats seemed to be becoming.

Ozzie loved me to be especially well dressed. He felt that for many years the image of a pastor's wife was too drab. He believed, I think, that this added to an overall impression that a minister did not have a very important or attractive vocation. And so, it was he who encouraged me to choose some outstanding outfits, some more costly than I would have chosen. Among his favorites were a black coat banded in black fur, worn with a black fur hat and black boots (very Russian), a brown ultra-suede dress with an ivory opposum-trimmed coat and opposum fur hat, a taupe wool suit with a huge fringed shawl that he picked out for me at Wanamaker's in Philadelphia, a burgundy dress and large, wine-colored hat, a green cowboy type hat that lassoed under my chin with a strap, worn with a tailored camel-colored dress, and a tricornered black hat that I purchased to surprise him in 1976, the year of our American Bicentennial.

This particular hat was expensive; banded with narrow dark red grosgrain ribbon and with a pearl-tipped tiny American flag tucked in the band. I had to have it! It seemed perfect to surprise my especially patriotic husband. That Sunday I walked into Ozzie's Bible study class, which preceded our second service, with that hat on, and a deep red dress that I already owned. As I walked down the aisle to my seat before class started, I heard my darling say, "Where are the fife and drums?" and his big smile and lit-up eyes told me that I had indeed surprised him pleasantly.

Many friends in and out of our congregation have told me they enjoy my hats, and if a period of time goes by without my wearing one, such as the hot summertime, I start getting inquiries as to what is happening. "Aren't you going to wear your hats, Mrs. Bertram? We love them on you!" As I had always enjoyed hats even before Ozzie (B.O., as we laughingly called this period of my life), I still enjoy wearing them; even though my most appreciative fan is now with the Father.

Soon after our marriage, I noticed I was choosing clothes that looked well with my husband's clerical garb, which was either the black suit in winter or the white one he looked so well in, in the summer. Many outfits I bought were meant to complement him. Black and white costumes, or clear, bright colors, or dresses with the small white collar that echoed his. I must confess that we were told that we were visually quite an outstanding couple—taller than the average, looking well in what we wore, and noticeably enjoying all the material and physical gifts that God so generously blessed us with.

We were told again and again how people loved to see Ozzie stop at my pew after every service and extend his arm to me. The two of us would then walk to the back of the church where we would greet the congregation as they left the church. I loved the way I would get a hand squeeze and an "I love you" whispered to me as the final chimes were being played. I always felt this was one of the ways Ozzie expressed his gratitude for my not only being a loving wife, but looking like one.

I had the joy of entertaining many delightful houseguests during my marriage. We had a lovely guest room, and I was always happy to have it occupied. Among the overnight guests through the years have been Dr. Theodore Raedeke of St. Louis, Missouri, Rev. and Mrs. Jerry Nichols of Ft. Wayne, Indiana, Mr. William Bertram (Ozzie's uncle) and his daughter, Gertrude, from Elmhurst, Illinois, Dr. John Tietjen, then President of Concordia Seminary, St. Louis, Missouri, and Dr. Jacob A. O. Preus, President of The Lutheran Church-Missouri Synod. Two young strangers (entertaining angels unawares?) who were stranded in our great Ohio blizzard of 1976 stayed with us one night, and blessed us by their delightful presence and conversation.

Our vicar one year, now Pastor Mark Schreiber, stayed with us for a couple of weeks until he found an apartment. I remember with amusement how he asked which side of the bed Dr. Tietjen slept on. He had reference to the much-publicized controversy that was going on at that time between two factions in the Synod. Ozzie had invited both men prominent in the rift in the Synod, Dr. Preus and Dr. Tietjen, here on separate occasions, so that the congregation could hear their views in person. I had found both men to be especially charming.

During the time Mark served our church as vicar, my darling husband and Lorna Lee subtly steered him toward one of our lovely young members, Connie Cramer, whom he later married, much to our joy. It has been such a pleasure to follow Mark's career as a minister. At one time, he was serving his Lord as a Navy Air Force Chaplain. He and Connie have three adorable little girls now and their own church to minister to.

Another young man came into our lives in an interesting way. The day by day experiences that happened to me because I was connected with O. H. Bertram, prominent clergyman and man about his Father's business, were varied, fun, and productive.

One Tuesday in December 1974, when I attended the Christian Women's Luncheon that was held monthly in Toledo, I heard an extremely tall, quite handsome young man sing forth his testimonies to the Lord in a startlingly beautiful tenor voice. His poise, charm, and especially his sincerity, "spoke to me," as born-again Christians are wont to say.

Ozzie had mentioned to me previously his desire to get some new type of musical talent on the television "Worship for Shut-ins" program. As I looked and listened to this young man, I knew that he would be it! After the luncheon and the speaker for the day were finished, many women were lining up to make comments, expressing their appreciation for this outstanding man's ministry through song. I had learned from my husband, who intensely disliked standing in line for any reason (he was always in "high gear" and standing still must have always seemed the least effective way to accomplish things) to think of an alternative. I quickly wrote a note: "If you would like to sing on my husband's television program, call this number." I added Ozzie's office telephone number and then quickly approached Chuck Olson, the professional Christian artist from Iowa City, Iowa. I thrust the note into his hand, flashed my most (I thought) brilliant smile, hurried out and drove to the church office to prepare Pastor Honey for the call I felt sure he would be getting. As I explained, after I arrived there, what I had done, Ozzie threw back his head, laughed, and said, "You must be catching what you call my holy boldness."

Chuck Olson did telephone, and the two men arranged a meeting. This was the beginning of a beautiful four and a half year professional and personal relationship, as Chuck agreed to teletape songs and hymns for the program each time he came to Toledo. These then would be incorporated into the "Worship for Shut-ins" televised service.

Chuck knew that the program was part of the outreach of our church. He also knew, as he visited the television studio that first time of teletaping the program, that it was an ecumenical, nondenominational type of service for shut-in people unable to get to a church. He chose his songs for inspiration and comfort for these listeners. And did they ever respond to his special talent! Letters like the following poured in.

Dear Rev. Bertram,
Please send me Chuck Olson's album that you are giving to your listeners.
Rev. Bertram, I want you to know that your wonderful sermons on Jesus, what He is, and what He can do for me, have been my life saver for three years now. I'm alone and unable to travel even to church . . . One has to give of themselves to truly receive the Spirit of God.
Again, I want to thank you for your wonderful work. In Jesus' name I ask for all things and His spiritual blessings

upon you and Chuck Olson. He, also, is a child of God and shows inspiration in his singing and his eyes."

Fostoria, Ohio

Over the years Ozzie had sent thousands of what I came to call his "holy handouts" to viewers who requested them. Among these were lapel crosses, crosses on chains, magnet mottos, bookmarks, crucifixes, plastic figures of the Good Shepherd, Portals of Prayer (a daily devotion booklet) in small and large print, Bibles, New Testaments, and copies of his newspaper articles. After the Sunday he offered one of Chuck Olson's albums of song, we were deluged with requests.

All the money ever received by the program was used for these free offerings, postage costs for mail, television tapes and mailing costs for what is called "bicycling" the films to the various cities that carried the program. Ozzie never asked for contributions.

Chuck Olson travels the country giving music workshops and concerts. Sometimes Enid, his talented wife, and their two young daughters, travel with him. Ozzie and I were privileged to have them as houseguests several times, but more privileged to have Chuck lend his especially blessed talents to Ozzie's television services. I was always teased and praised by Ozzie for being the talent scout for this handsome young musician. How grateful I am that my husband trusted my judgment so much that he arranged for Chuck to sing on his program before he ever heard his voice. And my intuitive sense about Chuck came from God, for He blessed the association of these two men greatly as time went by.

Besides the travels and personalities that came into my life in the day by day life with my husband and the spiritual growth that was occurring, other aspects of this life, more down to earth or average, made living with this unusual man a joy.

Our nightly walks of a mile route around the blocks near our home were a much looked forward to pleasure for me. Of course, this exercise was physically healthy for both of us—you may be sure they were brisk walks. I really had to stretch my legs to keep up with Ozzie's long ones; and he always held my hand. But there were other reasons I treasured our walks. As I told women audiences (when I was giving a lecture series on Christian womanhood one year), to have your husband to yourself, not sharing him with the television or newspaper, was a gratifying experience. Many heart-to-heart discussions and much communication, both verbal and silent, went on during those walks! I highly recommend it to my audiences of women, for growing closer in marital communications.

At the time I was giving these talks on Christian success in marriage, I didn't share another reason I enjoyed these walking times. It was the fact that Ozzie never failed to whirl me to him for a kiss as we were approaching our home. It embarrassed me when we were first married. "The neighbors, or people going by in cars might see us!" I'd exclaim. "We're married, aren't we?" Ozzie would say. As the years went by, I treasured these romantic gestures that kept us so much in love with one another.

In one of his newspaper articles he makes a reference to our walking jaunts:

"The other day while I was taking my daily walk, I heard the strains of the scale being played on a saxophone from one of the houses. Whoever it was must have been quite a fine musician, because the running of the scales was nearly perfect. Whether the player was excellent or mediocre was not the issue, but I could not help but realize again that to do anything well, one must start with the basics daily and work toward perfection.

"Christianity is much like this. The basic knowledge of Jesus Christ is to know that He is the Son of God and the Son of man. But to make Him meaningful is to believe that He is my personal Savior. To know this is to follow Him in love and work for perfection in a life which not only exemplifies Him, but one which brings Him honor and glory. "He that abideth in me, and I in him, the same bringeth forth much fruit; for without Me ye can do nothing" (John 15:5). To bring forth the fruits of holiness, we must be sanctified, or as it is expressed in 2 Corinthians 5:17, "Therefore if any man be in Christ, he is a new creature: Old things are passed away; Behold, all things are become new."

How privileged I was to experience these years as a new "baby Christian" with one of Christianity's finest teachers, as was my beloved husband. How gracious was our Lord to allow me not only the joy of discovering Him, but the day by day pleasures of a completely happy marriage.

It seems as though this would be a good place to include some observations about my husband's likes and dislikes in life. After all, this book is mainly about him, and what better way to really feel you know someone, than to know his opinions. I gleaned these from our day to day living and loving together experiences.

For a man who believed that one only appreciated life by its contrasts, Ozzie was the epitome of contrasts in his own likes and dislikes. He had strong feelings about most things in life, and the next, and made them known. These are a few of them. They served to make his personality all the more fascinating in its individuality.

HE LOVED:
New England, the ocean, mountains, lighthouses and seagulls.
Strawberries, lemon meringue pie, Kadota figs, oysters, and meat loaf.
"Deep Purple," "Body and Soul," "Close To You", "What Are You Doing the Rest of Your Life?" and "The Good Life."
John Wayne and Western movies.
Fashionable clothes.
Organ music, string instruments, hymns, barbershop groups, and the "big band" music.
Conversation with friends, an occasional glass of wine.
God, Jesus Christ, Martin Luther, Abe Lincoln, Dwight Eisenhower, Billy Graham, Peter Marshall, Norman Vincent Peale, Robert Schuller, and Walter Meier.
Eating in good restaurants.
Church work, preaching, TV and radio work.
Mental stimuli and working with his mind.
Ministering to his "flock," and proclaiming the Gospel.
A good intelligent clash of opinions.

HE DISLIKED:
Flat lands, old cars, bugs.

Any meat that demanded much chewing.
"Love is Never Having To Say You're Sorry", "I Did It My Way."

Science fiction movies.
Vulgarity in dress.
Hard rock.

Card games, hard liquor.

Trouble-makers.

Cheap food.
Not doing everything "to the glory of God."
Lengthy physical work.

Not being needed.

Opposition with no thought or experience to back it up.

Brisk walks and rides in the evening.	Inactivity and slow drivers.
Peaceful relationships.	Inharmony of any kind.
Saturday afternoon naps.	No time for "togetherness."
On television: Newscasters, "Hogan's Heroes," M.A.S.H., good detective series.	Blatant sex, profanity, soap operas, and violence.
Touching, hugging, physical closeness, teasing.	Coldness in people.
Neatness, order, cleanliness in person and home.	Untidiness, dirt, spots on clothes.
Children and plants.	Dogs and cats in the house.
Traveling, especially by plane.	Long periods without travel.
Loved to express affection and meeting and charming new friends.	Disliked no one.
Jewish people, blacks, Catholics, Lutherans, politics, and America.	Bigotry and ingratitude.
Being with people, his family, and his wife.	Being alone.
His profession, being led by Christ, and answered prayers.	Not understanding someone, his illness.

Daily life with Ozzie was not always the easiest experience one could have. I was continually striving to learn how to be a pastor's wife. I realized I did not only belong to my husband, but in part, I belonged and had a responsibility to the church he served. I found an entry in my husband's diary of Saturday, October 21, 1972, which reminded me of some of the things I did to enhance my Christian growth and my effectiveness as Ozzie's helpmate. He writes, "Nine persons were at adult membership class as enrolling for premembership, plus six members. Also my darling Sally was present with the refreshments she brings each time. She is certainly doing her utmost to learn Christian doctrine. She is also enrolled with me at the Toledo Bible College studying the Book of Romans."

On October 31, 1972, Ozzie wrote, "This is the 455th anniversary of Martin Luther nailing the ninety-five theses on the door of the Castle Church of Wittenberg. May our church always hold to these Bible truths."

"My angel Sally and I attended our class on Romans this morning. I am so grateful that she has such a love for God's Word.

How could we help but be happy when Christ dwells in our hearts. I love her so very much! I must be cautious for fear that I love her too much."

November 1, 1972, the entry was, "Sally did substitute teaching today. The house seemed so empty without her this morning. No one to stand at the door to kiss me and wave a sweet and loving good-bye."

"Had the good news that WDIM-TV will carry 'A Worship for Shut-ins' soon. This Lansing, Michigan station is already carrying 'Thought For The Day' (the thirty second spots). So God opens another door! If only we could utilize this medium even more to proclaim the Gospel. Will I ever reach the height of my ambition for the Lord?"

Our life together was filled for me, with the excitement of living with a man in love with his work for the Lord, and also deeply in love with me. What more could a woman ask for. He wanted me to accompany him everywhere, and only four times in our life together did I ever have any unpleasant or frightening experiences.

One summer evening, Ozzie received a phone call from the police. They were investigating a report of a break-in at the church, and wanted to inform my husband that they were going in after the person they were sure was still inside somewhere.

My husband pulled on his slacks over his pajamas, and I watched him walk off briskly to our church, which was at the end of the block and perpendicular to our street, so that I had a good moonlit view of him as he neared his office door. Suddenly two gunshots startled the soft summer night; and an icy fear gripped my heart. Should I "stay put," as he had told me to do? Or should I run down the street to be at the side of what I felt might be my mortally wounded husband? The decision was taken away from me as I found I was so weak with fright, I couldn't move anyway.

As the fearsome moments passed, I thought of how much I loved my Ozzie, and how I knew I would not be able to go on if anything happened to him. A time of paralyzed watching and waiting elapsed, and then I saw him walking toward me. He told me that the police had shot through the door at a retreating figure who got away, just as he had approached the church. After they had searched the church together, my husband returned home to his tearfully upset, yet grateful wife.

104

Another year, and another frightening experience occurred. I had become used to my Pastor Honey receiving phone calls for help; sometimes in the middle of the night. In the beginning of our marriage, I used to listen to his part of the conversation and marvel at his patience and wisdom, and the actual time he would spend counseling a troubled soul. As the years passed, I learned to turn over and return to sleep, knowing that another distraught person was getting the help he or she needed.

But this late night call was different. Ozzie asked me to dress and accompany him to the home of a woman who was being confronted by her angry, drunken husband who was waving a gun. To this day, I don't know where we went or who the people were. I do know that my always wise husband had called the police, and that they were pulling up to the house at the same time we were. He went in with them, and sometime later, came out to tell me everything was under control. You can imagine, I'm sure, the mental agony I went through as I waited in the car.

Ozzie never wanted me to go to the hospital in the middle of the night, as he was sometimes required to do. I felt that he was experiencing some fearsome possibilities as he coped with the thoughts of what might happen dealing with an alcoholic with a gun. That is why, I'm sure, he wanted me to be nearby this frightening evening.

The third unpleasant event in my otherwise happy existence as a minister's wife happened again as a result of a desperate phone call. A lovely and devout young married woman in our congregation had just taken a huge amount of pills. She was getting in her car and was driving to leave a letter of explanation under the church office door, she told Ozzie. She then planned to die in her car outside the church.

Of course, we dressed quickly—these things always seemed to happen after we had gone to bed—and drove as fast as possible the short block to our church. She was weakly getting into her car after placing the letter under the door. She would not get out so that we could get her to the hospital. Ozzie and I lifted and tugged and almost carried her into the front seat of our car. I held her in my arms, stroking her lovely, long hair and crooning all the love and encouragement to hang onto life that I could think of, into her ear. I thought, *This could be one of my daughters if she broke under seemingly insurmountable troubles.* She was slowly, but surely, passing into unconsciousness, and my verbalizing gave way to prayers for her life. Ozzie and I prayed together as he drove above the speed limit to the hospital.

The orderlies carried her in and pumped her stomach. She survived to thank my husband for his part in helping her realize that she did want to continue living, with the Lord's help. I never spoke of this incident to her. I don't know if she even realizes I was there that agonizing night, and I don't ever wish to embarrass her. Her problems have been resolved, and she seems to have a happy life now.

I was learning that the life of a pastor's wife was not always the delightful experience most of my friends thought it to be.

The only other horrifying experience in my life with Ozzie was his illness and death.

But he did indeed, as he promised when I agreed to marry him, make my life a "foretaste of heaven on earth."

14
Dropping Names in Washington

"Noble blood is an accident of fortune;
noble actions characterize the great."
Carlo Goldoni

The eighteenth century Italian dramatist Goldoni certainly said it succinctly when he made this part of one of his character's speeches in the play, "Pamela." I've always felt a person's value lies in his talents and achievements, not in dollars and cents accumulated, or an inherited family name. Therefore, you can imagine what a thrill it was for Ozzie and me to meet so many people in our seven years together whom I feel have contributed greatly to the betterment of human life.

We were exposed to many of these notables in our annual trip to Washington, D.C. to attend the National Religious Broadcasters' Convention, which was usually held at the Washington Hilton Hotel. Some 3,000 men and women connected with broadcasting through radio and television, converged on Washington from all over the world every January to meet, mingle, learn, and inspire each other. The program committee never failed to assemble a roster of distinguished speakers and musicians for the enjoyment and edification of the people serving the Lord through the electronic media.

Imagine hearing sing in person George Beverly Shea, Jerome Hines, The Bill Gaither Trio, Myrtle Hall, Anita Bryant, Norma Zimmer, Evie, Susanne Johnson, Doug Oldham, Merrill Womack, the "Up With People" group, and Rex Humbard and his entire family of singers, and many other prominent musical talents such as Dino Kartsonakis, who enthralled us all with his electrifying playing of the piano. We could always anticipate hearing the best in Christian musical artistry at the convention each year.

I had my personal thrills also. One morning in January 1977 I got on the escalator to ascend to the Washington Hilton coffee shop where I was to meet Ozzie. I sensed a tall presence who had stepped on the moving stairs immediately behind me. I turned to look right into the brilliant blue eyes of Dr. Billy Graham. I'm sure I reacted with a surprised and thrilled expression on my face. This prominent Evangelist, who was to give the NRB Thirty-Fourth Year Anniversary Banquet address that evening, smiled at me and said, "Good morning" in that familiar voice so known to me from years of hearing it on radio and TV.

In 1974, Miss Corrie ten Boom, author of *The Hiding Place* and other books, gave the opening program message on the first Sunday evening conference. The next morning I had arranged to meet a high school best friend, Jean Nelson Woodward, who had also married a minister, and whom I had not seen in years, in the Hilton coffee shop. As Jean (who had driven to Washington from Frederick, Maryland) and I sat at a table near the doorway, who should walk in alone, but Miss ten Boom.

I copied my husband's example of "holy boldness," drew a deep breath, and asked her if she would like to join us. She would, and did! While Jean and I had our coffee, she drank a glass of milk. She said it was the one thing she missed most in the way of food during her concentration camp experience. She also shared how the women in her building at the camp hid separate pages of her New Testament, rolled up like quills in their hair. She told us how she achieved her distinctive "hair-do." She put a loose rubber band around her head and tucked all her hair around it in a neat circle roll. We were entranced with her precious personality; meeting her was a thrill that Jean and I treasure.

Every year the convention planned special events for the women attendees. It has been my privilege to hear Catherine Marshall, famed author and wife of Dr. Peter Marshall, speak. I also received inspiration from Eleanor Page, prominent Bible study leader in Washington, D.C.; Millie Dienert, one of Dr. Graham's staff; Irene Conlan, the wife of Congressman John B. Conlan; Bert Lance's wife, LaBelle; Marabel Morgan, author of *The Total Woman*; Ruth Stapleton (Jimmy Carter's sister); Kay Huber, a Major in our U.S. Air Force; and many other prominent Christian women.

Each year Embassy teas are arranged, and it has been pleasurable through the years to attend, among others, the Embassies of the Republic of Korea, Liberia, Switzerland, the Republic of China (Taiwan), Equador, and the Russian Embassy.

It was on these bus trips to the Embassies that I met a most delightful lady. Every year we would look forward to going together to the teas and tours. Her name was Claire Killman, the beloved wife of Dr. Russell Killman, well-known director of the radio, "Heaven and Home Hour." Claire went to her heavenly home in January 1982, and I treasure my memories of this lovely lady, especially the joy of attending Ford's Theatre one afternoon together to see the play, "Mr. Lincoln."

Each year a women's reception was held for some of the NRB women at the White House to meet the current President's wife. Only one hundred could go, and as there were many who sought this honor, it was not until 1980, having been invited to attend the National Religious Broadcasters' Convention to accept a posthumous award for my dear Ozzie's thirty-seven years of broadcasting, that I was privileged to be invited to the White House to attend a reception given by Roslyn Carter. Having my picture taken with her, and having it appear in my local newspaper, was indeed an exciting event in my life. No matter what one thinks of former President Carter and his politics, his wife was the epitome of gracious charm—every inch the First Lady, and one to be proud of.

During Richard Nixon's Presidency, in 1975, a small reception was held for his daughter, Mrs. Julie Nixon Eisenhower, a newly reborn Christian, at the Washington Hilton. While I was standing in the reception line to meet her, someone admired the violets I was wearing on my suit. I had made them from yarn, and some of my friends have received them as love tokens through the years. Julie Nixon Eisenhower also admired them and I gave mine to her. This was more of a thrill for me, I'm sure, than for her. I like to think that she might still have them.

Each year on the Tuesday of the convention week, a huge Congressional Breakfast was held. Not only was it exciting to see all the Congressmen you ever heard or read about, filing in to the unbelievably huge International Ballroom of the Washington Hilton to sit on daises facing us; it was a joy to see and hear the invocations usually given by either Dr. Edward Elson, Chaplain of the United States Senate, or by Dr. Edward Latch, Chaplain of the United States House of Representatives.

I would usually get a nudge and a raised eyebrow knowing look from Ozzie after the chaplain's prayers. Perhaps it was only I who knew one of his secret dreams was to be the chaplain of either the House of Representatives or the Senate some day. He had had the honor of being invited to give the opening prayer for the U.S. Senate May 16, 1961, the opening prayer for the House of Representatives January 30, 1973, and also January 24, 1978.* This experience gave him a new goal in life. The people of our congregation sensed this love for Washington, D.C., and each time we would return after a visit, someone or another would concernedly take me aside to ask, "Is Pastor seeking a church in Washington?" Or, "You two aren't thinking of leaving us, are you?" I always reassured them that we were not considering leaving Toledo unless we were led some day to feel it was God's will to do so.

At the Congressional Breakfasts, we would hear many government notables speak. Usually the Mayor of Washington welcomed us. At one time, Mr. William Yopee, President of the National Indian Tribal Association sat at the same table with us. What a thrill when we all rose and joined hands while we were led in prayer.

Ozzie wrote in his "Clergyman's Corner" titled, "A Generation Of Peace," for newspaper release July 5, 1978:

". . . As I grasped Mr. Yopee's hand, I could feel the sincerity of the oneness between the Indian and the white man

---

*These prayers are included in the Appendix.

in a common faith through Jesus Christ. This is the secret of the possible unity of the world and the solution for the animosity between nations and people. It is this unity of which the Bible speaks, 'Eager to maintain the unity of the spirit in the bond of peace. There is one body and one spirit, just as you were called to the one hope that belongs to your call, one Lord, one Faith, one Baptism, one God and Father of us all, Who is above all and through all and in all' " (Ephesians 4:3-6).

The President of the United States of America, or his Vice-President, was sometimes there to give an address. Some years the President made his greetings to the thousands of broadcasters Sunday or Monday evening. Ozzie and I were privileged to hear Richard Nixon, Gerald R. Ford, and Jimmy Carter, in person. You may well imagine that my husband, whose second interest was politics, was highly enthralled with this aspect of the yearly conference.

Ozzie always arranged by phone calls or letters before the January of each year to hold taped televised short interviews with the Congressmen, or the Senate Chaplain, to interject into his Religion in the News or Worship for Shut-ins telecasts. One year an interview was teletaped across from the House of Representatives in the small park area there. I sat on a bench watching the televised taping, and was also checking out the recognizable personages that were coming out of the House. Hubert Humphrey passed me, and then my thrill for the day—Ted Kennedy walked by and gave me the famous Kennedy smile, complete with charisma!

Other interviews taped in Washington that I was privileged to watch were with Representatives Latta, Helms, Esch, Guyer, and former Congressman, The Reverend Walter Moeller.

Our Ohio Congressman Delbert Latta annually took us to lunch in the House of Representatives' Dining Room. Ozzie always ordered their special bean soup, just as I always managed to try some elegant dessert that I knew I shouldn't indulge in. One such luncheon day, we sat two tables away from Gloria Swanson, also a guest that day. She and I were the only ladies wearing hats. She looked elegant; and I hoped that people might be wondering what celebrity *I* might be.

110

My Ozzie knew so many "biggies" in the political and religious broadcasting scenes, that it was always exciting to be his consort. If he didn't know them, and wanted to, he always managed to meet them one way or another.

Back in Toledo, people would sometimes come up to him on the street and say, "I've seen you somewhere. Is it TV? Are you Bishop Sheen?" There was admittedly a resemblance: the thin, aristocratic face and nose, the piercing eyes, the rapid, intense delivery of thoughts, the black suit and the white clerical collar—and of course the appearances on television.

Ozzie would laughingly say, "No, I'm not, but thanks for the compliment." My husband admired not only the Bishop Fulton Sheen's messages, but also his zeal. Consequently, when after one NRB conference session, we were leaving the main speaking and musical attractions of the evening, and found ourselves walking out in the crowd with Bishop Sheen, Ozzie seized the opportunity to introduce ourselves to him. He told Bishop Sheen how he was sometimes mistaken for him. I remember Bishop Sheen tipped back his head to look up at my husband and laughingly said, "You poor man, mistaken for me! I certainly wish I had your height!" Humble, vital, attractive, and a true man of God. There certainly *was* a resemblance between these two.

One year our famous Lutheran Hour speaker, Dr. Oswald C. J. Hoffmann, was to give an after-banquet main speech. As the preliminary speakers addressed us, I nudged Ozzie. "Look," I whispered, "Ozzie Hoffmann ate too much. He's dozing!" Dr. Hoffman's head was on his chest, his eyes closed.

"Oh no he's not," was my husband's reply, "he's probably praying!" Just then Dr. Hoffmann was introduced and he quickly arose to give a brilliantly vital and animated talk. I was impressed and proud of the impact one of my denomination's "boys" was making on this huge group of broadcasters.

Another exciting incident occurred the evening Anita Bryant gave a program of speaking and singing. I remember thinking, "What a truly gorgeous woman she is!" and, "I never realized how powerfully and beautifully she could sing." The years of hearing her singing the Florida orange juice commercials had not really shown off that beautiful voice. Suddenly we were all being asked to leave the gigantic ballroom; there had been a bomb threat! Before this moment, a noisy intruder had been removed from the scene. We hurried out to one of the lobbies to watch from a glass doorway the large candlelit parade of the homosexuals of Washington, D.C. who were circling the Hilton in protest of Anita Bryant's appearance there. Although this was extremely interesting, it was somewhat frightening to experience.

One of Ozzie's special favorites among his friends was the late Dr. Eugene R. (Rudy) Bertermann, President of the NRB in 1974, then associated with the Far East Broadcasting Company, and then Associate Director of the Lutheran Bible Translators. I feel sure it was upon Dr. Bertermann's recommendation that my Pastor Honey's "distinguished ministry" (in the words of Dr. Ben Armstrong, Executive Director of the National Religious Broadcasters) was recognized posthumously at the 1980 NRB by being given a commendation for his thirty-seven years of being continuously heard or seen on the radio or TV. It was at this particular conference, which I attended alone, that I received a direct call from the Holy Spirit to write this book, to the glory of God, and the memory of my beloved husband.

Dr. Ben Armstrong, before mentioned, Dr. Thomas Zimmerman, well known among evangelical leaders, Dr. Robert H. Bowman, President of the Far East Broadcasting Company, and Dr. Martin J. Neeb, Jr., former Executive Director of the Lutheran "This is the Life" honored TV series, who served on the National Lutheran Church-Missouri Synod Board for Communication with Ozzie, were also treasured friends. Each year, Dr. Billy Kim of the Far East Broadcasting Company in Korea, and the Korean interpreter for Billy Graham, would remember us and greet us by name.

This conference was where my Pastor Honey met Owen Carr, Award of Merit winner and Emmy Award recipient Channel 38, Chicago's first and only Christian television station's owner at the time. He sold himself to Mr. Carr and the Channel 38 President, Jerry Rose. By that, I mean they were impressed by him personally, and agreed to try out Ozzie's "Worship for Shut-ins" TV program. Thus began a wonderful association and the continued airing of the program on Channel 38. It was to become one of Ozzie's largest viewing audiences. The station felt that quality programming was a vital prerequisite for effective TV ministry, and I was especially proud of my husband's program being shown on this channel. He was just beginning to acquire a huge and

112

growing appreciative audience of listeners when he became ill in 1978.

A few other notables that I feel aided me in growing in Christian knowledge and faith through hearing them speak, were Dr. Billy Graham, Pastor Ben Haden of the historic First Presbyterian Church in Chattanooga, Tennessee, and speaker on the nationwide radio-TV program, "Changed Lives," Jerry Falwell, Bill Bright, Pat Robertson, Dr. D. James Kennedy, and Dr. Paul Freed, President of Trans World Radio. The brilliant author, Dr. Francis A. Schaeffer from L'Abri Fellowship, Switzerland, Dr. Stephen Olford, Dr. Abe VanDerPuy, Dr. Russell Killman, and Tim LaHaye were also unforgettable speakers.

One evening Ozzie and I were honored to sit at the same table with Mrs. Walter A. Maier, the lovely widow of Dr. Walter A. Maier of "The Lutheran Hour" fame. She was at the conference to accept a beautiful trophy given in her husband's honor, which entered him in the National Religious Broadcasting Pioneers "Hall of Fame." She remembered my husband, and they had a delightful conversation reminiscing about shared memories.

With her was the wonderful singer, Miss Kim Wickes of Seoul, Korea. Kim had shared with her audience the previous evening the story of how she was rescued by Christians, after having been thrown away in the river after her birth. You see, she had been born blind. She was brought up in the Christian school there, and God has blessed her with an exquisite singing voice. "To sing his praise," she told us. What an inspiration, I thought, to hear how God works!

My all-time personal favorite among the religious world notables was Malcolm Muggeridge, the famous English writer and former managing editor of the British journal, Punch, widely known for his television appearances. He was then in his eighties. I first became acquainted with him through reading his book, *Jesus*, a birthday gift to my husband from our good Toledo friend and assistant church organist, Eileen Nupp. When I read that he was to speak at the 1978 NRB, nothing would do but that I take the book in my suitcase, on the chance that Mr. Muggeridge would autograph it. I've never been interested in obtaining autographs, but I began to see its use now. It would give me a legitimate excuse to speak to the famous personality and writer.

While I waited for him to leave after his talk, I rehearsed what

I would say. When he suddenly appeared before me in the hallway, what came out was, "Mr. Muggeridge, I love you and your
writings. I've lugged this heavy book all the way from Toledo.
Would you write in it, please?" He laughed, asked my name,
and seemed delighted as he wrote, "To Sarah with love, Malcolm
Muggeridge, January 23, 1978." Each day afterwards if he caught
sight of me in the meetings or hallways, he would gaily call out,
"Sarah!"

The day he left, Ozzie and I saw him leaving the hotel with his
assistants and luggage, and I was able to introduce my husband
to him. When I wrote to him three years later telling him of my
husband's death, and requesting permission to quote him in my
book, I received a lovely note saying, in part, "Of course you may
quote from me as you suggest."

God bless you, my dear.
Yours sincerely,
Malcolm Muggeridge

15
I Married a "Wanderlust"!

"How shall I know, unless I go
To Cairo and Cathay,
Whether or not this blessed spot
Is blest in every way?"
Edna St. Vincent Millay

Before promising to marry the Reverend O. H. Bertram, I had
planned a trip abroad with a teachers' group. But what red-
blooded woman would not prefer to travel with her beloved, new-
lywed husband for a first European adventure.

Before our June wedding, I told Ozzie of my previously made
plans. I also told him I would much rather be with him than go
anywhere without him, and I would cancel the trip. He had a
wonderful idea. He would purchase my ticket for the tour through
Europe, and if I wanted, my wedding present to him could be his
ticket. That way he would feel that he was giving me the trip of
my dreams, and I, conversely, would be giving him something for
us both to build future memories on.

Our honeymoon in Washington, D.C. was less than a week, and Ozzie was intrigued with the idea of a real vacation two months hence. "A *real* honeymoon," he would exclaim, as he enthusiastically told our family and friends. I had by now experienced how exciting traveling could be with a man on fire with life and the joy of his Christian beliefs. My Pastor Honey was fifty-four years old when I married him; but about him clung an air of strength, purpose, and vitality that made youth seem like an "awkward dream." As Charles Dickens said of someone in *David Copperfield*, Ozzie was the type of man for whom "Life unrolled itself like a red carpet before him until the last."

I knew that this would be a thrilling tour. I realize that many people believe group tours are confining. But looking back on our three separate trips to Europe and the trip to Israel and to Greece, we came to the conclusion that to see *all* one has desired to see in the way of points of interest or historically significant places, one must be guided and cared for, as the tours do. Unless you have time to hunt and seek and randomly wander, a guided tour is the way to go.

The third time we went to Germany and Denmark in 1978, we were on our own, and this turned out to be our least successful travel experience. Ozzie wrote a post card to Lorna Lee from London the night before our return home saying, "The visit to Germany was fair. Mingled with the people, but had enough of that type of vacationing." I knew he preferred sight-seeing, not visiting.

With tour plans made, excitement building for our first plane flight over the Atlantic Ocean, trepidations calmed by a prayer together on our knees at the altar of our beloved Good Shepherd Church, we set out August 8, 1972. Not only our Lord, but the whole world seemed to be smiling on us—remember, we were newlyweds much in love. Even though we were middle-aged, our hearts were young, and so in love that we felt nothing could help but turn out beautifully for us.

We met our tour group in New York and boarded the huge jet plane that would take us to our first foreign city, London, the scene of what turned out to be our first disagreement. This was one of only three that ever occurred in our years together. I remember each vividly, as they were so rare, our thoughts usually being in accord.

Our first interesting incident occurred that first night. On board the plane was a man whom we later recognized from a magazine picture as Prince Alexis Obolensky. As the long night flight continued, the Russian-born Prince known as "lord of the backgammon boards" continued to play his favorite game with members of his party. He was at least six feet four inches tall, and he had a craggy, rugged, unforgettable face.

As my husband tried to get his long legs comfortable for dozing, it seemed as though Obolensky was continually going down the aisle to get orange juice or whatever—each time bumping into my husband's legs or shoulders just as he had settled down for napping. This was one of the rare times I ever saw Ozzie visibly annoyed, and I began to fear for what might happen if the Prince jolted Ozzie one more time. Fortunately, the incidents ceased.

I've often wondered if the man had a feeling against "men of the collar," or whether the obvious bumps were, after all, purely accidental. In any case, it made an interesting occurrence for us to recall, especially when my brother recognized the man (from our description later on) in a magazine picture and article. We shrieked with recognition when we saw that rugged, unforgettable face again.

The flight continued, and morning finally came. We saw the sun float up from the ocean's edge, and everyone rushed to the left side of the plane to see it. This caused me a moment's concern about too much weight on one side of the plane, but I was assured that the pilot would compensate for any effect this might have. We were soon flying over the white cliffs of Dover, and then landing at Heathrow Airport, London. Our tour guide met us and we gathered with our group to go to the hotel, an old world sample of European hostelry near Piccadilly Circus.

Instead of a travelogue, I've chosen personal anecdotes to write about—one that show the other sides of the many-faceted character of my Pastor Honey. Our disagreement started with Ozzie's disappointment at seeing twin beds in our room. He grumbled about having to sleep clear across the room from his bride. This was to be a running comment all through our trip. We rarely had a double bed, and my husband could not sleep well, he said, without me "snuggling" his back. We were so tired from our first day's sight-seeing and the previous night's lack of sleep, we prepared for bed early.

I submerged myself in a giant of an English tub to steamingly reward my tired body, when what to my wondering eyes should appear just over the tub's rim but a push-button at eye level. I thought. Would the water run out? Would a towel drop down out of nowhere to cover me? I had already discovered my first bidet, that wonderful European fixture that I had been prepared for by friends' numerous stories of the reactions of the uninitiated. And now, a tempting button; what new wonder might appear at its bidding?

And appear she did! A precious gem of an English girl whose job, it appeared, was to help the elderly out of their tubs. More English charm clothed in a delicious cockney accent.

I fell into a deep sleep, but I was awakened around four in the morning by a husband who wanted to talk because he could not sleep. I confess I was not too thrilled at this, and our first disagreement occurred.

The ensuing years mellowed me to this occasional occurrence, and I must say, I improved in my reaction to being awakened now and then, especially as Ozzie made it clear that he never wanted me to not wake *him* if ever I had the "terrors in the night," or could not sleep. Because he was so kind, it was difficult for him not to find this same degree of kindness in others. But I scolded my new husband of only two months, and then I felt badly.

It was all forgotten in the morning and our sight-seeing continued. At four o'clock that afternoon, after seeing many of the places and sights London has to offer, we decided to treat ourselves to a traditional "high tea" at our hotel. They really do serve the exquisite thinly sliced cucumber and watercress on buttered bread sandwiches that you've always read about. Oh, the delicious English tea, and oh, that dessert cart that came to us, loaded with the most appealing sweets! To top off our pleasure, an elderly man in white tie and tails appeared, to tinkle out the teatime music on the grand piano. How English we thought, and we treasured that restful moment in our busy day.

One of our photos later developed shows Ozzie standing at the wall overlooking the Thames River, with the huge Westminster Clock in the Parliament tower in the background. What I did not realize as I snapped the picture, was that behind Ozzie, facing the other way, was a huge man with the largest stomach encased in a yellow sportshirt—that one could ever imagine. Ozzie never failed to say as we later showed our pictures, "Guess which one is Big Ben?"

Another incident that involved picture taking occurred when Ozzie wanted to snap my picture standing next to a Britisher dressed up in the famous "Beefeater" costume on guard at the famous Towers of London where the crown jewels are on display. As he obligingly stood close beside me for the picture, he said softly out of the side of his mouth, "How are things in the Colonies?" Ozzie overheard the remark and retorted, "Oh, haven't you heard? We're independent now!"

The tour continued to Amsterdam where one of the experiences besides canal cruising, was exploring a Gouda cheese factory in a small village in the countryside of Holland. Nothing would do but that we have a newly made Gouda cheese to take home. I placed it in my suitcase, surrounded by my clothes for padding, and off we continued on our tour. Although the cheese was encased in its characteristic quarter-inch layer of red, waxy substance, and wrapped in cellophane, the rich cheesy odor permeated my clothing. For several days afterward, people on our tour were known to make remarks when I drew near such as, "I smell cheese. We must be near a restaurant." We never explained, and eventually my "eau de Gouda" dissipated.

We saw all the sights tourists characteristically see, enjoying every moment together. My tall, aristocratic-looking husband and I became the center of much discussion and conjecture among our fellow tour bus traveling companions. "Have you two been married long?" they'd ask. "Do you have any children? How old are they?" We would say, "Twenty and twenty-four," and they would shake their heads in amazement at the seemingly long-married couple still acting like newlyweds. For some unexplained reason, we never told them we had only been married two months. Our happiness seemed contagious, and we enjoyed the fact that our traveling group seemed to derive pleasure from being in our company.

It wasn't until we were on the plane back to the states that we told our group we had just been married in June. I still can clearly see in my mind the facial reaction of one of the older ladies. "Humph," she snorted, "I knew it all along. I can tell newlyweds when I see them!" How I wish I could tell her now that my husband continued to act in the same attentive, loving manner up to the end of his earthly days, almost seven years later!

118

The motor coach trip through Dutch masterpiece country proved to us that the scenery really does look like those beautiful Dutch paintings we are all familiar with. Along we went, past farms, dikes and stork nests in chimneys into Germany. We were awed by the beautiful and famous Gothic Cathedral in Cologne, intrigued by Berlin, but the highlight for me of the tour through Germany was the cruise down the Rhine River on a steamer. The hills of the Rhine winelands were lovely, and above the vineyards we saw villages and castles dating from the Middle Ages.

Soon we were told we were about to approach the famous Lorelei rock, the spot where sailors were, as German legend has it, lured to their destruction by a lovely siren who sang as she combed her long golden hair. Ozzie hurried me out on deck on the left side of the boat. As he positioned me for a snapshot with the Lorelei in the background, an observing ship steward said, "Gebe ihr einen kamm!" Ozzie took out his pocket comb and snapped me pretending to lure him as I combed my hair. This seemed to delight both the steward and my husband, and they laughed at their cleverness at staging the picture. Ozzie's ability to speak German fluently added greatly to the pleasure of our German and Austrian travels.

After the lovely Rhine River trip, I wondered if anything could be more beautiful; but that was only the beginning of a hundred beautiful sights to come. We continued on to Frankfurt, the city rich in historical memories of Goethe. Then Hanover where memories of the unforgettable formal gardens of the Palace called Herrenhausen are still vivid in my mind.

On this trip to Germany we discovered there really was a village of Hamelin, southwest of Hanover, where the Pied Piper traditionally rid the town of rats centuries ago. We purchased small wine bottles shaped like rats; and then wondered when we finally arrived back home why we had purchased them, who we had bought them for, and whatever we had seen in them. All travelers, I'm sure, have experienced the "foolish purchase syndrome," and we were no exception.

Heidelberg Castle on the Neckar River proved to be as charming as we had thought it would be. There we added a lovely print of its courtyard and well, to our growing collection of engravings, prints, and watercolors of the various countries we were experiencing. We planned to frame them all and form a grouping on one wall of our home. This we did, and ever afterwards enjoyed their stimulus of pleasant travel memories.

As we drove through Bavaria into Alpine Austria, Ozzie continued to express verbal delight at the land of his ancestors. He determined at this time to come back again some day for a Lutherland tour. And so, as usual, my husband had a way of making dreams come true, and our second trip abroad was in July of 1976. Ozzie had realized that traveling in Germany was something he wanted to experience more of, having just had his appetite whetted in the travels through "Das Faterland" in 1972. He became the tour host for a trip through the cities of Germany that are known as "Lutherland."

In the travel brochure, part of his letter to interest people in traveling with us said, "Not only will we be enjoying the scenic beauty of Europe, but also many of us will be touring the areas in which our forefathers lived, the land that helped formulate the pattern of our lives and helped influence us in many ways . . . May God's blessing rest upon us as we travel together, enjoying the beauty of His nature and refreshing our vitality."

One could see Ozzie was looking forward to his own pleasure at not only seeing all the traditional places so important in Martin Luther's life, together with sites where the Reformation began, (so important to a Lutheran clergyman) but to seeing his own ancestral land again.

Our trip together through Hanover, Kassell, Whittenburg, Worms, Wiesbaden, Rothenburg, and Munich, enriched our picture of Germany. Can I ever forget watching my husband get out of the bus to walk along the Berlin Wall to experience first hand the emotion that this deterrer of freedom can cause. Will I ever again experience heat like the day we traveled to the site of the concentration camp at Dacchau, or the fierce emotions of hatred and sympathy I felt. I hope not! I experienced great pleasure at seeing Ozzie's delight in entering the church of his grandfather at Hermansburg, making it truly "Das Faterland" for him. Recalling excited comments when he saw the place of the famous trials at Nuremberg, the huge deserted field where Hitler spoke to thousands, and later on the place called the "Eagle's Nest" where Hitler vacationed, are memory treasures.

My birthday was spent touring Vienna—with a chocolate torte, a trip to Demel's, world famous and historic tea and torte house, and exploring Schonbrunn Palace and, the highlight of the day, attending *"Die Lustigie Widwe" (The Merry Widow)* at the opera. The next day we shopped, ate, toured, and walked through the State Park in the evening, where my husband waltzed me around to the music of a small Viennese orchestra that was playing there. This was the only time I ever danced in public with Ozzie. He was not in his clerical garb, and felt it was the perfect evening to enter into the gay and beautiful spirit that we felt in this city. Our trips together always seemed one pleasurable experience after another. We were blessed through the years by never experiencing the inconveniences, troubles, or difficulties that others had told us we might encounter.

16
Traveling Right Along

"The use of traveling is to regulate imagination by reality, and instead of thinking how things may be, to see them as they are."
Samuel Johnson

The hotel rooms in Europe continued to intrigue us on our 1972 tour. The stop for the night in Innsbruck, Austria, site of the 1964 Winter Olympics, was at a small inn obviously planned for the winter sport enthusiast. The huge bath had heated pipes for the towels, and we could imagine snow dampened sport socks and scarves hanging from them also.

We enjoyed the evening's entertainment of Tyrolean singers and dancers. The cuisine was great and the ambience warm and cozy, but the high point of the night was crawling into our first real feather bed, complete with a puffy down comforter. As we sank deeper into its billowing bulk, we suddenly realized it was August, it was warm, and this type of sleeping was for cold winter nights. We solved our dilemma by stripping the comforter of its sheet-like covering and used this for our lightweight topping for the night. When we finished our nightly prayers, Ozzie said, "Darling, this is the life!" He obviously was enjoying the fast pace and varied experiences we were having. So was I!

The next morning after some sight-seeing, we all settled down in our tour bus, prepared to climb the Alps and cross the historic Brenner Pass into northern Italy. The most astounding sights I had ever seen began to appear—the Dolomites! I had never even heard of this particular division of the Eastern Alps. Huge mountains that appeared to be made of solid rock arose on each side of our route. They fascinated me more than the snow-topped Alps we have all seen photos of. I had never realized that there could be such a variety of colored rock strata, and that mountains of rock could rise up so high, so huge, so breathtaking in their gigantic beauty. Small lakes were dotted here and there, and we perilously rounded sharp turns as we climbed, some so sharp that the back end of the bus seemed to hang out over the edge of a drop that appeared to go straight down. I was somewhat amused by the tiny barbed wire that was strung along the road, as the drop appeared to start about a foot away from it. I wondered what was its use if one were to start to slip over. I confess to being so frightened at one point, I exchanged seats with my husband so he would be by the window. There was no logic to this, but it made the danger seem less.

Finally we were arriving at the mountain resort of Cortina D'Ampezzo, called the "Queen of the Dolomites," where a lunch outside in the sun, at open air tables, revived us.

We had heard that this resort, site of the 1956 Winter Olympics, has the country's best ski hotels, the best slopes, and the most exciting people. In Cortina, princesses (Windsch-Graetzes and Furstenbergs), movie stars (Mastroianni, Gassman), and industrialists (Pirelli, Burtoni), ski hard, eat lustily, and dress *beyond* the hilt. Of course it was the wrong time of the year, so we saw no famous persons we could recognize.

As you might remember from your literature classics in school, these beautiful Dolomites are the distant mountains Romeo referred to when he gazed out of Juliet's window in Verona and said, "Night's candles are burnt out, and jocund day stands tiptoe on the misty mountain tops." It was rumored that the 1988 winter games might again be hosted by Cortina—and we could understand when we saw the beauty of this magnificent ski terrain.

Then it was on to Venice, the city Ozzie could hardly wait to see. "I've heard they walk or float, but never drive," he commented. "Save some crackers for the pigeons in St. Mark's Square. We're staying at the Bauer Gruenwald. That's a German name if I ever heard one. Did you know, darling, that Venice was invaded by the Huns at one time?"

I could tell by the running remarks that he was getting more and more into this traveling spree. Ozzie's boyish quality was never more evident than when he was traveling, seeing new sights, experiencing new thrills. I was looking forward to seeing Venetian glass (the world's thinnest), Venetian lace (the daintiest), and to the tour's promised evening gondola ride complete with serenade.

I was unprepared for the beauty of the glorious pink and white stone Doge's Palace, its luminous pastel facade set airily on multitudes of delicate arches, in turn resting on dozens of sculpted columns of marble. I fell in love with the bridges everywhere, the tiny lace, glass, and embroidery shops, the magnificence of the grandiose Piazza San Marco. We fed the pigeons, hundreds of them, as all tourists do, and literally gawked at the glittering mosaic splashed fantasia that is the Basilica of St. Mark.

But the hotel room! That was the pièce de résistance. It was huge with a wood floor that you knew must have been waxed for a century. Venetian glass shaded electrical fixtures. There was a tiny escritoire where you could imagine an Italian countess sitting and writing secret notes of passion; and a bathroom as large as our bedroom back in Ohio. I leaned out as far as possible from the grilled window overlooking the quietly gleaming small canal and thought, *Could anyone be as fortunate as I.*

Such sights, and the best was yet to come! We were on our own for lunch and chose to eat at the hotel. We had been told that the building had been a former palazzio, and the outdoor restaurant bordered the Grand Canal. We were ushered to a small table for two at a balustrade overlooking the Canal. It was apart from the rest of the people, and we wondered if the waiter thought the "priest" wished privacy with the lady. My husband had worn his clerical clothes that day. He had noticed the looks we received from the predominantly Catholic Venetians while sightseeing, and was enjoying the questioning glances we were getting.

Then ensued the finest service you could imagine. We were pampered with not just a small plate of fruit, as we had seen on the other patrons' tables, but a huge basketful. Knowing smiles occurred between the waiter and his assistant as we traded bites, as was our habit when we each ordered a different ethnic dish.

After lunch we each received a glass bowl the size of a small dishpan. "To swish our fruit around in," we discovered when we asked what it was for. We giggled and agreed we were glad we had asked, and hadn't started to use them as finger bowls.

I reached into my bag for our camera, wishing to capture the lovely experience, when the waiter who was watching our every move offered to take our picture. Another treasured photograph was taken to add to the growing collection of beautiful memories.

When Pastor Honey was given the bill for our lunch, he almost paled visibly. Yes, it was exorbitant; yes, there were no prices listed on our "special" menu; yes, we had been pampered for a price. But then he threw back his head and laughed. We had been overcharged, but it was worth it, he said. Years later, we still laughed at the memory of that extravagant luncheon on the Grand Canal in Venice, Italy.

As we climbed into the gondola that evening with another couple on our tour, the Curtis's from Philadelphia (a lovely black couple that we had so enjoyed conversing with on the bus excursion), we felt our cup of joy "runneth over." The gondolier was a young opera student, and he put his heart into his love songs as he poled the sleek, shiny black swan of a gondola on liquid history; between high dark walls, by wrought-iron gated courtyards, where the gleaming cobblestones were polished with age and moonlight. Yes, the moon was out, and we were blessed with a night to remember.

The launch took us back to the reality of mainland Italy the next morning as we set out for Florence. One could write for hours on the splendor of the art treasures of Florence; to tell of only a few memories seems inadequate to do justice to this historic city. As the tour bus traveled along, the high water mark on buildings from the disastrous floods of a few years ago was pointed out. In the Accachemic Museum we turned a corner and gasped! There in front of us, in its own separate rotunda was Michelangelo's David. It was larger than we had anticipated, and we marveled at its beauty. Ozzie said, "Look at his hands, Angel. The one he is holding up is smooth; the hand down at his side shows the veins standing out. What a man!" He meant Michelangelo's skill as a sculptor. I confess I was thinking the same thing about the beauty of David.

A later version of the well known Pieta was interesting, as it was sculpted in a reddish marble, and a self-portrait of Michelangelo as an older man included in the grouping. Other partly finished statuary by this sculpting genius left the unforgettable impression of hands, arms, legs, parts of bodies struggling to get out of the entrapping marble.

Other travelers will recall with me the pleasure of seeing the famous Cathedral, the East Door Michelangelo himself called the "Gate Of Paradise"; the Medici Chapels, Giotto's Belfry, and the Ponte Vecchio, or Old Bridge, lined with shops. And then, as all roads really do lead to Rome, we began to anticipate seeing this monumental city.

Every evening Ozzie would take out a small notebook and make notes about what he had been seeing; spiritual "tie-ins" with incidents, sights, art works, and people for his future newspaper articles and sermons. He seemed to have a knack for drawing analogies from our experiences to make a spiritual point for use in his life's work. One somehow sensed that even though completely submerged in the activity of the moment on our travels, his mind was always on the importance of the grandeur, ability, wisdom, and grace of his Triune God.

17
Some Roman and Parisian Memories

"The fool wanders; the wise man travels."
Old Proverb

Impressions and memories of Rome are humorous, awe-inspiring, and one was rather painful for my husband. As usual, he wore the clerical collar in Italy, partly out of respect for this mecca for Catholics, partly because he was human enough to enjoy the deference paid to a man in the priestly collar.

One time we were the last seated in the bus. All took turns sitting in the back, and we hurried out when it stopped and began to run to catch up with our group. Ozzie had his arm around my waist as we ran. He was laughing at my efforts to keep up with his long legs. A twosome of elderly Italian ladies dressed in black stopped with open mouths, to cross themselves in horror at what they thought was a priest running with his arm around a blonde hussy!

As we paused that afternoon to reflect on the magnificence of the Vatican, and St. Peter's with its breathtaking Sistine Chapel, we were standing alone deciding which of the cafes on the Via Veneto we would patronize. All of a sudden, one of the small deadly bees that are indigenous to Rome, stung Ozzie on the neck. Ozzie said, "I guess the Pope hasn't forgiven Martin Luther yet. He sent one of his emissaries to remind me."

We looked for a pharmacy to buy some type of salve to relieve the pain and the swelling, which was becoming quite red and noticeable on my husband's neck. We spoke no Italian. The pharmacist spoke no English. In desperation, I buzzed like a bee and pretended to sting Ozzie's neck. The man threw up his arms in understanding, laughing at my play acting, and went to get a tube of ointment that worked beautifully.

Later on we threw a coin into the Trevi Fountain; for we were assured that it would guarantee our return to Rome. We did return a few years later, but weren't able to toss in a coin this time, as the fountain was being drained for cleaning.

The beauty of the Spanish Steps was marred for us by the hordes of hippies that were sitting, standing, or just hanging around. We gathered that this was a popular meeting place for them.

The "illumination" tour (nighttime sight-seeing) that evening was outstanding, almost unreal in its beauty of lighted fountains, buildings, and statuary. We felt anything after this would be anticlimactic.

But of course we were wrong.

We were driven to the Roman colosseum after observing all the cats that populated the Forum. As we stood looking down on the open rooms that had been under the floor of this amphitheater built about 80 A.D., Ozzie remarked, "When you think of all that was suffered here by the early Christians, I wonder what have I ever endured for Christ." The archway in which we were standing was lit by a single bare and hanging light bulb. The shadows created an eerie atmosphere for our reflecting. I stubbed my toe on a small rock, put it in my pocket, and even now, wonder if an early Christian sandal might have trod on it centuries ago.

Each city we visited had its own special thrilling delights. Milan, vital and bustling financial center of Italy, allowed us to see the LaScala Opera House, and the world famous old Gothic Cathedral. It was here that Ozzie conversed with a caretaker who showed us a golden cask purported to contain some of the bones of the wise men who traveled to Christ's birthplace. I was awed and excited until Ozzie told me many a cathedral had been built around a relic that was made out to be authentic, but whose main purpose was to inspire the building of a needed church. I was crushed. I wanted to believe those bones were the real thing.

Ozzie teased me about my gullibility, and said, "Well, perhaps this relic is an authentic one." Always mindful of other's feelings, he never wanted to hurt anyone, especially me. This constant awareness and interest in another's feelings or thoughts was a great part of his charm. It was this character trait that led to one of the funniest incidents of our trip. I will tell you about it later on in this chapter.

After an eye-filling drive by Lake Como into Switzerland, we continued through the Alps to Lucerne, where we promenaded on the fourteenth century Chapel Bridge, viewed the lion monument, and did some extensive shopping. After a good night's rest, we continued on through Berne and Neufchatel into the fertile farmland and quaint old villages of France on our way to Paris.

Oh, how I loved Paris! Our hotel was a brand new one this time, a few blocks from the Arc de Triomphe. Ozzie was fascinated by a small refrigerator in our room, which automatically totaled up via a computer system each can of juice, or small wine bottle removed from its inner racks.

Our last night in Paris, after two days of sight-seeing, we relaxed in our room and discussed the beauty we had seen, I particularly enjoyed the Palace at Versailles with its gardens all in flower and its balcony where Marie Antoinette, had stood. What sights the upper smoky glass panels in the ballroom must have reflected back in the days of Louis XIV!

Ozzie had seen his most favorite cathedral in all Europe, Notre Dame. "How would you like to see that in our church!" he asked me while gazing at its famous rose stained glass window. "Remember our first night's walk in the mist by the Seine?" (How could I forget it, remembering the sight of my uninhibited husband unabashedly wearing a clear plastic hotel shower cap in the rain.) "And wasn't our early morning walk great?" Ozzie asked. Little old men with long brooms were out cleaning up the sidewalks of Paris as we strolled under the trees leafily leaning over the walks. We saw a building under construction, obviously of contemporary design, contrasting starkly with the man who was lighting up a charcoal brazier of water that already contained tin lunch boxes, a task we were sure must have been practiced for centuries so that workers could have a hot noonday meal.

We decided to have our final dinner in Europe in the beautiful main dining room of the hotel. Ozzie wanted me to wear his favorite long white crocheted dress, and he changed from the sport jacket of the day's excursions to his formal attire, the black suit and clerical collar, which became him so well.

During dinner he attempted conversation, as was always his pleasure, with our very French young waiter. "What is your opinion of Pétain?" he asked. The young man's eyes widened and he turned to look me up and down. Ozzie again said, "What do you think about Pétain?" Again the waiter's eyes expressed some shock, and he looked at me, this time out of the sides of seemingly very embarrassed eyes. "*Je ne comprende pas, Monsieur*," he said shyly.

Ozzie finally realized the boy was probably too young to remember France's traitor of World War II, and explained who he was. "Oh, oh, Monsieur, oui!" the young man said, in obvious relief. "What did you think I said?" asked my Pastor Honey. "I thought you said 'putaine,' " our waiter retorted. "What does that mean?" Ozzie asked. "Oh, Monsieur, that is very bad word similar to what you call prostitute!" he said. No wonder the young waiter had looked me up and down in embarrassed horror. He had thought the "Father" was asking his opinion of his prostitute!

Next morning we were to jet back to New York. Ozzie snapped a picture of me at Orly Airport sitting in the middle of a long row of our tour group's luggage. He later titled this shot, "Angel with her Paris purchases." He had said I should pick out a Paris gown, or some other special purchase besides the small things one invariably gets when one tours foreign places. Instead of clothes, I had already chosen a beautiful hand embroidered table cloth and napkins in an embroidery shop in Venice as my special large purchase. It was to be embroidered to specifications by nuns to match our china, with one red rose to the left of every place

128

setting, and on each napkin. It arrived three months later, to my great joy, just before Christmas. I still treasure it and consider it something to be handed down to my daughters.

We were so thrilled at our going home to the United States. "It's great to travel, but greater yet to be getting home!" Ozzie commented. We had had just enough of "le grand tour," and we were looking forward to being back in the world's most prized place to live, our America!

18
The Holy Land

"Art thou only a stranger in Jerusalem, and hast not known the things which are come to pass there in these days?"
Luke 24:18

The land of Christ's birth, death, and resurrection seems always to be caught in sporadic violence. During our ten-day tour there in October, 1975, we experienced evidences of a life continually overshadowed by the presence of soldiers. They watched with guns slung over their shoulders from the roof tops. Our purses were searched upon entering a department store in Tel Aviv. Because of an El Al (Israel's airline) strike at this time, I had a complete body search in a small booth by a woman in army uniform as we were preparing to board our plane to Rome after the Holy Land tour.

Nevertheless, Ozzie and I agreed that this trip was the most outstanding, the most meaningful of all our trips. There is almost no possible way to convey to the reader the feeling one experiences as one really does tread the paths of the Savior. I kept saying to myself, "My eyes are seeing the same sights He saw. My feet are touching the same stones that His sandals touched." It was awesome at times to see all the places you had ever read about in the Bible. Instead of just being names, like the Valley of Gehenna, you actually saw and smelled this long, narrow valley outside the South wall of the old city of Jerusalem. You realized why our Lord mentions it in at least eleven different verses in the New Testament; using it as a synonym for hell. It was and still is used as a receptacle for refuse, fires continually being kept up to prevent disease. As the smoke rises seemingly a half a mile, one realizes the inelegant phrase, "stinking to high heaven" must have had its beginnings here.

Again, instead of a descriptive travelogue, I feel some impressions and anecdotes would be an interesting way for me to convey to you the personality of my husband. A man's words reveal the man. Through his words, you come to know him more intimately. So I include some thoughts written by Ozzie during our trip. On the back of a picture of the Garden of Gethsemane he wrote, "Stood here this morning and meditated. Then on to the place of Christ's scourging, Jericho and the Dead Sea. What a humbling experience to be here! The Bible comes alive, and one feels truly awed. What a price Christ paid for us! Tomorrow we plan on being in Tiberius, and then a trip on the Sea of Galilee. The olive tree in the picture is thought to date back to the time of Christ."

Upon visiting the Church of the Nativity, just the two of us wandered a bit away from our group to stand at a portion of the grotto wall under the church, undecorated and uncovered by the beautifully decorated hangings. There, alone and unseen, Ozzie knelt with his hand on the bare cave wall and had a silent prayer. He told me that he knew Jesus could have been born in any portion of these caverns, and felt the need to experience an undecorated place. He believed it would be more like it was at the time of that miraculous birth. He wrote, "This is a soul-searching experience. We visit so many places and everything I have read seems real now. Knelt here in humble adoration."

In Hebron, in the ancient land of Canaan, we visited the cave of Machpelah where Abraham, Isaac, Jacob, and their wives are buried. Of course, the inevitable massive building is built over the tombs. I found it hard to believe that this immense shrine was the work of King Herod's stonemasons around 40 B.C. It is a place revered today by Christians, Jews, and Muslims, and it is a gorgeous feat of architecture and engineering. Once inside, I was especially drawn to stand at the grillwork looking down on the spot where Sarah lay.

I had always teased Ozzie about us having a baby. "The world needs another little O. H. Bertram," I'd say. The thought of us having a child at our middle age would fill him with mock dread. And so, as I gazed down at that Sarah whose name I carried, I became visibly overcome at the similarity of our lives. I, too, had experienced great changes in my life, just as she had. My eyes teared up in emotion, as I thought of the miracles in her life and mine.

Ozzie walked briskly over to me from where he had been looking down on Sarah's husband's tomb. He said, "I know what you're doing! You're praying for a miracle to happen so you can have a baby in our old age, just like Sarah. Well, I just cancelled it. I told God, 'Her name may be Sarah, but mine isn't Abraham!' "

An eerie incident happened as we visited the traditional place of the Last Supper, called the Upper Room. A group of fifty or so people had crowded into the center of this place. Under the leadership of their minister, and attempting to follow his example, they were all babbling loudly—I suppose they felt they were "speaking in tongues." One poor woman looked embarrassed at it all, but made a valiant effort to join the others. What came out was a continual repetition of "lah, lah, lah."

I mean no insult to these dear people who, I'm sure, felt they were honoring God by doing this. However, a strange, almost evil feeling was experienced by me and others of our group. I actually shivered. It was as though Satan were influencing these people to dishonor this traditionally sacred place by having them utter these animalistic sounds in the misguided belief that they were doing God's will. It was not that Ozzie and I doubt the existence of the "speaking in tongues" phenomenon; it was just an insurmountable feeling that this we were seeing and hearing was not an example of it being inspired by God.

The day we traveled to the Dead Sea, one of my dear and supportive friends, Eve Rockwood, and I decided we would wear our bathing suits under our skirts and blouses. We wanted to experience the salt and mineral laden shimmering waters, surrounded by craggy desert landscapes, broken by the mountains of Moab on the east and the hills of Judea on the west. We had heard that it was impossible to sink because of the high concentration of minerals. We decided we were going to walk down the road away from the small refreshment tables and bathhouse where our guide took us. It was very hot and we walked away, exploring for a suitable place to do our private wading without an audience.

As we prepared to step over a barbed-wire fence, suddenly an Israeli soldier with a huge (it seemed to us) machine gun stepped out from a sign we were unable to read. "No, no, ladies," he said in English. How did he know we were Americans? "You must not step out there. This is the closest point to the Golan Heights. There might be land mines on this beach."

We retreated back to where our group was. At this time of year the water was low, and we waded in silt up to our knees, with much squealing, until we reached water deep enough to float. When we returned to the small bath house we were seated on a bench and treated to having our legs lifted into small buckets of water and scrubbed down by young boys in Muslim attire. I couldn't remember having my legs washed by someone other than my mother since I was a little girl. What a nice custom, I thought. On our return to our husbands, we told them of our experience. "Just how old *were* these boys that washed your legs?" smilingly asked my suspicious husband, and was reassured when we guessed they were around ten years old. Eve and I still giggle about our Dead Sea bathing adventure.

Another unforgettably vivid memory was of my leaning out of our fourth or fifth floor window of the hotel where we stayed overnight on the shore of the Sea of Galilee. Pastor Honey was already in the large double bed, anxious to go to sleep after a full day. "Come to bed, Angel," he called to me several times, as I continued to gaze out from the screenless window upon a yellow gold path on this beautiful sea, made by a full moon. The path seemed to come straight to me, and I could clearly picture Jesus coming toward me, walking on these very waters. It drew me, it fascinated me. I could not tear myself away from the beauty.

I could see why Jesus frequented this lovely body of water. There were no insects; it was cool and lovely after miles of seeing arid desert lands. What a fascinating land of contrasts, I thought. How could I leave this sight. I eventually did, of course. Others experienced the drawing fascination of this beautiful place, I realized; as early the next morning, upon looking out of this same window, I saw Mary Lou Gaffke, another member of our group, sitting with her Bible on her lap, reading and gazing out over the water intermittently.

We were fortunate to have undoubtedly one of the finest guides in the Holy Land. His name was Joseph Jahshan; he was handsome, very knowledgeable, and he was a Christian Arab. He would burst into Christian hymns as we traveled along. He stopped the bus on one occasion to get some pomelos, an odd fruit similar to grapefruit, for all of us to try. On another occasion, as we were heading toward the River Jordan, he jumped out to purchase a bottle of wine made by a group of Bethlehem nuns, so that we could all have a taste; and so that Pastor Honey and I could have the empty bottle to dip out some River Jordan water to carry home. We wanted it to baptize our new little grandchild, Holly Moulton. Ozzie's daughter, Lorna, and her husband, Gary, had made my husband a grandfather a month before, a source of great pride for Ozzie. I managed to get it safely home in my carry-on bag, with never a drop spilled. I boiled the life out of it before the formal baptism so that no germ would touch Ozzie's "little sweetheart," as he called her.

That evening saw us taking off our shoes and stockings and wading in the River Jordan. Ozzie wore size thirteen triple A shoes. His feet were extremely long and narrow. Again I teased him about them and said, "Darling, if anyone else besides our Lord could walk on water, it would certainly be you with those feet." He loved me to tease him, and always loved to tease me about something. Such was our relationship. He always made life joyous for me.

One of our tour days we climbed the steps trod by Jesus as He was led to Caiaphas, the high priest who presided at His trial. A priest showed us around the traditional place of the palace. He led us down steep steps into the dungeon where tradition says Jesus spent that last night. The Father recited parts of Psalm 88 to us. I was so touched I again shed tears; and stepped back and scratched my bare shoulder on the stone wall. I didn't want anyone to see my being so moved in this place. The priest did. Later on, he brought my Ozzie and me a soup can in which he had quickly planted a small passionflower vine. Our group said I could not possibly take it back into the United States. They said, "Hide it between your clothes in your suitcase. Perhaps it will be undiscovered." I didn't. I carried it boldly in plain sight, wrapped around the bottle of River Jordan water in my carry-on flight bag. When the customs officer asked what it was, upon our return to the United States, I told him, "It's a passionflower vine given us by a priest in Jerusalem because he recognized in us a mutual love for our Lord!" The officer said nothing, and nodded me on. Such was my reward for honesty!

Ozzie was fascinated with the plains of Armageddon—that place of a great battle to be fought out on "the great day of God," between the powers of good and evil (Revelations 16:16). He told me he had pictured it to be a vast arid plain. He was surprised to find it cultivated into many acres of beautifully planned green-growing gardens.

Our brief stay in Greece, before we came to Israel, proved to be very successful. In Athens we were allowed to crawl all over the Acropolis by moonlight—one of the last years that this was allowed. Our hotel was right on the Saronic Gulf of the Aegean Sea. "What a view!" Ozzie exclaimed as we set out for a quick tour of ancient Corinth. He wrote on a postcard, "Toured and retraced St. Paul's visit here as in Acts 17 and 18. What an experience . . . This is mythology and Christianity combined." He imagined Paul writing to the Corinthians as we walked over the excavated old streets, and was impressed with seeing the ancient Pirene fountain excavations. How much meaning, I felt, for Ozzie to see these statues of the "unknown Gods," and remember what Paul had said to the people of Athens when he had seen, as we had seen outside of Athens, the self-same altar to "the unknown God" that Paul had mentioned in Acts 17:23.

I must end what could be an endless recitation of outstanding remembrances, with an experiment my husband conducted at the sight called the Mount of the Beatitudes on the Sea of Galilee. We had a delightful boat trip across to Capernaum, and then went to a most exquisite church built on the sight of the place where Jesus preached his sermon on the mount. Ozzie asked us all if we would stay where we were while he ran to a likely spot for speaking. He spoke in a normal tone of voice and yet we could all hear him. "Christ knew about sound and how it travels. He knew just where to stand. I have always wondered about that," my communications-minded husband said.

When we returned to America, Ozzie never lost his enthusiasm when he spoke of this particular trip. We were thinking of planning another tour there when his illness struck. Oh, how grateful I am that I persuaded him to conduct a tour to the Holy Land. He had thought he really didn't want to go there—perhaps fearing it would not live up to expectations. He never ceased thanking me for encouraging him to go, whenever the subject came up.

Ozzie was still mentioning our Holy Land trip in a portion of our printed Christmas letter a year later. He wrote:

"The year 1976 has been diversified in our activities. In July, we led a tour through Germany, Austria and Switzerland. This proved to be a very stimulating trip, both spiritually and politically. It was an entirely different trip from the previous October journey to Israel and Greece. The latter brought us in close perspective to the life of Christ, and it gave us a feeling of sacredness to walk the paths where Christ had walked. On the trip to Europe, we learned firsthand the state of affairs in the Church in Germany, both West and East. The persecution of the Church under Communism is of such proportion that makes us thank God for our many freedoms, especially of worship. The subtle undermining of religion by atheism is thorough, and it is well that Christians support their fellow brothers and sisters with their prayers and financial aid. "The cement curtain," which engulfs the communist-dominated nations, is depressing and frightening; it is one large concentration camp.

"On the other hand, we were privileged to see where the two grandfathers, Bertram and Castens, went to the seminary in Hermannsburg. The historical knowledge that we gleaned from that trip in general is invaluable."

19
A Year of Peaks and Pits

"But at my back I always hear
time's winged chariot hurrying near . . .
Let us roll all our strength and all
our sweetness up into one ball,
and tear our pleasures with rough strife
through the iron gates of life."
Andrew Marvell

"Those blasted feather mattresses in Germany!" Ozzie said one morning after our return from our last trip abroad. It was September 1978, and the travels through northern Germany and briefly into Denmark had been marred slightly by the backaches that seemed increasingly annoying to him.

"I know that this is the reason I didn't sleep well throughout our trip. My back was not supported well in any of those beds," Ozzie continued, "I think I'll start seeing the chiropractor again." In August Ozzie had not seemed quite his vigorous, cheerful self as we visited his sister, Clara Schweitzer, and my brother, Dr. Richard Breck, in Connecticut. The stress of the trip there by way of Quebec City and Montreal, Canada, proved to be greater than either of us imagined. Pollyanna me had made light of some wrong turns, but Ozzie was visibly distressed at the incidents. This was unlike him, but at the time I attributed it to the letting-down process one experiences at the start of a vacation after a particularly distressful, though successful, year's work.

There had been a quiet uproar, if there can be such a thing, from a few people over Ozzie allowing an elderly man and a younger man, both highly respected in our community, to join our church. You see, they were members of the Masonic Lodge. There are some regulations in the Lutheran Church-Missouri Synod concerning lodge members and holding church membership. It has been not only the written regulation, but also the understood practice that each minister is allowed to make a judgment on each individual person's request to join the church. Even with the obtained permission of the "higher ups" in Ozzie's Synod, some people were distressed by the admittance of these two into church membership.

This, together with the worry caused by a persistent unwholesome love for Ozzie by a most attractive woman who had come to my husband with her troubles, had made for a year that seemed to him more distressing than most years.

As we traveled to Connecticut after touring Quebec City, a place I had never visited before, and highly enjoyed, Ozzie confided his worries to me. A member of the family was drifting away from her faith, he felt. The television station he most desired to accept the "Worship for Shut-ins" program was proving to be illusive and expensive.

The hurt of having his judgments questioned after thirty-five years of experience in the ministry preyed on his mind; and he seemed puzzled as to how people who knew the Lord was first in his life, could doubt his motives and actions. I must confess I was finding it difficult to understand also.

As I look back, I feel it was at this time that the disease that was to end Ozzie's life began. Subtle changes were taking place that caused Ozzie to not feel up to par, and he sought reasons for this in the exterior world.

When his sister and brother-in-law, the Reverend and Mrs. Ernest Laabs from Napoleon, Ohio, suggested that we accompany them to visit cousins in Germany, it seemed to my husband a chance for a much-needed change, as the vacation in the East had only been for a week. Ozzie truly hated leaving his beloved work. As many people who love their vocation feel, he loved going away, but could hardly wait to get back.

It has been an old church-related joke that if some people came to church, the roof would fall in. I must include here an item from The Toledo Blade that appeared in Don Wolfe's column of interesting bits of news concerning the people of Toledo. He reported, "After the Rev. O. H. Bertram left for vacation last week, the roof fell in. Ceiling tiles along the hallway of the education wing of Good Shepherd Lutheran Church came tumbling down." Quite a switch on the old cliché.

This story illustrates the reputation that Ozzie held—one who really lived for his beloved church work, and one upon whom many depended. Thus, it took a real temptation to leave his work, as was the invitation to visit the town in Germany to see the seminary where Ozzie's grandfathers had obtained their ministerial training, and the church where one of his grandfathers met and married the girl who was to be Ozzie's paternal grandmother.

Passports were quickly checked, passage by air obtained, letters exchanged, and Ozzie began to prepare a sermon in the German language for preaching in a small church in Kiel, Germany, from whom he had received an invitation to preach upon visiting the area.

We left with high hopes of experiencing what we had experienced before on our trips to Europe and Greece and Israel; relaxation, new experiences and sights, together with the pleasure of being in sister Irma and brother-in-law Ernie's company. Both these relatives had always expressed much love for Ozzie and me, as we always did for them, so there was never any strain in being together.

Our practice of strictly following a low cholesterol diet was almost impossible to adhere to. Torte every afternoon was the custom, with real whipped cream. Every distant but dear relative

137

in the several different small German villages of Satrus, Husby, and Wankendorf seemed to vie with each other in showing us the culinary treasures of German cookery. The food was different—more animal fat than Ozzie and I were used to, but oh, did we both enjoy it. We carried a sugar substitute with us, but it was insignificant, I'm sure, in relation to the rich foods that were prepared for our visit.

It is interesting and almost prophetic to note that in a sermon given by Ozzie in 1976, he said,

"Dr. Hans Selye of Montreal, Canada, claims that practically all disease is caused by stress . . . and if a person drives himself, becomes filled with tension and stress, fear and guilt, the glands that produce protective hormones cannot produce enough to protect the body from attack by maladies, which strike at the weakest point."

I've often thought the combination of prolonged stress and a different diet had something to do with Ozzie's illness. Until cancer research finds an answer some day, this is only a personal observation. Most psychologists and physicians agree that stress can cause illness, either real or psychosomatic. When several nights were interrupted by Ozzie's inability to sleep, caused by the recurring backaches, I extracted a promise from him to have a real going over by his physician upon our return to the United States.

Upon the finding of his doctor that nothing seemed to be seriously wrong, Ozzie determined to get some relief from what was considered an arthritic back problem. He started going to his chiropractor, which did provide a measure of relief, and he planned to join a local health spa for a concerted plan of exercise.

One of our church members, Aaron Mattes, who was a highly esteemed teacher of physical therapy at the University of Toledo, mapped out a program of exercises for Ozzie. We began to go to the University twice a week; Ozzie wanted my companionship and encouragement in every venture. I enjoyed watching him go through these athletic paces, and prayed they would be the answer to the ever-increasing discomfort of the back pain.

Rita McGinnis, Ozzie's very capable and beloved church secretary, afterwards told me that it was around this time that she would sometimes go into my husband's office to find him stretched out on the black leather couch in what I called his "consultation corner," and he would dictate letters from there while catching some brief relief from his back problem.

In November, through the suggestion of one of our church members, Dr. Joachim Dressler, who was a prominent pathologist in Toledo, plus the added encouragement given by a cardiologist church member, Dr. Earl Perrigo, Ozzie made an appointment for a CAT-scan. The doctors and Ozzie felt this should definitely be the next step in determining what was causing the increasingly intense pain.

The indepth X-ray scan revealed a small, one-inch or so growth or shadow on the pancreas—the gland that lies deep in the upper abdomen in the proximity of the spine. Now we were told the reason for the pain. The gland itself has no nerve endings, so it caused what is called referred pain. In retrospect, we know now that the intense pain was due to the invasion of the cancer into nerves in his back.

An appointment was made for surgery in December. We obtained the skills of a highly qualified surgeon, Dr. Paul Carter, who had also the blessing of being a Christian. On the morning of Tuesday, December 12, 1978, Ozzie underwent surgery of four hours' duration at St. Vincent's Hospital in Toledo.

The year was quickly drawing to its close. My husband was at the peak of his career. Our church had grown greatly in membership, and the television possibilities for expanded coverage in city after city seemed to be unlimited. Ozzie's sermons and writings had mellowed, as he had in life. His messages were richer, deeper, with the insight and talents gained through the passage of time and experience.

Our love for each other had grown with each year, and we looked forward to the days when our golden years would be spent in each other's company. The loss of our dream for a future together seemed almost as intolerable as it was impossible.

20
The Approach of the D.A.

"Tho' devils all the world shall fill,
All eager to devour us,
We tremble not, we fear no ill,
They shall not over-pow'r us.
This world's prince may still scowl
Fierce as he will,
He can harm us none, He's judged;
The deed is done,
One little word can fell him."
                    Martin Luther
                    from the hymn,
                    "A Mighty Fortress Is Our God"

The hours of waiting for the medical news that surgery would provide, proved to be one of the greatest ordeals I had ever endured. I adored my husband; my life was wrapped up in him and his well-being. I willed that all would be well. I prayed that Dr. Carter would find a small tumor encased in a "membrane baggie" so that he could just lift it out.

I am so grateful now that I did not know anything about cancer of the pancreas. If I had medical knowledge of the deadliness of this particular type of cancer, I think I would have immediately fainted when I was told that the operation had revealed a cancerous growth that, though small, had entwined itself so utterly around important veins, nerves, and the spinal column itself, it was impossible to remove.

I only remember Dr. Earl Perrigo, the cardiologist, and our young Director of Christian Education, Dennis Liebich, being with me as they broke the news to me as I waited in Ozzie's hospital room. I can hear myself saying over and over again through my tears, "This isn't the way it was supposed to be; this isn't the way I wanted it to be." It seemed as though I couldn't grasp what they were telling me.

Then Dr. Carter came in and beautifully, lovingly, and patiently told me of the "by-pass" surgery he had performed on Ozzie, so that there would be no blockage from the liver and no chance of Ozzie's developing jaundice.

140

I had a mixture of feelings during these moments—joy and gratitude to the Lord for allowing my Ozzie to come through the surgery with no other complications—abject disappointment over the fact that the tumor was cancerous and could not be removed. The moment of joy I felt when I had that beloved man back in the hospital room again after the long hours away from me in the recovery room was a feeling only one who has shared the same experience will fully understand.

Our church congregation, together with many people who knew and admired my husband, were waiting for the news. I'm sure more concentrated prayers were going to God during these days than anyone could imagine. Cards, plants, flowers, and letters of encouragement started to flood in. The amount of expressions of love and encouragement were impressive to even the most casual of hospital workers and visitors.

Ozzie's progress and recovery from the surgical by-pass were enhanced and furthered, I'm convinced, by the public show of love and concern. Even the ones who managed to come up surreptitiously, as he was supposed to have only a minimum of visitors, served a purpose; they were the very ones who encouraged him the most by their persistent insistance that they must see for themselves that he was all right.

My only problem was with the many, many clergymen who visited. I'm sure they felt that they would perhaps be one of only a half-dozen or so who would stop to see their fellow clergyman. To Ozzie and me it seemed as though a dozen or more a day walked in the room to provide spiritual comfort to their brother in Christ. They were of all different denominations, calling on patients from their own congregation, and they all wanted to see and pray over my husband. So loving and kind they were, so loving and kind was he, that it was the nurses and I who finally had to call a halt to the steady stream of visitors.

I lettered a note and taped it to the door of the room, "Please stop at nurses' desk next door to see if you may visit." However, most felt they were the exception to this request, and we were truly grateful if exhausted by their loving concern. One of Ozzie's favorite admonitions of Christ was, "Behold how they love one another." And they expressed this.

The greatest joy we experienced (next to hearing that Ozzie could go home December 23rd), was the evening when our church

*The young Pastor Bertram, the people
in New Haven, Danbury, Wallingford,
Naugatuck, and Madison, Connecticut, knew and loved.*

The Rev. O. H. Bertram, representing the Lutheran Church, Missouri Synod, presents an award for "outstanding cooperation and public service in the field of religious programming" to Ray W. Welpott, NBC Vice President and General Manager of WRCV-TV, Philadelphia, Pennsylvania.

Rev. Bertram, as representative of the Lutheran Church, Missouri Synod, accepts the gold medal award presented to the church body for an outstanding episode in the "This Is the Life" series. The award is given by the Freedom Foundation, Valley Forge, Pennsylvania. In 1969 the Foundation chose WSPD-TV, Toledo, and O. H. Bertram, producer, for its highest honor, the George Washington gold medal for their outstanding patriotic TV program, "Lest We Forget."

Delbert L. Latta, Congressman from Ohio, with Sarah and O. H. after Rev. Bertram's opening prayer for a session of the House of Representatives in January 1978.

Congressman Delbert Latta, Speaker of the House Carl Albert of Oklahoma, the Reverend Bertram, and Dr. Edward Latch, Chaplain of the House of Representatives, on Capitol Hill in Washington, D.C.

The "Team" at Redeemer Lutheran Church, Philadelphia, 1960: Vicar J. V. Moyer (now Pastor of Good Shepherd Lutheran Church, Toledo, Ohio), Pastor O. H. Bertram, and Principal K. Kretzmann.

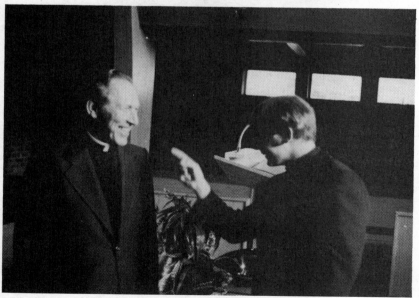

Having fun with his Pastor is Vicar Mark Schreiber at Good Shepherd Lutheran Church in Toledo, 1975.

Bishop George J. Rehring
and Rev. O. H. Bertram...

FAMOUS ON THE LOCAL SCENE!

DEADLINE 6 and 11 weeknights

WSPD TV
Toledo 13

An ad for WSPD-TV, Toledo, that appeared in the Catholic Chronicle and the Toledo Blade in the late 1960s. Bishop Rehring, head of the Toledo Catholic Diocese, and Ozzie were good friends, and loved to discuss Martin Luther together.

WNHC-TV, New Haven, Connecticut, was the first station ever to use the "split-screen" technique on the non-denominational program "Moments of Comfort" in 1953. The Reverend George R. Kraus of New York City "signed" the words as O. H. Bertram and various speakers and singers appeared.

In the 1970s Rev. Bertram presents an award of appreciation for WSPD-TV's religious programming— "Worship for Shut-ins," "Religion In the News," and "Thought for the Day" —to the station's vice president and general manager, Keith McKenney.

*"Sally" (my other nickname) at the
height of the fashion modeling days.*

*Loving every moment of the teaching
years at Monac School, Toledo, Ohio.*

150

The Bride and Groom with the silver punch bowl wedding gift, June 21, 1972.

"Pastor Honey's" favorite photo of me. He kept it framed on his church office desk for all of our seven years together.

The newlyweds at Heidelberg on the Rhine River in Germany.

That special lunch on the Grand Canal in Venice.

"Pastor Honey" and "Angel's" 1976 Christmas card photo.

My favorite photo of Ozzie, with that certain smile that charmed.

Having a laugh together at a church picnic.

*With my three favorite people: My brother,
Dr. Richard Breck of Wallingford,
Connecticut, and daughters Sally Amos
(1) and Leslie Boudouris of Toledo and
Sylvania, Ohio.*

Our last vacation together, on Sanibel Island, Florida, in 1979, after Ozzie had had his radiation treatments. He is feeding his favorite birds, seagulls.

As Pastor Bertram's Recognition Dinner and Program after fourteen years at Good Shepherd Lutheran Church. Radiation and chemotherapy treatments are taking their toll. (I loved that hand on my knee!)

Widow receives posthumous award from broadcasters

Attends breakfast

Mrs. O. H. Bertram, right, is welcomed to the White House by Mrs. Jimmy Carter. Mrs. Bertram was in Washington to receive a posthumus award for her husband from the National Religious Broadcasters. Rev. Bertram was widely known for his television appearances and as a columnist in the area.

Sarah at a tea given by Mrs. Jimmy Carter at the White House in January 1980.

Sapphire Ball (Toledo Opera Guild). The committee woman in her gown—1988.

Still going—Sarah, Christmas 1992.

choir gathered around the doorway of our hospital room. I say "our room" because Ozzie wished me to be with him at all times, and the doctors gave permission to have a cot placed in my husband's private room so I could stay with him even at night. You could arrange with the hospital kitchen for guest trays, so I could eat three meals a day there, chattering away to my husband, amusing him with whatever I could think of in the way of conversation to make his stay seem shorter.

The almost two weeks spent sleeping and living at the hospital were an ordeal for this very private lady. The main problem was, I hadn't any. Privacy, that is. One incident illustrates the experience well. I did quite a lot of reading, as television understandably was annoying to my husband as he was trying to rest or sleep. The light bulb in the lamp over my cot burned out, and I requested that it be replaced.

That night I slept lightly. How else does one sleep in a hospital when comings and goings of the nurses taking vital signs, blood, checking equipment, and hall noises one doesn't notice during the day become seemingly louder at night. I sensed a different presence in the room. I opened my eyes just in time to see a hairy male arm reach over my head to the floor lamp above it and twist in a new bulb. As the new bulb lit up my horrified expression, I don't know who was more embarrassed—the owner of the hairy arm who had just illuminated a lady in a very feminine aqua nightie, or the lady who had previously thrown off the sheet in the warm hospital room! After a hasty apology, the man left, leaving me to check out just what he had seen. My guardian angel was working that night as I discovered that the lacy nightie was doing a good job of covering parts of me that discretion would not have me reveal.

The incident gave Ozzie a good laugh the next morning as we breakfasted, he on liquids and just the beginnings of some soft cereals, and I on my favorite bacon and eggs. We rejoiced together as I read our morning's devotions from *Portals of Prayer*, as was our practice every morning of our married life together, even on trips. We especially rejoiced that even though the tumor was inoperable, he was recovering from surgery, and that we had the hope of treatments that would perhaps diminish or rescind the tumor.

December 23rd came, and I drove Ozzie home. We both were so

happy Dr. Carter had allowed him to come home for Christmas. We gave grateful thanks to God as Ozzie returned to our bed in our own room at home.

That night we cried in each other's arms as we thought of what the surgeon had found, and of the days and weeks ahead of radiation treatments and chemotherapy, to arrest and perhaps encourage the cancer to go into remission. But they were not tears shed in despair, only tears of a mixture of joy at the homecoming and sadness at the outcome of the surgery. We little dreamed that the D.A., as I called the dark angel of death, was beginning his flight to claim Ozzie's physical body.

21
Winter Sets In

"God rest ye, little children;
Let nothing you affright,
For Jesus Christ, your Savior,
was born this happy night; . . ."
D. M. Mulock
Christmas Carol

We had a joyous Christmas Eve at our Church of the Good Shepherd in Toledo, together with our beloved congregation and members of our family. As usual on Christmas Eve, we had two services in order to accommodate the many who wished to come. Ozzie delivered the Christmas Eve message seated on a tall stool behind the lectern at the front left side of the sanctuary. He was not yet strong enough to stand any length of time, so he decided against speaking from the pulpit.

I never saw him look so handsome. The rosy flush of impending pneumonia (of which we were unaware) gave a glow to his face and a shine to his eyes. He sat tall and spoke as always, hardly glancing at his notes, and his soft brown-grey hair was fluffy and wavy like a halo of light around his head, and the things he said were wonderfully joyous as he told of the birth of the Savior.

I stood in the doorway of the sacristy, that small room where ministers don their robes, and watched and listened to him. I needed to be close to aid him if necessary. I looked at the faces of the people as they listened with love shining from their eyes, and wondered if they were remembering other Christmas Eves together at our church.

Four or five years before, Ozzie had been struck with an idea. He would teach me two verses of the favorite Christmas carol, *Silent Night,* in German, and we would sing them at the Christmas Eve services. This would be a love gift to our congregation. He struggled patiently to teach me to sing in German, but oh, the fun we had doing it. We'd practice together as we drove to and from places, or as we took our nightly mile walk.

I'm afraid my German was not perfect, nor were our voices all that good, but the people seemed to love our rendition of this beloved Christmas carol. They would beam as we performed, and I suspect their main pleasure was not in the actual singing they were hearing, but in the love they saw so obviously expressed as Pastor and Mrs. "B" stood singing to them with their arms around each other; I in my long, dark blue velvet gown and Ozzie in his best dark suit with the clerical collar.

This duet of *Stille Nacht* became a tradition each year. People would start asking us if we were going to "do it again this Christmas Eve" early in December. Ozzie would set me wondering, as he would say with a twinkle in those sea-blue eyes, "Are you sure, dear, that they don't just want to know if we are going to sing so they can make other plans for the evening?"

He noticed the good reactions of our own church, however, and so for two years before his illness, we also taped our German version of this carol for the television service of "A Worship for Shut-ins." Many wrote their thanks for this; most stating it brought back memories of their childhood, or mothers or fathers long gone to heaven. They would write that seeing and hearing us sing the old German *Stille Nacht* would bring tears to their eyes. Again Ozzie would tease me and say, "Probably the tears were because it was so bad."

I looked out at our beautifully decorated church this Christmas Eve of 1978 and wondered if our congregation would miss,

Stille nacht, heilege nacht,
Alles schlaeff, einsam vacht.
Nur das heilege eltern paar,
Das Im stalle zu Bethlehem var,

Bei dem himmlischen kind,
Bei dem himmlischen kind.

Stille nacht, heilege nacht,
Hirten erst kund gemacht,
Durch der engel, "Hallelujah",
Toent es laute von verne und nah,
Christ der Retter ist da,
Christ der Retter ist da.

If they did have a fleeting sense of nostalgia, I'm sure it was forgotten in their joy at seeing their beloved Pastor back in church again, looking so radiantly well.

The following week Ozzie continued to rest, and I dressed his still-draining surgical stitches and derived pleasure from waiting on my darling's every need.

Dr. Earl Perrigo came by every day to check on Ozzie and noted an alarming rise in temperature and other symptoms, indicating pneumonia. He knew how distressing it would be for Ozzie to have to go back in the hospital, so he allowed him to stay at home in bed, and came several times a day to give the necessary injections. I will never forget this kindness of a busy cardiologist with a practice and all that it entails, caring enough to come to the house, not once a day, but morning, afternoon, and evening.

Dr. Perrigo was, I'm convinced, the physician with the perfect personality to care for Ozzie these last remaining months. I saw him many times on his knees beside the bed with his arm around my darling—cajoling, teasing, loving, caring, joking, and sometimes in serious conversation with Ozzie. I can still picture him as he asked Ozzie to turn over so the medication could be administered in that special strategic spot called the derriere. He would tease him about this part of his anatomy and give him a loving "spank" after the shot has been given. I can't imagine a morose, silent type of physician caring for Ozzie during these harrowing days. God even knew the type of personality that would help Ozzie get through the difficult days ahead, one that would be completely honest, but would temper the unpleasant outlook of cancer of the pancreas with the uplifting attitude and convictions of a committed Christian.

161

It seems as though God thought of everything—even the "just right" men who were to figure largely in this, the last act of the beautiful drama of my husband's life. Most prominent were Dr. Carter, the Christian surgeon, Dr. Perrigo, the Christian cardiologist who became the attending physician, and Dr. Dressler who initiated the inquiry into what Ozzie's health problem was, Dr. Roland Skeel, Chemotherapist, and Dr. Gerald Marsa, Oncologist. Fellow clergyman and beloved friend, Otto Schultz (who became the interim pastor for our church after Ozzie's death), and young Dennis Liebich, the Director of Christian Education for our church, were also the "just right" people to handle the difficult situations and problems that arose as the life of a prominent, effective church leader was coming to a close.

These men, together with Rita McGinnis, Ozzie's secretary, and the men on our church council, served to hold our beloved Good Shepherd Church together during these difficult days.

When complete recovery from pneumonia was achieved, Ozzie was to begin the radiation or cobalt treatments.

22
That He May Raise

"So in His purple wrapp'd receive me, Lord,
By these His thornes give me His other Crowne;
And as to others soules I preach'd thy word,
Be this my text, my Sermon to mine owne,
Therefore that He may raise, the Lord throws down."
John Donne
"Hymn to God My God, in My Sickness"

Ozzie was X-rayed, mapped, plotted and peered at, as the plan for his course of treatment continued. Radiation therapy was decided upon as the first step in the battle against the progress of the cancer. Marks with food coloring were made on his back to indicate the area to be treated, and a pleasant young man and woman escorted my husband to the Cobalt machine. We had both been beautifully and lovingly prepared for the mechanics of the radiation treatments by Dr. Gerald Marsa, Head of the Oncology Department at Flower Hospital in Sylvania, Ohio.

I was allowed to look through the glass in the door as the huge steel machine, marvel of man's engineering skill containing the tiny mystery of radioactivity, zeroed in on my husband lying strapped to a moving table. The treatment was brief, and I realized that we would be doing this for six weeks, and that it wasn't at all as frightening as I had imagined it to be.

Twice a week I would drive Ozzie to the hospital. We would chat with the other patients in the cheerful waiting room. They all seemed to derive a degree of comfort in talking about what type of cancer they had, what their reactions to the cobalt treatments were, and how glad they would be when they were over. By the time the six weeks of treatment were completed, all the wives or husbands, or sons or daughters who accompanied or brought the patients for their treatment had become like old friends. Waiting room acquaintances, and yet what a common bond we shared in our mutual concern, love, disbelief, and anxiety. We would pretend to thumb through magazines as our loved one was in the cobalt room, but each, I'm sure, had deeper thoughts as we mutually endured the waiting time.

I questioned Ozzie as to his feelings during the treatment. "I didn't feel a thing," he would say. I noticed as the weeks went by that his back looked as if it were slightly sunburned. The intern and nurses were especially gifted with the most exquisite tact and courtesy; and they explained that this was normal. As any middle-aged man would be, Ozzie was concerned about whether he would have hair loss. "God was good," he'd say, "I didn't lose my hair!"

He did experience a growing weakness and nausea.

Another physician, Dr. Wassaf Mikhail, who had become a good friend of Ozzie's through their being seat partners on a plane flight at one time, had a beautiful surprise for us when my husband had completed the radiation treatments. He invited us to spend a week at his lovely condominium on Sanabel Island in Florida. What a thrill to look forward to! We flew there in January 1979 on wings of hope and gratitude. Ozzie, though deep in the throes of intermittent nausea, could rest in the sun as I scampered about on the beach collecting the shells that Sanabel is famous for.

One of my favorite snapshots is of Ozzie throwing a handful of bread and cracker crumbs up into the air over his head as thirty or forty seagulls, his favorite birds, circled him.

Frequent medication of different kinds became our way of life from then on. My job was to write down in a small notebook the time each one was taken so we would not get them mixed up. Nothing seemed to control the growing nausea, and we flew home; Ozzie visibly weakening and I nursing a broken toe that occurred when I was wading for shells.

It would certainly be remiss of me if I did not mention the encouraging love of our many friends at this time. In every hug, smile, touch, pat, and reassuring word, we felt the love of Jesus Christ expressed. I wanted Ozzie's healing so badly. I had prayed for it, I knew it would happen. I was blind to any other thought. People reinforced me by saying positive things I wanted to hear. *God cannot help but perform a miracle of healing for such a good man,* I thought.

I was human and filled with fear at times. I felt that time and a life was swirling around as water does when it runs out of the bathtub. It seemed to swirl and race around me and have no other way to go but down, down, and gone!

The hardest part at this time was to allow Ozzie to be a man and handle his own situation—that of a man with the growing realization that barring a miracle of healing, he was going to die in a matter of months. We both began to pray for the strength to accept our human weakness and fears and try to give them to God to deal with. We realized if we could do this, we would break the power of fear.

Ozzie could, and did. I never heard him question or complain about God's will for him. He was the ideal of husbands still, even in the illness that was progressively worsening. Loving, considerate of me, appreciative, cheerfully going about the semblance of his regular work as long as it was physically possible.

He firmly believed in all he had ever preached. What St. Paul said in II Timothy 4:6-8, seems to say it as I feel Ozzie thought and believed. "I have fought a good fight, I have finished my course, I have kept the faith: Henceforth there is laid up for me a crown of righteousness, which the Lord, the righteous judge, shall give me at that day: and not to me only, but unto all them also that love his appearing."

He lived his belief that God's grace was sufficient for him—that

God's power is shown the more perfect in human weaknesses (II Corinthians 12:9). It shone out of his eyes and his still charming smile. The pathway to our door was continually trod as friends came to call and see for themselves how this dearly beloved man was progressing physically and mentally. No one left, I'm sure, without being uplifted by his calm, accepting attitude. There was a strength inherent in his beautiful patience and outlook.

Hundreds of cards and notes poured in. Encouraging, loving, strengthening words from all of God's saints (fellow Christians). The letters of Robert Carson and Tom Scher, two men of our congregation, were especially uplifting to Ozzie, and he thought of them as his special ministering angels. Ozzie's sister Irma in nearby Napoleon, Ohio, visited every week, and her visits were also beneficial to Ozzie's outlook.

It was I who faltered at times. The strain of coaxing him to eat, giving injections for pain every few hours day and night, being responsible for giving the right medication and keeping a record of them, taking him for the chemotherapy which had now started, fixing four or five small meals a day, began to be felt. I wore myself out keeping up a good, cheerful front. And I loved him so! To see him in pain was torture. And I felt fear, doubt, and worry as I had never experienced in my life before.

The moments of closeness we shared these last three months are something I treasure. Every single evening, our chairs would be close together. If the arm of my little rocker was not actually touching his tweed reclining chair, he would tease me and say, "What are you doing so far away?" We talked, planned for "in case something should happen," and watched television or read to one another. We'd reminisce about our trips, or special happenings at our church, such as the recognition dinner given the previous February honoring my husband's fourteen years of being Pastor of Good Shepherd.

This surprise dinner had touched and thrilled him. People had literally come far and wide to honor the man they were beginning to realize might leave them. The church overflowed with love and the usual tributes and testimonies for a much beloved man.

I'd like to quote, in part, Kay Heilman, chairman of this event, as she introduced my husband. I took them from the cassette tape that was made at this time.

She said, "The Scriptures tell us that Jesus said to His disciples,

'Go ye therefore and teach all nations.' And we at Good Shepherd
are extremely blessed to have as shepherd of our flock, a man
who embodies that scripture, and has for the past thirty-five
years, over radio and television and in getting the message forth,
and in knowing that the Word shall not return void, has never
neglected his flock and those of us who need him. He has always
been there for us."

Our congregation's president at that time was a young lawyer
named Craig Covrett, and in his comments he said, "Just an-
nounce a recognition dinner for Pastor Bertram and you will have
a full house." Keith McKinney, then the Vice-President of WSPD-
TV, Toledo, said, "First time in my life I've ever stood taller than
you," as he stood on the step above Ozzie after calling him up for
a tribute for his contributions in the "Electronic Media" and a
spontaneous hug. Dr. Joseph Schradie, head of the Pharmacog-
nosy Department of the University of Toledo, another very active
church member, and appointed member of the National Board for
Evangelism for the Lutheran Church-Missouri Synod, read letters and telegrams from prominent persons. Among these were
expressed appreciations from Dr. Oswald Hoffman of the Lutheran Hour, and Dr. J. A. Preuss, then President of the Lutheran
Church-Missouri Synod.

Twelve hundred dollars was presented to my Pastor Honey to
carry on his television and radio ministry. We were both close to
tears at this expression of love and encouragement.

Again, Ozzie's ecumenism was in evidence as a letter from a
prominent Christian Scientist, Edgar Hawkins, was read, nuns
from Lourdes College, Sylvania, Ohio, were present, and a letter
from a Toledo Rabbi was read.

My husband's voice was strong as he made a short acceptance
speech. None of us thought that in three more months that strong,
thrillingly vital voice would be stilled.

I was delighted to be included, as Kay Heilman presented me
with a dozen roses in gratitude for what she said was "the loving
support you have given to Pastor, and because you have shared
him so often with the congregation." Ozzie was pleased that I was
remembered, too, and in a snapshot someone took immediately
after I had returned to the pew, one can see his hand on my knee
in pride as I gazed down at the armful of roses.

This was typical of the man. He was a "toucher," but only of those in his immediate family. He always either had me by the hand, or had an arm around my shoulder or waist. I loved it, as we were perfectly matched in the showing of affection.

I did not feel we could be closer than what we had always been, but the following March of 1979 appeared to bring a type of togetherness that was bittersweet. It seemed the sharing of what we were facing brought a new dimension to our love; a greater appreciation for each other's personalities and traits.

The Veres family, one of the loving and dear families of our congregation, had sent a card-like book to us the Christmas before my husband's death. It contained some inspiring quotes, and Ozzie and I talked and thought about them in the last few months of his life. This seemed another link in the chain of growing support that came from everywhere, and it helped me realize how God was working in our lives to prepare us for what was to happen.

One of the quotes from this little book, which we discussed, was written by Marcel Proust: "Time, which changes people, does not alter the image we have retained of them." How wonderful to talk about, in a seemingly detached way, the way we felt about the physical changes my darling was experiencing. Slowly, but oh so painfully obvious now, was the fact that my already slim husband was losing much weight. He needed to know how I was reacting to this, and of course it was a perfect moment for me to tell him that when I looked at him I *always* saw the same dashing "man of my dreams" as he had appeared to me in the pre-radiation and pre-chemotherapy days.

Another one of our favorite quotes, anonymous, was, "Time is too slow for those who wait; too swift for those who fear; too long for those who grieve; too short for those who rejoice . . . but for those who love, time is eternity." This led to a discussion of each point, with the emphasis on grateful agreement with the comment on those who love.

Ozzie and I were sure of each other's love—what a valuable memory that is to me now. We both knew that no matter what the outcome of this illness was to be, we would always be together in eternity through this mutual love, and through the promise of Christ and the Bible. The strong conviction I have of a life hereafter in heaven was one of the most valuable concepts Ozzie left with me.

167

How subtly he led me to a discussion on the debilitating effects of fear and long grieving. I am grateful for these seemingly casual mental preparations he was making for me. Ozzie reminds me of the type of man Longfellow wrote about when he said,

"Lives of great men all remind us,
We can make our lives sublime,
and departing, leave behind us,
footprints on the sands of time."

The thousands whom this man's life touched will agree with me, I feel sure.

Ozzie's often quoted, and one of his most favorite passages, was Philippians 4, verse 13, "I can do all things through Christ which strengtheneth me." He and I both knew that the reason he was able to cope as well as he did with the knowledge that (barring a miracle of God's healing) death was imminent, was that the power of Christ within him gave him the strength to endure and accept, and have the same spiritual contentment that Paul had throughout his trials and testings.

23
Here Comes Our Beloved Pastor

"I praise thee while my days go on;
I love thee while my days go on;
Through dark and dearth, through fire and frost,
With emptied arms and treasure lost,
I thank thee while my days go on."
Elizabeth Barrett Browning
"DeProfundis"

In May, after a beautiful spring and Easter season, when Ozzie was still preaching as much as his strength would allow, phlebitis in his leg caused it to swell badly. I was instructed in giving the Heparin (blood-thinning) injections that were to help dissolve the blood clots causing the swelling. These had to be given in Ozzie's abdomen, and I would almost faint after giving each injection, as they were difficult to administer. Ozzie would hold me, praise me, and thank me, and I would regain courage for the next time.

Mother's Day our family had planned to join us at The Chalet, Ozzie's favorite dining spot. Leslie and Pastor Don Mossman from Ann Arbor, her guest, Sally and her husband Mark Amos, Lorna and her husband Gary Moulton, and their little daughter Holly, Gary's parents, Bob and Ruth Moulton, his brother Jeff and his wife Linda, all sat down for our last supper together. I believe that subconsciously we all felt it was our last family gathering, but of course, this was not mentioned.

Dr. Perrigo, his wife, Carlyn, and their two little girls, Christa and Kari, had decided to come to the restaurant also and sat at a table nearby.

I know now he wanted to be near in case he was needed, as my Pastor Honey was getting so weak. Ozzie wanted this occasion to be celebrated this way. It pleased him so to be with his family in a restaurant setting.

The next day I took him to the hospital, as the leg swelling was not improving, and he was extremely weak. Dr. Perrigo said it was now time.

As I walked into St. Vincent's Hospital, the place I had taken Ozzie two times since the December surgery for intravenous feedings, each time for two days, I had a distinct premonition. I dismissed the thought, but it kept returning, seemingly to prepare me for what lay ahead. I felt I would not be taking Ozzie home.

Marilyn Scott, one of the several R.N.'s who helped care for Ozzie, had some interesting things to say to me when we talked after my husband's death. I said I had noted a change in the nurses as the two weeks Ozzie was in the hospital progressed. At first they were cheerfully, detachedly efficient; going about their business in a typical hospital fashion. Then as the days passed, they began to linger longer in my husband's room. They started to converse in more than just a professional and respectful way. Heads of hospital workers began to pop around the doorway "to see how Pastor is today."

"He was especially lovable," Marilyn said. "Uncomplaining, always in a good mood, always had something pleasant to say, joking, accepting, grateful for whatever was done for him, and his spirituality just shone out."

Instead of just caring for Ozzie's physical needs, the hospital workers grew to care very much for the man himself. One lovely registered nurse, Jennie Gargotto, who had cared for Ozzie back

169

in December and had come to see him with a special anointing oil and prayer for his healing, also was a visitor. She and Ozzie reminisced about several discussions they had had then about what the Bible has to say about anointment, and how my husband had come to believe that it was something he wanted to have done.

Ozzie knew his life here on earth was ending, I realized. He would say, "You know it doesn't really matter if one's prayer for a physical healing is not answered, because we already have God's greatest gift, life through Jesus Christ." The realization of what a tremendous faith can do to help a human being accept his humanness, and carry him courageously through the valley of the shadow of death, came over me as I listened to him speak.

I always knew my husband was "special," but as he was going farther and farther away from me, physically drawing nearer the heaven he looked forward to, I realized just how strongly special he really was. I knew why so many were always drawn to him. It wasn't merely the beautiful smile, the attractive personality, the supreme and utter kindness of the man. It was the strength of God expressed through a human being. People had always recognized his strength, this courage of his beliefs, and although I'm sure that sometimes they did not analyze why they loved and admired the man, I knew it was the fact that he expressed a living Christ to them. He made our Lord alive and real to them because he lived and spoke and expressed all they had ever learned about Christ's teachings. They saw Christ through and in Ozzie.

I had a fleeting thought of a story one of our young mothers had told us a few years before. Linda Chappelear White was sitting with her three beautiful children in church on a Sunday when my husband and I were out of town at a conference. Little Andy, about four years old, looked up at her and said, "Mother, where's God?" Linda thought, "Here's my chance for some good theological teaching," and began to explain that God is around us at all times, He can be everywhere, and is ever present. Little Andy seemed content with this answer and settled back for the rest of the service.

The following Sunday we were back in Toledo, and Pastor Honey came out of the sacristy in his robes, for the regular service. Linda told us, "Andy looked up at me and said, 'Oh Mommy, God is back!' " She realized that her little son had his own beliefs about who God was. I thought at this moment, in my dying husband's hospital room, how many had seen God more clearly through my husband's convictions and life.

Some strong belief that I must conserve my strength for what lay ahead had kept me from sleeping in my husband's private room as I had done before. He had been disappointed in my decision to go home each night, and for the first time in our married life he was, as the expression goes, "put out" with me. He began to tease me about visitors who came after I had left or before I came in the morning, knowing this would distress me as he was weakening so very much.

Ozzie was very human, and I don't think he really knew how tired, how frightened, how frantically worried I really was. I was always able to put on a good act of cheerful strength to everyone. As I look back on those two weeks, I realize what horror I was going through. I admit that my strength was not all in God. My strength in spiritual matters was lying in that hospital room with all kinds of tubes feeding him, sedating him; with a machine around his leg pulsating it to loosen and break up the blood clots that were causing his leg to still be very swollen. My spiritual strength and belief was all wrapped up in that beautiful, emaciated human being who was dying a little bit more each day, right before me, and I was without power to do anything about it.

One night I fell asleep in the hospital bed, with Ozzie's arms around me; under and amongst all the tubes attached to my darling. We still loved to snuggle, the habit of years together at bedtime, I suppose, and our love for each other needing to be expressed in this normal, everyday way.

We were awakened by two nurses standing over us and giggling, "Look at our two love bugs. Do you suppose we'd better awaken them before the doctor makes his night rounds?" Ozzie enjoyed this little episode, and then typically expressed concern over my having to leave the hospital at such a late hour. I must call him the minute I arrived home, he said. Imagine, he so very ill, and yet concerned about my driving home late at night. I had a moment's regret about my decision not to stay at the hospital.

I now know how beautiful God's plan for these days was, as I would not have been able to cope with the weeks that were ahead of me, had I not had these blessed two weeks of uninterrupted sleep each night. This was something I had not had for six months.

Monday, May 28, 1979, was Memorial Day. Lorna's husband, Gary, was to celebrate his birthday at a family noon dinner at his parent's home. Ozzie wanted me to go to represent him and carry our birthday wishes. As I came out of the small hospital bathroom, having fixed my face and hair preparing to leave, I said, "Should I really go? I'd rather stay here with you. How long shall I stay? When should I come back, Dear Heart?" He looked at me, eyes still able to twinkle mischievously, and said, "Ten minutes after you leave this doorway."

I understood that although he felt I should go for the family's sake, and for my own need of a break from my long stays in his room, he really didn't like me out of his sight for very long. I treasure the memory of his bright, alert, aware mind up until the moment of his death. God was so good to His beloved servant. He gave Ozzie this gift of mental ability, awareness, and lucidity right up to his last minutes on earth.

After the birthday dinner Lorna told me that she and Gary would be coming to spend that evening with her dad, and that I should go home as soon as I wished after having dinner with her father. Ozzie was eating practically nothing by this time, but the intravenous feedings were sustaining him. That night I remember thinking that this was the first Memorial Day that I had ever washed clothes. The laundry had begun to make a noticeable mountain in the basket after several weeks of neglect. I made a telephone call to Ozzie to wish him a good night's sleep, and to say our nightly "I love you's" and then went to bed.

I was awakened around five o'clock in the morning by a phone call from one of the nurses, saying my husband was having difficulty breathing and that I should come. I phoned Lorna to tell her I was leaving for the hospital as soon as I dressed, and that I knew her father would want her to come too.

My body was clenched like a fist as I traveled to the hospital in the early morning fog. Our car did something it had never done before, nor has it happened since. It made a weird screeching sound in the area of the front right brake section as I sped along. *It must be the dampness*, I thought. Then as the sound continued, it seemed as if the world were crying out in protest of what was happening.

172

As I arrived in Ozzie's room, the nurses were just beginning to give him oxygen to ease his visible gasping for breath. He grabbed my hand and I his, and he held on with the same familiar hard grip as I had felt the first time he had held my hand seven years ago. The oxygen mask prevented him speaking, and I could see he was fighting for each breath. I kept thinking, "This can't be it. The blood clots in his lungs will soon dissipate."

Lorna arrived soon and held her father's other hand. The two people in this world he loved the most were with him. Soon Dr. Perrigo came in. Time passed and I kept pressing my cheek against his and whispering, "I love you, my darling; you'll be all right soon," in his ear.

Gary Moulton, Lorna's husband, and Dennis Liebich arrived, and I was aware that one by one, four or five nurses had come in and were standing against the wall in silent respect. Dr. Perrigo and I had agreed that no unusual life prolonging machines were to be used at my husband's time of meeting the Dark Angel face to face. Dr. Perrigo began a prayer out loud, and I remember feeling how appropriate it was for him to be having one at this time.

The prayer went on and on. I glanced at Dr. Perrigo. He was watching my husband intently as he prayed. I began to wish he would stop, as it seemed overly lengthy to me. Then he said, "And now, and now . . . and now, Lord Jesus, open up Your loving arms because here comes our beloved Pastor." Ozzie took one breath—and no more. It was done. My beloved was with his Maker in Paradise at 7:58 a.m. on Tuesday, May 29, 1979, with my kisses on his cheek to comfort him into eternity.

I had determined before that I would not scream, cry, throw myself upon him, or in any way act in such a manner as to cast any doubt upon where I knew he was at this moment. My youngest daughter, Sally, had arrived and held me in her arms, and I glanced back at my Ozzie's body before she led me from the room. The dear Father in heaven knows I mean no disrespect, but at that moment Ozzie looked exactly like a painting I had seen somewhere, either at our beautiful Toledo Museum of Art, or perhaps in Europe, of Christ at His moment of human death.

His eyes were cast heavenward, and his handsome, emaciated face with the aquiline and aristocratic nose had a saintly look on it—like the face in the painting of that Christ on the cross. I

173

will never forget this expression, nor can I forget Ozzie's most beautiful gift to me; that of forever removing whatever fear of death I might have had.

I knew beyond any doubt at that moment where my husband was: with his beloved Jesus. And I knew the transition was beautiful, and that I would never again think of the process of dying as something to be dreaded. I will always be grateful for all Ozzie gave to me, but this above all.

24
Afterglow

"... the healing process for ... sorrows can begin the moment we stop resisting them. Tightly closed hands are not in a position to receive anything—not even comfort. It matters little whether they are hands clutched in rebellion or just piteously trying to clutch the past."
Catherine Marshall
To Live Again

The days that followed are still dreamlike in my memory. Every molecule in my body seemed continually tense from fighting for my husband's life. I had coaxed and cajoled him into eating five or six little meals a day. I had been driven with the desire to make up for what he was losing every day. The injections for pain every three hours day and night relieved him so, but my energy was draining as were my hopes for his recovery. No wonder I rested and slept for a month after he was gone. Nature leads us to recuperate from mental and physical strain in a sort of natural numbness.

The funeral was held at our church, and it was alive with love expressed in many ways. My husband's favorite hymns were included, "How Great Thou Art," sung by Dr. and Mrs. Earl Perrigo and, "I Know That My Redeemer Lives"; Lorna Lee's favorite, "Jerusalem the Golden", and mine, "Abide with Me". Dr. Earl Perrigo sang the solo "I Wonder as I Wander."

Dr. Victor Halboth, Pastor of Grace Lutheran Church, Detroit, Michigan, the same fine friend who married us, gave the funeral address, and Dr. George Bornemann, head of the English District of the Lutheran Church, Missouri Synod, also spoke. My dear brother, Richard, and sister-in-law, Verne, had flown in from Connecticut, as had Ozzie's sister, Clara Schweitzer, also from Connecticut. Ozzie's sister, Irma, and her husband, Pastor Ernest Laabs of Napoleon, Ohio, were also there, and hundreds of others. I was told later that the procession of cars to Toledo Memorial Park where the entombment was to be, held up traffic for twenty minutes.

I was in shock, and felt as though I were in slow motion, in a dream sequence from a movie about someone else. This couldn't be me going through this. It wasn't really my darling who had died.

I do remember going up to Ozzie the first time after his death in the hospital, seeing him in his beautiful coffin, and pushing his hair into a less flat position. I touched those soft greying waves of hair that I had fussed over many times before, and thought of how he loved me to care for him.

At one time early in our marriage, I noticed that he shampooed his hair while he bathed, and I had offered to wash his hair for him. He took me up on this, and about every other shampoo was done by me at the kitchen sink under the faucet, with much tender loving care and conversation, plus scalp massage with a towel. He loved the extra attention, just as he loved me to come into the sacristy before church services to "straighten his stole."

I scolded myself for thinking of things that were making me start to cry, and made a conscious effort to think of present decisions to be made, and I prayed for strength.

Lorna Lee and Gary Walker, another dear friend who was director of the funeral home, came up to the coffin, and I agreed with them that Ozzie looked well, though very thin. I wanted the coffin to be left open as I knew so many would want a last look at their beloved friend.

I have the tape of the funeral service and the lovely tribute and emphasis on triumph of Dr. Halboth's message to us all. At the time I knew it was a great address, and appreciated the strong consoling words. But later, as is normal I suppose, I was unable to remember what he said. I was hearing another voice, a beloved voice whose tone and timbre I longed to hear say, "Good morning, beautiful!" (accent on the "morn") just as he did every day of our seven years together. I could not concentrate on the present, it

175

seemed. Ozzie's voice and words were filling my ears and heart. "True love has its source in Jesus Christ. It is the fruit of faith in Him" (John 15:12), I heard him say in my heart. "I can do all things through Christ who strengthens me," (Philippians 4:13). "Love for another is evidence that we have passed out of death into life," (1 John 3:14). It was Christ's words spoken in my husband's voice that were filling my ears at the moment of that walk down the aisle of our church behind Ozzie's coffin after the service. I thought of the many times we had gone to and from the altar of our church; and of how I must not dwell on this being our last walk down our church's aisle together.

Somehow I got through the trip to Toledo Memorial Park and the short entombment service; and afterwards the generous lunch back at our church, provided by so many loving hands. And then finally I could go to our home and crawl into bed. People came and went, relatives left one by one, and then the life alone began.

Friends are always especially treasured at a time of great grief. They help to keep you occupied and busy; making efforts to take you out of a lonely environment into a busy world. I treasure these times when friends were thoughtful enough to make the time to be with me. I especially valued the calls and letters from the other dear men of God, the ministers of various denominations who either came to see me, or wrote beautiful, comforting letters containing words I needed to hear over and over. My former minister, Dr. Robert Croskery of First Congregational Church in Toledo, where I had first invited Jesus Christ into my heart, came to see me one day when he passed through the city, and he was most helpful with suggestions for my future life and attitudes. He was now living, studying, and ministering in another state. He was dear to me for three special reasons: he was the first minister to inspire my desire to become a Christian, it was he who had special prayers with me during some difficult days before Pastor Honey came into my life, and it was he who wrote this unforgettable P.S. to a letter releasing me from my job as secretary to the Christian Education Board at First Congregational Church when I became engaged to Ozzie and planned to join my future husband's congregation.

> "P.S. One Sally should be worth about a dozen Lutherans. So I hope your Oz is planning to make restitution for my sheep he has taken!"

176

The retort from my darling when I showed him the letter was to forever remain one of my favorite quips. Ozzie read the congratulations on our forthcoming marriage and the postscript to my letter of release, and then, with those twinkling blue eyes sparkling, he said, "I know just the twelve I'll send him."

Dr. Croskery and Pastor Otto Schultz of King of Glory Lutheran Church in Toledo, Pastor Phillip Giessler of Cleveland, Ohio, and Dr. George Bornemann came to offer comfort through the sharing of special Gospel words, encouragement, and shedding of the sympathetic tear together. Pastor Earl Key from Luckey, Ohio also came to see me.

I had first met Pastor Key when my husband and I had just become engaged to be married. Ozzie was invited to speak for a special occasion at Pastor Key's Zion Lutheran Church. We were both impressed at that time with the sweet sincerity of the man, his obvious love of the Lord that was so discernible. This quality was especially appreciated by my husband. His low key delivery and the integrity of his feeling always came through clearly when he spoke. It was a "blessed day," as Ozzie called it, when Earl Key said he would serve regularly as liturgist for the television "Worship for Shut-ins" service. His personality proved to be the perfect balance for Ozzie's. Many listeners complimented his well thought out and sincere prayers. I always called them the "dynamic duo," as each in his own way made his impact on the television audience. Pastor Key's calls on me in my bereavement time were most appreciated. I always felt that he in turn appreciated the fact that I had encouraged Ozzie to have a regular liturgist instead of a different guest each week that the programs were taped for television.

The letters from many other brothers in the Lord's work were pouring in; assuring me of prayer, support, love, and sympathy, and containing treasured paragraphs lauding Ozzie and his work in the Kingdom. Some of these are included in another chapter.

I continued to love and trust God—not going through a loss of faith or any anger at God for allowing Ozzie's death, knowing that "His ways are not our ways, for they are higher than our ways and understanding," (Isaiah 55:8, 9). But, pacing the floor one night after moving from the parsonage to a new little condominium, I remember crying out in my loneliness to Ozzie, saying,

"How dare you die and leave me!" I learned later that anger at God or a spouse is one of the normal stages of grief. I also remember thinking, "I must be slightly crazy to say something like that," and recall being relieved when I heard widows at my first THEOS meeting express that they had said similar things when their husbands died.

THEOS was a widowed persons' support group, which came to mean much to me in my "working through" my grief. I had read in our Toledo Blade newspaper about this national group the letters in whose name stand for They Help Each Other Spiritually, an acronym that formed the Greek word for God, THEOS.

I began to attend the monthly group meeting. From this faithful attendance came many good things. I learned about the grief process and the different stages that one might expect to experience. I received the sympathetic understanding that only others who have gone through the same kind of loss of a mate can give. I made treasured friendships within Jaqui Fellabaum, Layla Foos, Virginia Riker (who became my special pal and partner in grief) and several other women who grew dear to me. After two years, my role of receiving understanding, sympathy, and first aid for my sorrow, changed. I still attended, but found that I was giving help to the newly widowed, the same loving help that I once took. I try now to extend this help to others. And so the support is passed on.

As I grow beyond the extreme sorrow that seemed to immobilize me at times, I find I am entering the speaker's circuit again. Speaking and encouraging "Woman Alone," the title of a topic in a seminar for women I am participating in, helps me to feel I'm doing something worthwhile. I now find that instead of crying when I am preparing a talk, or when I go over moments that I write about, I take joy in the happy memories they revive.

This morning I am going through the big brown folder of notes that Ozzie wrote to me throughout our years together. It was his habit to get up early on Sunday morning and have a simple cold cereal breakfast alone. He desired that I stay in bed so that he could prepare for the morning's service without the distraction of conversation. Studying the outline for his sermon, and quiet prayer alone, were, he felt, the most conducive preparations for his "big" morning of two sermons for two services, plus his teaching of the adult Bible study class between the services.

When I arose, each Sunday after he had left the house around 7:30 a.m., I would invariably find on the counter next to the stove: my coffee cup, the jar of instant coffee, a spoon, and a note.

I saved almost every one of these notes I'm happy to say. They mean much to me, and also serve me now as an indicator of changes that were occurring the last year of our marriage. As I contrast the first few years of sentimental love notes, with the ones that Ozzie wrote in 1978, one can plainly see that he felt something was wrong, but just couldn't put his finger on the problem.

I feel the inclusion of some of these notes will be interesting to the reader:

"Angel Mine,
Thank you for the fall season of New England. You were thinking of my longings. I love you!"

"Darling,
After 5 a.m. I could not sleep. Got up at 6:45. See you in church. God bless you. I love you."

"Angel,
I love you! Overslept by a little. Feel better. Tired out, I guess. Yours."

"Good Morning,
Thanks for asking how I felt in your waking moment this morning. I love you for your concern. Remember that I do love you."

"Darling Angel,
As the months and years move on into eternity, I love you more. I am grateful for your help in making my life more pleasant."

"Angel,
Slept badly. Feel sort of washed out. Pray that I do well today. Thanks for your nice note. Love you!"

"Dear Angel,
The pursuit of happiness is the seeking after of making others happy. I do hope that we achieve such a quest. I pray daily that I can do my part to make our marriage a very happy event in our lives. The next thing to heaven is a happy home.
I love you, and may this be a good day for you."

179

"Good Morning, Dear,
Hope that you feel rested. I begin this day with an extra prayer for strength.
Love you!"

"You are a Darling!
Getting up in the dead of night and 'cracking' my back, which did the trick, was a real act of love. You are the greatest wife!
I love you so very much—within twenty-four hours we will be on vacation, God willing. Happy day! May it prove to bring us relaxation and good health with better sleep."

"Darling Angel,
You have been a real source of strength to me this past week. I love you."

"My Darling Angel,
Thanks for that loving note. Your love for me is expressed in so many ways, and I hope that you feel the embracing affection I have for you. Day by day, I love you more and am grateful to God for such a precious wife. Darling, I love you so very much.
Your Oz"

The last note Ozzie wrote to me was in April of 1979, one month before his death. It was on an Easter card, and he wrote:

"Dear Angel,
Many thanks for all deeds of kindness you show me. I am blessed to have you as my wife.
With all my love,
Ozzie"

I have the last Easter card I sent to him on which I wrote:

"Dearest Ozzie,
May this Easter be a true "resurrection" for you, too, my darling; with a beautiful new physical "you" happening!
You *are* so dear—not only to me, but to *many*.
All my love,
Your Angel."

I was so praying for a physical healing. I did not know that a few weeks later he truly would be a new creature with his Lord.

180

About a month after Ozzie's death, Rita McGinnis, a good friend and our church secretary, presented me with a file folder, fat with every note or card I had ever written to my husband. He had placed each one in the folder as he received them through our seven years together. Although we were married just one month less than seven years, I like to consider the month before our marriage as making a complete seven years together. We were so close every waking moment that it was only the sleeping hours of night time that separated us that month before our marriage, he in his home and I in mine.

What a treat to re-read all my words to him, and how I loved him for treasuring them enough to keep them. Rita was correct when she said as she gave me the overflowing file, "Now don't open this until you get home, because you'll cry." I did, but with gratitude and joy for having them.

It was my oldest daughter, Leslie, who pointed something out to me when I was moaning one day about only having had seven years of marriage to this extraordinary man. "Mother, don't you realize that seven is a special number in God's word, the Bible? It stands for completion—like the world being created in seven days." My curiosity was piqued and I looked up the word seven in Strong's Concordance. Sure enough! Four columns in fine print telling of the appearance and significance of this number. How lovely and how blessed I was to have my number of years with Ozzie mean perfect completion. They were perfect, and complete in every satisfying area.

25
Lorna Lee

"With eyes so blue and tinted cheeks,
A newcomer appears with pinkish feet,
To make her abode within the fold,
Of the O. H. Bertram's expectant household."
From Lorna Lee's birth announcement

I could not possibly write a book about O. H. Bertram without showing the side of him that was pure "father." The years I spent as his wife revealed him to be a man who had nothing but the
181

highest hopes for, and pride in this only child. Brought up with the greatest of exposure to Christian ideals, nourished spiritually by parents who knelt by her bedside to pray each night of her baby and childhood years, she could not help but be the innately good person she is.

I can imagine with what joy the birth of their little eight pound, four ounce daughter filled the hearts of Lorna Marie Kern Bertram and O. H. Bertram! Snapshots of childhood days and snatches of conversation left me with the definite impression that this little girl, born September 5, 1947, was loved and idolized from the very moment of conception, let alone birth.

One picture shows her at around eight months, sitting on her daddy's chest while he was lying down holding her, with her little feet on his face. He was loving it, as shown by the expression of sheer delight. Another snapshot shows a one-year-old Lorna Lee smashing her little hands into her birthday cake, to the obvious amusement of her father.

As I looked at pictures of Lorna Lee, named for her beloved mother, I see progression from a high-spirited little girl doing all the normal things parents take pictures of, to a young lady, always beautifully dressed, who seemed to exude the utmost confidence in herself. There was much closeness evidenced in the way Lorna Lee and her mother were posed in numerous photographs, usually with arms around one another, or looking fondly at one another.

There were also frequent photographs of Lorna Lee with her father. Their loving regard for each other was apparent. How proud Lorna Lee must have been of her daddy when she heard him preach from his various pulpits, and knew that she was the daughter of the "main man" in each church he served. She could not help, I'm sure, being indulged by not only her parents, but by each congregation. Such is the life of the "P.K." or "preacher's kid" as they are commonly called.

This is not without its disadvantages, as we all know. It must be very difficult to be brought up always under the surveillance, not only of one's immediate family, but the extended family of one's father's church.

How difficult it must have been to tear herself away from the middle of her senior year in high school in the Mayfair area of Philadelphia. She was compelled to do this in 1964 when Ozzie, after much prayerful thought, (he told me) decided to accept the call extended him by Good Shepherd Church in Toledo. My heart always went out to her, as I felt great empathy for what must have been an extremely traumatic experience for her. To also lose her mother in an automobile accident a few years later, seems almost more than one young woman should have to bear.

This is, I felt, one of the reasons my Pastor Honey was so delighted with finding a wife who was experienced with daughters. My oldest girl, Leslie, was in the same senior class with Lorna. Ozzie wrote, in our first Christmas greeting printed letter in 1972, "Lorna Lee is happy again; she not only has a mother, but two sisters. Our families get along very well and have combined into one."

I remember vividly my first meeting with Lorna Lee. Several people had come to me with dire predictions about our getting along. "She's the apple of her father's eye," they said. "She'll always come first, as she can do no wrong in his eyes," they warned. "She will never accept you," they predicted. "She and her mother were so close; they were all such a close-knit threesome." I really did not know what to expect from this young woman about whom I had heard so much.

Ozzie and I stopped one night before we became engaged at the Holiday Inn where Lorna Lee was "moonlighting" in the cocktail lounge from her regular job as a Toledo Trust bank teller. She was dressed in the attractive garb of a short white mini sailor dress and white boots, and was expressing the outgoing, uninhibited fun-loving personality that she was, as she served the customers.

After the introductions were made and we all conversed for a while, Lorna Lee and I went to the ladies' room to "freshen up," as they say. She looked at me and said, "My father has gone out with lots of ladies since my mother died, but you're the only one I love already." I have never forgotten her saying that to me. It meant an approval of her father's choice for a wife, and I felt all would be well in our future relationships.

If I wondered about her choice of extra work at that time, and how Ozzie reacted to his daughter working there, I was soon to find out that Ozzie was always tolerant of her choices in life. He understood her rebellion against being categorized as a "prissy" type minister's daughter. He was proud of her college experience at Concordia College in Ann Arbor, Michigan, and of her choice of a banking career. I feel he saw her as she was, understood her

183

way of thinking, and although he might have preferred another type of extra job for her, he was accepting of her choices in life. After all, she was over twenty-one, he had brought her up "in the nurture of the Lord," as he used to quote, and he prayerfully left her in God's hands.

Ozzie's greatest hurt seemed to be that Lorna Lee wanted to move into an apartment of her own a few months before we met. My role as a sort of "go-between" started even before we married, as I tried to explain how I felt a young girl needed to do this, especially if she felt overly clung-to, after her mother died. Again, that character trait of a mediator that I seem to possess, whether for better or worse, gave me complete understanding of both viewpoints.

There are many of us who need, enjoy—yes, even love, constant attention! And there are those who can do very well with little human companionship and even enjoy more than a few minutes of solitude. Ozzie was one of the former. He never liked to be alone.

After his first wife's death, his daughter needed time, as would any other young woman, to go to various activities of her own interests; times that would not include the presence of a father, no matter how beloved. She often would arrange to have one of her closest girlfriends over, and then would feel freer to leave her father to attend whatever function she desired. Perhaps it would be a basketball game in which one of her boyfriends was participating that night, or another activity or engagement. The girlfriend would stay with Ozzie, amusing him with "daughterly" conversation, until Lorna returned home. This seemed to me a conscientious desire to be helpful to an extremely lonely man who needed much attention at this trying time of life. If Lorna was drawn quite normally into her own activities, Ozzie would sometimes interpret it as a loss of affection, or even a callous lack of loving understanding.

There were times when his loneliness became unbearable, even for a "man of God." Ozzie was very human. Sometimes his much-loved, elderly black housekeeper, Carrie Hill, was able to stay overnight so that he would not be alone in what must have been excruciatingly silent evenings. Only one who has lived with this unique man would be able to comprehend his need for continual visible expressions of caring. And only those with twisted minds

184

would have construed this need of his to never be alone in his sorrow into something evil, as they did sometimes, upon hearing about the evenings when Lorna provided a "father sitter."

Many times after our marriage Ozzie would ask me to speak to Lorna Lee about something that caused him concern. I always said something like, "No, darling, *you* talk to her. She would accept it better from you. I don't feel it would serve to bring us closer. She would hate me attempting to be Mother."

I feel now that I erred in not forming a closer "pal" type relationship with my step-daughter. I always encouraged Ozzie and Lorna Lee to be free to be alone together, sometimes even declining to go with them on an errand. I felt Lorna would prefer not always having me there listening to their father-daughter conversations. I bent over backwards to not intrude in their special relationship. In the doing, I realize now that I was not building a close relationship with Lorna Lee myself. I was overzealous in my attempts not to be an interfering step-mother.

Later on, after her marriage, it was my heartfelt joy to be able to take care of Lorna's and her husband Gary Moulton's little baby girl, Holly Marie. I did this two or three days a week, so that Lorna Lee could continue her job as bank teller. This little baby brought so much love and joy into my husband's life that even if I had not grown to love her for her precious little self, I would have wanted to care for Holly just for the pleasure it gave him to see and experience her in our home.

Marion Gust, one of our church members, told me a dear story about Holly when she was around three years old. Holly had said, "That's my Grandpa!" to another little child who was nearby. The child said, "That's my grandpa, too!" The small argument continued until Marion said to Holly, "Yes, he really *is* your grandpa." Marion received a beautiful smile in gratitude that someone knew and understood that Holly really was the one and only grandchild. "The whole point was that the children of the church all wanted to claim Pastor as theirs," Marion said.

Ozzie and I took little Holly many places with us. I can almost experience again in memory the joy we felt in taking her to feed the ducks at a nearby pond, or to lunch with us in a restaurant, or to a Kern Family picnic in Frankenmuth, Michigan. I could not have loved her more had she been my flesh and blood granddaughter, and so one can imagine the momentary shock I received one day when she told me, "My mom and daddy told me you are not my real grandmother." I guess I had just felt so strongly that I was.

Lorna Lee and her father seemed to me to be so similar in personality. She possessed many qualities that Ozzie had: she was outgoing, outspoken at times, super-confident, able to talk to anyone and everyone, ambitious, hard-working, and physically good looking. This in itself was enough to make her attractive to me. I have never seen anyone whose hair I admired so. When we met, it was waist-length, dark red and thick; sometimes piled on her head in a most becoming hair style. No wonder after Ozzie's death I enjoyed seeing that face with the same aristocratic "Barbara Streisand" nose, and the same beautiful blue eyes as her father possessed. It was as though I could see him again when I looked at her.

I've often thought it must have been difficult for Lorna Lee to see her father so much in love with someone other than her own mother. But she never indicated this, only expressed joy that he had someone to make him happy. I know she must have felt extreme gratitude for my care and love for her father those last six months of his life; and that the unspeakable sorrow of losing both parents was almost unbearable. How happy Ozzie would be to know that she now has a son, Todd, to also fill her life.

It is extremely difficult to live and face life alone, and I am grateful she has a family around her and a mate to help bear her life's tragedies. I know that Lorna Lee would be happy to know that the love I had for her father, O. H. Bertram, has been replaced by a closer love and dependence on Him to whom I gave my heart, my life, my allegiance years ago, Jesus Christ. Though this book is written in memory of a truly singular man, I write it for an even greater purpose—for the glory of my Lord and Savior Jesus Christ.

Lorna Lee, my dear husband's only daughter, will remain special in my heart always. Not only for the reason that she was so special in his eyes, but because I genuinely always enjoyed her so much the years that I was his wife.

26
Letters, Lauds, and Lashings

"To him whose elastic and vigorous thought keeps pace
with the sun, the day is a perpetual morning."
Henry David Thoreau

"The files! The files!" I'd forgotten about them, and the sudden
recalling one morning that they would still be in the church secretary's office elated me at the thought of the rich source of extra
information I knew I would find there.

I was unprepared for the volume of letters that my husband
wrote and received. I knew he was an extremely articulate man
and had hoped for some examples of letters that would express
this volubility in communicating with others by writing.

Besides copies of letters to the TV and radio studios, friends,
former parishioners, relatives, his video audience, and business
letters, I discovered many letters to political figures and others
in the news that had captured his attention for the moment. He
loved to praise someone for a job he thought particularly well
done. Here is a sample of one such letter written April 27, 1972:

The Honorable Richard M. Nixon
President of the United States
The White House
Washington, D.C.

Dear Mr. Nixon:
Your leadership of our Nation is becoming more superb
as your term of office lengthens. Certainly, your address
of last evening should be the conviction of every freedom-
loving citizen in the world. I am certain that the patriotic
American supports you.

If only something could be done to put restrictions on
mass communications, which seem to be more communist
infiltrated and oriented now than ever. They play into the
hands of the enemy and oppose those who would defend
the rights of freedom and justice. Could not legislation be

implemented to muzzle the news media that would play into the hands of the enemies of freedom-loving America? God bless you and give you strength to carry on your tedious and difficult work.
Sincerely yours,
O. H. Bertram

It is interesting to recall how Ozzie finally changed his attitude of admiration for this former President. After the written transcripts of some of the much publicized tapes came out, my Pastor Honey had to confess complete disillusionment with the person of Richard M. Nixon. I noticed that he expressed this by an overt action one day when I dropped by his office. The picture of the President had been turned to face the wall!

Another letter dated March 30, 1977, was informative in its constructive advice.

Mrs. Glenn C. Dougherty
1808 Sinclair
Fort Wayne, IN 46808

Dear Mrs. Daugherty:
"Received your letter of March 25, which assured me that you are among our faithful listeners to "A Worship for Shut-ins."

I can well understand that certain things in church life today may trouble you and have therefore sought advice regarding leaving a considerable sum to some worthy cause. I would like to suggest that you designate your gift to the Board of Evangelism of the Lutheran Church-Missouri Synod, 500 North Broadway, St. Louis, MO 63102, expressly indicating that you would like to have it used for the mass media, such as television, radio or newspaper. I feel that the church at large has not had this vision from the standpoint of a direct outreach for the Gospel of Jesus Christ.

Also, since I assume that you are middle-aged, I hesitate to indicate that the gift be designated for "A Worship for Shut-ins," since it may not continue after I leave the scene of the present world. However, as long as God gives me strength, we seek every avenue to share the comforting message of Christ from coast to coast.

If, on the other hand, you would prefer indicating your gift to be made out to the foreign missions of our Lutheran Church-Missouri Synod, that would also be worthwhile. We in our parish have adopted three missionaries, since we feel this is a direct means of conveying the message of salvation, which we hold so dear with those in India, Ghana, and the Middle East.

Enclosed you will find a Lamplighter and a Sunday Bulletin giving you a little information regarding our church and its activities.

Yours on the upward trail in Christ,
O. H. Bertram

In the fourth paragraph of this letter, I found the startling reference to the fact that he might not be around when the lady left her material gifts. I suddenly realized that this letter was written March 30, 1977, two years before his demise. Had he some inner knowledge or awareness of the shortness of his years left on this earth? Or was it just the lovely gift he possessed of always thinking ahead so wisely.

The bulk of his "fan mail" type letters was handled and sorted by volunteer members of our church. Mr. and Mrs. Harold Marquardt were the last couple to take care of this job. They found it interesting to keep track of the different parts of the country from which mail was received, and how many pieces. Ozzie answered, with the help of his secretary, as many letters as possible that needed personal replies. Other letters that requested the giveaways (holy handouts) mentioned on his programs were handled by various volunteers. Harold and Erma Marquardt informed the church that they had answered a total of 6,760 letters since November 6, 1976, a period of two and one-half years. They indicated the letters came from fifteen states and parts of Canada. When I think of the tremendous job of mailing they handled, my heart fills with gratitude.

There were also hundreds of letters that my husband and his secretary answered personally. At the time of his illness, audition tapes of "A Worship for Shut-ins" were being prepared to send to the General Operations Managers of television stations in San

Francisco and Los Angeles. Correspondence relative to these plans for more Western program expansion was ended two months later, at Ozzie's death.

I came across a letter Ozzie had written in the 1960s. He was reminiscing about the fact that when his TV program began November 5, 1952, he received 6,500 letters the first twenty weeks of its airing. The Nielson rating at that time almost thirty years ago was estimated to be 500,000 listeners weekly. This number must have quadrupled as the years went by and the program expanded to many other cities! How encouraged I am in my writing to think that some day all the people who loved and derived benefit from my husband's programs will be able to read about him in this book.

The files reveal incidents of which I was unaware, such as the following.

A small furor occurred when WKVG-TV, Fort Wayne, Indiana, took "Worship for Shut-ins" off the air for a month. Mr. Calo Mahlock, Assistant General Manager wrote to Ozzie that forty-five phone calls in protest were received, plus many letters. Three letters are outstanding in their description of the program, and I include them because they expressed the love and zeal that was felt by all of Ozzie's regular listeners. One was from a lady in Van Wert, Ohio, who was a regular viewer of the Fort Wayne station.

WKVG 33
Fort Wayne, Indiana

To Whom it May Concern:

I seriously question the moral sense of values of a program director who will cancel a religious program for a football review broadcast.

Worship for Shut-ins is the one program free from theatrical gimmicks and fanfare. I remember you did this last year but it came as a shock this morning that a program of such popularity and prestige was canceled.

The simplicity of it is its appeal. One can close ones eyes, lean back and imagine being in one's own beloved sanctuary. And for shut-ins that is therapeutic.

Yes, you have what you think is a good excuse that I

won't buy. With all the football on the air (and I watch college games) surely a half hour could be given over to religious worship.

Sincerely,
Mrs. Roy P. McConahay
Van Wert, Ohio

Another was from a listener in St. Mary's Ohio.

Dear Rev. Bertram:

I want to let you know how much I appreciate your message on Worship for Shut-ins. I try to watch your program before I go to church. Your message brings out the beautiful light of the true Gospel, in especially referring to a personal relationship to Jesus Christ. I attend a church in Ohio, but the messages we hear are pathetically bland, contradictory, and all-inclusive. Possibly you cannot understand what I am talking about but please continue your very effective, "Christly" messages. By the way, the camera work on your program is great too. God bless you and your staff and I pray your fruits will be many.

Another came from Riverhead, New York.

Worship for Shut-ins:

I pray for you all every day, Rev. Key and Rev. Bertram, and everyone that works so hard to bring the church into our homes. I pray for strength, God's guidance and that He may give you good health to carry on the good work you do so well. Being in a hospital bed with pain and suffering, I realize how much I need your beautiful church services, to strengthen me with faith and hope.

One could literally fill a book with fan letters; especially poignant are the ones describing personal heartaches, problems, or illness. Most were seeking wise advice from the man who projected spiritual wisdom to them as they watched the television service each week. All express gratitude for the emotional and spiritual blessings gained from "Pastor O. H. Bertram's insight into God's directives for us."

Ozzie answered all the mail—by personally directed letters or forms. One such letter is included now, as a typical answer to an admiring viewer. The promptness indicated by the dates, was right in character with Ozzie's always businesslike procedures.

August 4, 1977

Dear Mrs. _____,

Thank you so very much for your letter of July 30. I thoroughly enjoyed it. I am so grateful that "A Worship for Shut-ins" serves as your means of spiritual invigoration and revitalization. Also, please accept my thanks for your generous gift of $10 for the support of this program.

Regretfully, I did not have the opportunity of speaking with you on the airplane on March 23. I wish you had pulled at my coat sleeve! I always enjoy speaking with people who are part of our unseen congregation.

Since we had to use a repeat program (which I seldom do) on July 24, I am unable to send you the sermon. However, we are enclosing several of our newspaper meditations which may serve a similar purpose or might even touch on the subject about which I preached that Sunday.

May God's richest blessing rest upon you.

Yours on the upward trail in Christ,
O. H. Bertram

Of special interest and deemed worthy of editors of many laudable news stories, was the venture into creating a television program that could be enjoyed by the deaf. One such newspaper, *The New Haven Register*, Connecticut, devoted almost a half page news story in 1954, on Ozzie's beginning TV programs, which were entitled "Moments of Comfort." The headline and first paragraph said,

Moments of Comfort, Religious TV Program Aids Deaf, Attracts Listeners

"Moments of Comfort," a non-denominational, Bible-centered religious program originating here is attracting nationwide attention as the only program designed for both the deaf and those with normal hearing facilities. Every other Wednesday, the Rev. Oswald Henry Bertram, pastor of St. Paul's Lutheran Church, Naugatuck, preaches in a low, well-modulated voice on the one side of the screen. His words are immediately interpreted in the sign language by the Rev. George Richard Kraus, whose image appears on the other side of the screen. A split screen carries the message. The program will begin this Wednesday over WNHC-TV, the regular outlet.

In Philadelphia, the interpreter for the deaf was the Reverend C. Roland Gerhold. In Toledo, Ozzie was aided by the Reverend August Hauptman who did the sign language for the deaf.

Articles taking note of the television program appeared down through the years in publications such as *Christian Life Magazine, The Springfielder Magazine,* Illinois, *The Lutheran Witness,* Missouri, *The Lutheran Accent,* Michigan, *The Danbury News,* Connecticut, *English Channels,* Michigan, *The Fort Wayne Lutheran,* Indiana, *The Gospel Voice,* Missouri, *The Waterbury Sunday Republican,* Connecticut, *The Spotlight,* Chicago, *New Haven Register,* Connecticut, *Chattanooga News Free Press,* Tennessee, *The West Toledo Herald* and *The Sylvania Herald* and *The Toledo Blade* of Toledo.

In checking the last two and a half years' "mail answered" report by our church members Harold and Erma Marquardt, I found that they responded to over 2,000 letters sent to Pastor Bertram and the "Worship for Shut-ins" program. This does not include the hundreds that my husband answered personally through dictated letters to his secretary. Letters of personal problems, questions about theology, or the outreach of the program were always answered thoughtfully.

Communications to the congregation in Toledo, by Ozzie were included in the monthly church publication "The Lamplighter." They often contained paragraphs pertaining to Ozzie and me. One from the June paper of 1972 refers to our honeymoon week. It said, "The English District Convention will be conducted at River Forest, Illinois, from June 23 to 25. I will be using the quotation of Luke 14:20 as the reason I will not be attending. I have married a wife and therefore, I cannot come.

Our first Christmas letter to friends in 1972 contained these two paragraphs.

Dear Friends,

What an entirely different 1972 Advent-Christmas season this is for both of us compared to that of last year! How true is the phrase, "The house is not a home when there is not a complete family." The unhappy situations of my life make a person re-evaluate the better side of life. Tragedies are meant to direct our thoughts heavenward and loneliness can force us to our knees to seek God's help. We are mutually agreed that our prayers were answered in 1972 and that God's love was abundant in our lives when He directed our pathways of life to meet, which culminated in the exchange of solemn wedding vows on Wednesday, June 21. It made us happy when our children wholeheartedly accepted each other in love and rejoiced that Mother and Dad had found mates.

For those of our friends receiving this Christmas letter that are not acquainted with my wife, I should like to give you a little sketch of her life. She is by vocation a wonderful Christian and by profession a wonderful school teacher. In 1970 she was chosen "the outstanding teacher of the year" out of 560 teachers in the township. She has two daughters, age 25 and 21. Lorna Lee is happy again. She not only has a mother but has two sisters. Our families get along very well and have combined into one.

In another letter in "The Lamplighter" Ozzie wrote, "During the summer months I have been actively engaged in calling on prospective members. I have found these calls very profitable. I am grateful for my wife's consideration in my not taking many days off this summer. Many families want to be together, especially in the evening hours. I am reminded of the statement she made: 'I don't want you to serve the Lord less because of me,' I am grateful for her attitude."

Together with the thousands of fan letters received were letters to and from the men prominent in America's political scene. At the beginning of this chapter the disillusionment with former President Nixon was mentioned. In a file of early correspondence

I found a personally signed note from "Dick" Nixon from the office of the Vice President, dated December 16, 1960.

It showed me that even in his early forties, my husband took the time to do the unexpected—write a letter to encourage a man whom he admired for his Christian principles, who had just lost an election. I include it to show a side of Richard Nixon that has endeared him to many, despite the Watergate debacle.

Dear Reverend Bertram:

Pat and I want you to know how very much we appreciated the letter which you sent us after the election.

A message of congratulations after winning an election is of course always appreciated although not unexpected. But nothing could have meant more to us than to receive such a warm and thoughtful message after losing.

In the years ahead as we look back to 1960, the disappointment of losing the closest election in history will fade into the background. But your act of thoughtfulness will always remain close to our hearts.

Pat joins me in sending our very best wishes for Christmas and the New Year.

Sincerely,
Richard Nixon

In 1976, before the then Secretary of Agriculture, Earl L. Butz fell from the favor of many, Ozzie enjoyed a lively two-way correspondence for about nine months. Then Secretary Butz began it by writing to Ozzie. The letter in part said, "Last weekend we were visiting my 91-year-old mother who lives on the home farm near Albion, Indiana . . . On Sunday morning she tuned in to your 'Worship for Shut-ins' as is her custom every week. This means a great deal to her. She is unable to move out of the house so you provide her Sunday morning church service . . ."

Later correspondence, after the death of Mr. Butz's mother, stated, "Thank you so much for your kind note following the passing of my mother. You will never know how deeply she enjoyed your services every Sunday morning and because she enjoyed them, all of us are grateful to you. Hers was a beautiful Christian life, with a faith so unyielding that it is impossible to

195

grieve in death... May I thank you for all you meant to her through the years she attended services with you."

I include these quotes as typifying the many who shared with us how much the older generation who were house-bound enjoyed Ozzie's special formal church service. They considered him to be "their Pastor," and one lady told us of how her tiny elderly mother would dress, take her purse and white gloves and sit in a chair in front of her television set every Sunday; just as though she were attending church.

Among the voluminous files of correspondence with political figures were the requested and granted three-minute interviews to be included in Ozzie's Religion in the News half hour program that preceded the "Worship for Shut-ins" for several years. Some of the interviews were teletaped in Washington, D.C., and some were made when the dignitaries were in Toledo for some occasion. Among them were Governor George Wallace, Senators Mark Hatfield, Sam Irwin, Harold Hughes, Delbert Latta, Tennyson Guyer, Walter Moeller, Jesse Helms, and Vance Hartke.

Always interested in government and current happenings, my husband expressed his views. He either lauded or lashed out at Presidents of the United States, Vice-Presidents, Congressmen, the Chief Justice of the Supreme Court, the chairman of our national parties, members of our city council, our city mayor, and on several occasions the Editor of our hometown newspaper, *The Toledo Blade*.

Ozzie wrote letters on several occasions that lashed out at items in the news that were against his principles. In a day when "anything goes," it was refreshingly encouraging to many to have someone speak up for morality.

May 5, 1975 to the Editor of The Blade:
Your insinuations that the church and honorable and decent citizens should not raise their objections to the drama, 'Hair', which is scheduled to be presented at the University of Toledo, indicate that your moral principles are certainly at a low ebb. If we as adults and as upright citizens overseeing the welfare of our community do not raise our voice against immorality, then we deserve to suffer under the degeneracy which is rapidly creeping over us.

I would certainly think that you would hold the banner of morality and decency high and set the pattern of constructive and beneficial entertainment for our community. If the adult does not set a wholesome pattern for the youth, directing them and guiding them to higher principles, what will be the outcome for the future? I doubt that my objections will change your mind, but I certainly hope that you would refrain from encouraging activities which would demoralize humanity.

The University of Toledo is a state-supported school, maintained by the taxes of adults. Should they not have the right to object?

On another occasion the *Sylvania Herald*, Ohio, carried this news item:

Hair Length Included in New Police Manual

Long-haired patrolmen may run afoul of a new police rules and regulations manual now being prepared by the administration, Chief Duck said.

The chief said he has been reluctant to start an "interdepartmental hassle" on hair length because of the existence of more pressing problems.

But there is a section on grooming in the new manual which will deal with this matter, he said.

The question arose when the chief was asked about a letter from the Rev. O. H. Bertram, pastor of Good Shepherd Lutheran Church, who complained that some patrolmen need haircuts.

Mr. Bertram also suggested air-conditioned police cars, an idea which Chief Duck said that he is studying. "The proposal is a good one, but the major question is whether the city can afford it," he said.

Notice how the criticism about the long hair was tempered with the suggestion of air-conditioned cars. Usually a compliment or a constructive suggestion would accompany a criticism.

I found a letter from Congressman Thomas Ludlow Ashley dated March 20, 1967, before I was privileged to know my husband. It said:

197

Dear Reverend Bertram:

Thanks very much for sending me the copy of your letter of March 15 to Defense Secretary Robert McNamara concerning the proposal of one Richard L. Bast of a firm known as Redex-Vietnam to send topless go-go clubs to entertain our servicemen in Vietnam.

Frankly, Reverend, I would be very surprised if our Defense Department would put its official approval on any such undertaking. The Special Services Branch of the Defense Department provides outstanding entertainment in excellent taste for our men serving throughout the world. In any event, I have asked Defense Department officials for a report on this matter and will be in further touch with you just as soon as it is received.

Meanwhile, this takes my best wishes.

Sincerely,
Thomas Ludlow Ashley, M.C.

How I would have loved to hear my Ozzie indignantly express his feelings about the topless go-go girls and their effect on the morals of the servicemen. No doubt they would have been accompanied by humorous remarks. My husband was human, male, and could always see two sides to most everything. His opinions were valued, and requested on numerous occasions, and were on both the serious and facetious subjects, as you can see by his answers to two polls that were taken in the Toledo area, and which appeared in the newspaper.

One asked a group of people if they would favor a suggestion that the United States pay the North Vietnamese $2.5 billion for reconstruction as an investment in peace. Ozzie's published answer was, "From a Christian standpoint we have an obligation to feed our enemies, to show them kindness. We can win them over by showing them love. Yet, to give with supervision and discretion is essential. Perhaps they have never understood that the American motive for involvement was helping people. The expenditures for rebuilding food, homes, hospitals, and industry should be supervised by people appointed by our government."

Another inquiring reporter asked if area residents approved of the idea put forth in a news article about a California woman.

198

Concerned about the souls of her pets, she insisted that her minister perform a wedding to sanctify the union of her prolific puppy-producers.

At the end of numerous expressed opinions, my husband's remarks were printed. He said: "I would discourage it. A dog is not like a human being with an immortal soul. Dogs do things by instinct, but humans, we hope, act based on reason. The Bible says about man, 'and the Lord God breathed the breath of life into his nostrils and he became a living thing.' But when it refers to the creation of animals, God just said, 'Let it be' and it was."

Merl Blay, superintendent of the Toledo House of Correction, a workhouse prison for minimal offenders, is quick to give credit to Ozzie's efforts toward the building of a rehabilitation center to house classrooms, chapel, gymnasium, and a recreation room. In the *Toledo Blade* of February 4, 1973, Mr. Blay is quoted as saying the building project will come about "mainly through the efforts of the Rev. O. H. Bertram, pastor of Good Shepherd Lutheran Church. The building was Mr. Bertram's brain child, and the clergyman is intent on making it a reality." And it became so!

Ozzie was always concerned about the welfare of prisoners; had brief services in as many towns as the churches he served as pastor. My least favorite activity was to accompany him, and he allowed me the privilege of "to go or not to go." *The West Toledo Herald* added this information about an educational program, which was started in 1972.

Clergyman Works for Rehabilitation

A West Toledo clergyman has spearheaded a program to motivate and rehabilitate inmates at the Toledo House of Correction, Whitehouse.

Rev. O. H. Bertram of Good Shepherd Lutheran Church, working with contractors, architects, and a representative of the Toledo Department of Education, has launched a project which will construct a pre-fab building 200' × 800' housing classrooms, vocational and recreational equipment.

Rev. Bertram has been chaplain of the institution and has taken a personal interest in the welfare of these men.

Since January, 1972, when he requested the Adult Education Department of the Toledo Public schools to undertake an educational program, ten diplomas have been granted.

City Welfare director J. Michael Porter has endorsed this project which has received government funding. Rev. Bertram points out that this is an opportunity for the public to contribute. Checks in support of the project may be sent either to him or to Mr. Porter.

In Ozzie's sermon of March 6, 1974, he said, "One of the most interesting experiences during my ministry has been the following incident. Several years ago, an extremely resentful anti-God, anti-social murderer was sentenced to the electric chair. It was in death row at the prison several months before his execution that I met him. He was reading Julius Caesar instead of the Bible, and had no need of prayer, he said. Upon leaving him I said, "We will never meet again, for you're going to a different place than I."

The following letter was written by that prisoner when Ozzie was serving as the chaplain of a state correctional institution. It was written after the Reverand Bertram's first visit, while the prisoner was awaiting the death sentence. In this letter to his sister, the young man tells of Pastor Bertram's visit. It contains one of the most accurate character analyses of my husband that I could hope to have. Many have told me of the effect he had upon them and their lives, and this letter characterizes the strain I hear over and over again, "There was just something about the godlike sincerity of the man—to know him was to love him."

Dear _____,

The good Reverend paid me a visit yesterday. And am I undone! He has penetrated where others couldn't even scarify the surface. O woe is me! I now find myself more unhappy than at any time before, for he has deliberately tampered with a mind I had thought set to meet an unjust fate. Last night I was unable to fall asleep as has been my wont. Troubled thoughts streamed through my restless mind. It is as though he released an untapped source of misery within me. In a word, he has sabotaged my soul, which I had long since placed in the hands of God.

Even now I find it difficult to dispel that nameless but

troubling atmosphere he left behind him. What is it about the man that he leaves you with the impression that he had left a part of himself behind? Surely he is different from others I have met. He strikes me as being a man who feels your misery without show of outward emotion, as though a part of him seeped into you and then returned again to him in purity of spirit.

Why did he have to overturn the peace of mind I thought I had? Why couldn't he have left me as he found me—that is, looking forward to leaving this world with the belief that only my body was being sacrificed to the law? For a while he almost had me feeling like a human being—a feeling a person doesn't need in so dreadful a time. Prison chaplains one takes for granted, for they soon become hardened to the suffering about them. And, too, too many men try to use them in furthering their false beliefs. Perhaps it was my desire to talk with someone that has made me look upon your Reverend as different from other men. Even so, I still can't shrug off him or his words just like that. What it is, I don't know.

He talked to me of heaven and hell. Is there a worse hell than this I am in? It is hard for me to believe that God will punish me twice for my wrongs. To tell you the truth, I don't know what to believe. Yet I couldn't stoop to saying I do when I don't. Being a hypocrite is far worse than having no belief at all. I never in all my life deceived a person to do him wrong, although I have deceived people to cover up my background. It would have been an easy matter to impose on him, to pretend that I believed him in a matter of minutes. And now I really think that if I had condescended to so low an act, I should be repenting of it, for, as I have already noted, there is something about him that will not permit a person to take advantage of his godlike sincerity. He is the man I needed when first I blundered into the pitfalls of life.

His purpose of coming, I know, was to prevail upon me to let you come up here. I am convinced that things are as they ought to be. Seeing me won't lighten your heart. I have given myself up as already dead. The state police made sure I would be their sacrifice. In dying I help to uphold their reputation. I had no more chance of getting a fair trial than a hog has of coming alive out of a slaughterhouse. Please try to see my point of view. There's nothing you can do for me but pray. My weak prayers need plenty of solid support. The "higher ups" will carry out the desires of the state police in any event. (Your parishioners must have gone into mourning when Rev. Bertram was transferred!)

Your brother,

P.S. God bless and keep you and yours. Tell the Rev. that I should like to see him again when he has the time—to hear him is to like him.

Through my husband's efforts, and after more visits with the prisoner, a stay of execution was granted. A new trial was arranged and the sentence of death was changed to a prison term. Christ again worked through the Holy Spirit and changed a life through the human instrument that was O. H. Bertram.

I would be less of a woman if I were not to treasure the many love letters I received from my Pastor Honey, both before our marriage and after. I know the romantic side of my husband will be enjoyed as these two letters are read. The first one I received before our marriage.

My darling Sally:

There are periods in a person's life when all about you one sees only gloom, with a better day obscure and remote. It is then that prayer becomes the only means of hope. Then suddenly the Lord answers the petition and it is difficult to comprehend His goodness and kindness. This describes my life in recent months. You are the answer to those prayers and I find it difficult at times to fully comprehend the Lord's goodness. I am grateful and ever shall be for this unexpected blessing.

Rest assured that I will never take you for granted or that my love for you will ever fade as the years go by. I will ever hold you in high esteem. I can only see before us happiness and the type of happy and peaceful home which will be a foretaste of heaven. Our love is based on something far higher than human love and some people

202

will never quite understand our devotion to one another. The flame of love which is now aglow will ever burn brighter.

Between now and that eventful 21st there will be those who will question us whether our actions are wise. Let us put our minds at ease that this is not an overnight whim but a true devotion of love which has been thought and rethought, prayed about and then directed by God. We know the higher Power which has brought us together. So many things in the past have proven this fact.

I love you with all my heart!

With deepest affections,
Your Ozzie

The second one for a birthday several years after we were wed while we were vacationing at the Northfield Inn in Northfield, Massachusetts. The large old Victorian Inn is no longer in business. It was a favorite former vacation spot in the days before I became Ozzie's wife, and he had given me the trip as a birthday present. I found the letter on my breakfast plate the morning of my birthday July 19.

My darling Angel,

As I look out upon the beauty of this area, I am reminded of the beauty you have brought into my life. It is the joy of knowing that I have the most loving and charming wife walking on the face of the earth. As each time I return to this part of the country I find it more beautiful, so with each day I find you more beautiful and lovely.

On this your birthday, I see in you an answer to my prayers, the request of a wife with spiritual depth, keen understanding, and physical charm. You are all these in one beautiful package that God has created for me. May this day be the beginning of even greater joy for you, deeper satisfaction of a life being spent in total dedication to God, and of blessings far beyond your expectations. May the Lord shower you with good health and more happiness than you have ever had in life.

Although this life at Northfield is the next best thing to a Utopia, you have helped to make it the next best thing to heaven. These days have been a fulfillment of a dream I have had for many years. Now we have enjoyed them together. They are also my gift to you on this your birthday. May we long remember them as a token of God's love for us in making them possible. They have welded us even closer together. As the years go by may each day seem even shorter because of our growing love and affection.

 Darling, I do love you!

  Your Ozzie

 The gift of expressing feelings for another is more precious than gold in the opinion of most, I feel sure. I must call attention to the beautiful spiritual vein that runs through the letters from Ozzie. Before we were married he told me when convincing me I should marry him, "You'll love me more after marriage!" At the time I did not understand what he meant. Later I realized he was right. I did! And it was because Christ was in the center of our union, enhancing our love for one another. In a Thursday, October 6, 1966 notation from Ozzie's Pastor's Desk Diary appointment book, I find, "Speak at Monac School Mothers and Teachers' Tea on 'The Basic Needs of Children.' " I was teaching there. I attended the tea.

 I don't remember a word he said, I'm ashamed to say. At that time the clergyman, even though tall, good looking and an intelligent speaker, did not register in my consciousness as someone who would eventually prove to be one of the most important and influential forces in my life. What fun to be reminded of a previous exposure to this man that I had forgotten!

 The appointment books of each year of our marriage provide a rich source for my remembrance of activities in which I was involved. Tucked in the page where our wedding "appointment" was recorded was a letter I had written to to congregation at the request of my Pastor Honey. He felt it would serve to acquaint the membership with me, and so published it in "The Lamplighter" a year after our marriage.

FROM THE PASTOR'S WIFE, SARAH
 A year ago I received a special gift from God—my husband. It was a miracle of God that brought us together,

and it is God who helps me make our marriage meaningful and happily fulfilling. It seems that God keeps proving to me that He really has a beautiful divine plan for marriage. "Except the Lord build the house the builder's work is useless" (Psalm 127:1).

Besides being a dear sweetheart, I consider my husband my best friend. We really enjoy each other's company—and the days are never long enough. Someone remarked the other day that I'm usually smiling. The secret of my life and joy is my relationship with my husband, which we know God brought about and is still helping to grow. I thank God for the privilege of being his wife.

There is a special lesson one learns in marriage. Love should not be according to the performance of the other person, i.e., if he would change I would love him more. That isn't God's kind of love. If you are trying to change your partner, stop! Instead ask God to change you.

I really think of our marriage as being the triangle my husband speaks about. God, Pastor, and me. If one is ever out of fellowship with our Lord, a marriage can suffer. A little prayer helps me, "Oh God, I feel so grumpy and self-centered today. It's going to take a miracle to change me. But I know that is what you specialize in, so I'm trusting in You. Amen."

> "No matter what life brings to you
> You'll have the strength to bear it
> As long as you have love to give
> And someone who can share it."

I am meeting so many wonderfully loving people here at Good Shepherd, I can truthfully say I no longer miss my former church. Many thanks to you all and a special thanks to our wonderful Pastor.

A communications researcher, Dr. Gerald M. Goldhaber has stated that, "Charismatic personalities fall into three distinct types:

Hero, who is an idealized person, talking and looking the way we wished we would.

Anti-hero, who is a 'real' person, talking and thinking the way we do.

Mystic, a person we can't quite figure out."

"Hero" is a title, I feel, that should be awarded to those who, given a set of circumstances, react with courage, dignity, decency, understanding, and compassion. It should be a person who makes us feel better for having known them, or having been touched by them. It is obvious that Ozzie's charisma was felt by many. I have noted with great appreciation some of the beautiful writing in condolence letters that Ozzie's demise inspired.

It was not said enough during his ministry, but it must be said now. Only eternity will reveal the number of lives his ministry touched, and those whose praise and thanksgiving to God for such a blessing will certainly look to your husband with thanks. Not only was it what he said about Jesus as his personal Savior, but it was how he lived and died reflecting his trust in God that will be remembered.

> J. A. O. Preus
> President of Lutheran Church-Missouri Synod

Few men in our synod enjoyed such a full and active ministry. Years ago when I first met him as he brought his confirmation class to Washington, I noted that there was something different about him. He seemed to want to give all the members of his flock the best experience possible. Then, too, his radio and television ministry was unique in our circles. I know it took much of his time and energy to do it all, it was done again for others. That is a mark of a true servant of the Lord.

I have related to many of my colleagues in the ministry that he was one of the few men in synod that I know who usually had more people attending a Sunday worship than the number of his communicant members. That really says much about the man.

> Walter H. Moeller
> (Former Congressman)

June 11, 1979

Dear Mrs. Bertram:

I don't believe that you and I have ever met, and I knew

206

your husband, Ozzie, only briefly by meeting him at the conventions of the English District. Still, however, I do feel that I knew your husband and enjoyed him very much.

He was such a friendly, outgoing individual; and we enjoyed our table talks very much. My heart goes out to you at the loss of your husband. Please accept my heart-felt sympathy.

Seldom have I met a person who seemed as alive in the Lord as Ozzie was. Since the life that we have in Christ goes on forever, however, there's no need to speak of his vibrant faith relationship in the past tense. It continues.

Allen A. Gartner
Lutheran Church of the Messiah

We will long hold in grateful remembrance the distinguished ministry of Ozzie. In addition to all of the other aspects of his Gospel outreach, he for many decades maintained a special outreach, by means of radio and television. He is truly one of the pioneers of Gospel broadcasting.

Eugene R. Bertermann
Associate Director of
Lutheran Bible Translators, Incorporated

We had counted Ozzie a friend ever since the period of our happy association with him during the time of his ministry in Mayfair, Pa. Our parish was in Levittown, between Philadelphia and Trenton. We had interests and concerns in common; we were on the same theological frequency. We have followed with admiration his work in the mass media, the "Moments of Comfort" program, etc. The Lord used Ozzie mightily in bringing the Gospel to many throughout the years of his ministry.

Lea and Walter A. Maier
Concordia Theological Seminary

I mourn your deep loss with you. I loved Oz in a unique

way—from a distance I guess. What a man! What a servant of ours—and his—living Lord! And so, while I shed tears last week, and with misty eyes even now, I also rejoice in his eternal salvation.

Don Mossman
Clergyman and Professor at Ann Arbor, MI

June 4, 1979

Dear Mrs. Bertram,

It is difficult for me to express in words the deep sense of loss which I feel at this time along with you. I not only lost a fine and worthy colleague, but a good and gentle friend, one whom I was able to share a beautiful fellowship with.

How much greater must be the loss for you and members of the family who saw him and were with him each day. I mourn his loss with you.

Reverend Bertram helped so many, giving them strength and the ability to look past anxieties and troubles of the present. May you, too, find that solace and comfort.

In our tradition, when one is known for kindness and humility, he is compared to Aaron, the high priest, as it states in our Talmud: "Be of the disciples of Aaron, loving peace and pursuing peace; be one who loves his fellow men and draws them near to God" (Ethics of the Fathers 1:12). This, to me, was Reverend Bertram.

May his beautiful memory ever inspire each of us to more righteous and nobler living.

In sincerity and with sorrow.

Sincerely,
Ed Garsek
Rabbi at the Congregation Etz Chayim
Toledo, Ohio

The lauds from one's fellow man are rewarding. I trust my husband somehow knows the love and esteem he inspired in those who knew him.

I knew him to be a Christian who spoke out, even lashed out, at things he felt were wrong. I'm proud of the strength he revealed in every aspect of his life.

27
Angel Analyzes

"Trust no Future, however pleasant,
Let the dead Past bury its dead!
Act—act in the living Present!
Heart within, and God o'erhead!"
Henry Wadsworth Longfellow
"A Psalm of Life"

I read an interesting thought by W. J. Toms in the *Detroit News*. He said, "Be careful how you live; you may be the only Bible some person ever reads." It seems to me that Ozzie continually strove to live as his Lord wished through the direction of the Bible. The amazing thing to me is that he always expressed godliness with such ease.

I suppose this was due to many things; his family training, the inspiration of the minister grandfathers he adored and emulated, the influence of his church, and the seminary training, and a natural tendency toward finding it easy to be especially good and kind. His attractive looks, manner, voice, and behavior made him a "natural" for the ministerial profession.

Whereas most, myself included, need each day to make a conscientious effort to practice their Christianity, Ozzie seemed to embody all that the phrase "born to the cloth" means. He was a natural for his calling as a minister, in the sense that all he did and spoke was what most people believe a Pastor should do and speak and live. It took no effort for him to be this way. He simply was the embodiment of a truly good man in the opinion of all who knew him.

In the years we were together, I never knew him to scold, be critical, slur, ridicule, be derogatory, slant wrongly, or get angry. Of course, he had definite opinions of people, but always with understanding of "where they were coming from," in the jargon of our day. He also was not afraid to take a stand on things or issues that he felt strongly about. He was no "wish-wash" (one of

209

his own expressions), and could become righteously indignant about things he deplored. I'm sure that the church councils and elders who served with him were aware of his strong-mindedness, but were intelligent and wise enough to recognize his innate good motives and years of experience in the church. They benefited themselves and their churches by usually accepting his strong leadership; and profited by it.

One of the secrets of his marvelous relationships with people, I feel, is that he always allowed others their say. He respected their opinions and never made them feel wrong or guilty in their ideas. He might subtly suggest alternatives, or changes—but always with a strength-filled kindness.

I saw a strong love and camaraderie expressed by these men who served with him. They obviously not only admired him as their spiritual leader, they came to trust his influence in the decision-making for the church's good. I imagine the elders and church council meetings were laced not only with spirituality, but with a good dose of humor, too, as this was so much a part of Ozzie, the man.

I saw the good-natured teasing that went on between my strongly Republican husband and Robert Carson, a president of our congregation, who was just as staunchly a Democrat, and who lovingly teased Ozzie about only mentioning Republican presidents in his sermons.

Dr. Joseph Schradie, head of Toledo University's Pharmagnosy department, his wife Marjorie, and their four attractive daughters, epitomize to this day, the staunchly loyal, intelligently religious practising Christians who characterized our church. Encouraged by Ozzie, Dr. Schradie has served not only our church well, but has been elected or appointed to many synodical commissions. It has been a personal joy to see two of the Schradie girls, Cindy and Kathy, whom I taught as first grade students, blossom into beautiful examples of Christian women.

Another exceptional man and teacher, Dr. Nick Nypodym, also of Toledo University, has remained actively loyal to Good Shepherd Lutheran Church since my husband's demise. His inspired Bible class teaching has been a contributing factor in not only holding the interest of a devastated church body, but holding the body of the church together, when the tendency seemed to be to

210

leave the environs of the edifice where there was no longer the beloved personage of Pastor Bertram.

The fact that this tremendous "sample of an excellent teacher" chose our church to attend, after visiting many when he first came to Toledo, is a tribute to the purity of Word being preached by my husband.

I observed the way, for example, Warren Myers, a church council member, could speak his opinions freely to my husband after service, knowing his views would be respected and taken into consideration after the humorous exchange of ideas would occur. Warren and Jean Myers love to remind me of how they had noticed a few years ago what looked like a couple "necking" in the parking lot of the neighborhood supermarket. How they laughed and were delighted when they saw it was their Pastor and wife who emerged from the car to do some evening grocery shopping together.

I love the story another fine gentlemen of our congregation shared with me, which expresses so well this closeness felt between my Pastor Honey and the beloved church "faithfuls." Art Meissner's story was that one day, while he and Pastor were driving somewhere together, they came to a red light. A lady who was obviously and conspicuously not blessed with physical beauty of face and form, was standing close by the curb. She was carrying an umbrella, and obviously was hoping for her ride to come—looking expectantly at each car as it passed her by.

Art said he shook his head in the universal gesture of unappreciation of a homely sight. Ozzie, who never said a hurtful remark about anyone, looked at the woman and said, "I'm sure glad she is carrying an umbrella; it's supposed to rain next Tuesday."

What you need to know to appreciate the subtlety of this remark is that it was then a Thursday, and the implication was that a woman with her lack of charms would have to wait a long time to get a ride with anyone. This was the closest Ozzie ever came to being derogatory about someone. If he was angry about something, only his family ever heard critical remarks about a personality. He was, after all, human.

In attempting to analyze just the right set of qualities that made Ozzie not only such a loveable human being, but a successful minister, I feel the sense of humor he possessed was very

211

crucial. As the Reverend Mark Schreiber, one of Ozzie's former vicars and now Pastor of Guardian Lutheran Church in Jacksonville, Florida, wrote me, "It seems to me most of Pastor's humor was made up of quick one-liners, which are quite funny at the time, but difficult to recall."

It was, however, very clear to all who were exposed to Ozzie's personality, that this just right sense of appropriate humor helped to make him the beloved and influential man he was.

In all honesty, I must confess he did not tell jokes often or well. One of his favorites had to do with, of course, church work. I can see him in my mind's eye now; blue eyes alight as he charmingly massacred this story:

"A pastor wished to purchase a new chandelier for the church. At the general meeting one of the congregation arose and said, 'I oppose this buying of a chandelier. First of all, we already have a piano, secondly, how are we going to find someone to play it, and thirdly, what we really need is new lighting for the sanctuary!' "

I'm sure the congregation in all my beloved's churches will recognize this story, and will recall with a fond smile his telling of it.

Jan and Jerry Boyers of Wauseon, Ohio, a lovely Christian couple whom Ozzie used many times as vocalists for his television program, told me this story about Ozzie: He called Jan one day and told her it was Billy Graham calling; he had heard her and her husband sing on TV and wanted them on his upcoming television special. Although the disguised voice puzzled her momentarily, Jan recognized Ozzie's voice as he began to laugh at the fun of fooling her.

The joy with which Jan told me this story shows with what special fond memories Ozzie remains in the heart of his friends.

Jerry then epitomized Ozzie as many have. "He was the kindest man I ever knew; and he spoke to everyone in the same kindly, courteous way, whether to a Mr. Astorbilt or a prisoner in a correctional institute." Jerry and Jan had been with my Pastor Honey several times at our Lucas County minimal offenses jail, to sing when Ozzie conducted one of his many services there for the inmates.

Two of the younger mothers in our congregation visited me in the new little condominium into which I moved after Ozzie's death. They shared stories of their personal lives with me. Helen

212

Felker reminisced about the great courage she derived from my husband insisting on her claiming Christ's promises at the time of her little son's death. She and Ruth Barker agreed that Ozzie's effectiveness in counseling them was, "He listened! He understood! He cared!"

Many have shared stories about my husband with me. I appreciate the ones who have done so. I feel their anecdotes are just the ones God wants me to include, to give a rounded-out picture of the character of this unusual man. The many who could have shared information with me, but for whatever reason did not, I feel are only acting as God would have it, as I could not possibly have incorporated 500 stories into this book.

I feel others can tell the many faceted personality of Ozzie through their experiences with him much better than I, who anticipate the reaction of some who will say, "Oh, she was prejudiced for the man, as any wife who loved her husband would be." And so you will find throughout this book many anecdotes from the people whom O. H. Bertram impressed in one way or another.

"What was Pastor really like, Mrs. B.?" and "Was he the man he seemed to be in day-to-day living?" These were questions the closest of friends and the most distant of the television viewers alike, asked me. They asked this verbally and by letter, both before Ozzie's death and after.

What they really want to know is whether the private person conformed to the public image. They are curiously ambivalent, for at the same time they want to believe he was the perfect expression of the ideal man of God, and yet not to believe. Human nature somehow psychologically derives comfort in discovering that a hero has feet of clay. Someone who seems more virtuous, more gifted, more inwardly and outwardly beautiful, brings out contrasting feelings in us. We want to be assured that he is really this way; yet we are almost hoping that he is not at all like the public personality.

Pastor's innate goodness, his attractive physical charisma, his intelligence, his true caring attitude, always came across to people, whether it was in person or over television. And yet he, too, experienced incidents of being regarded by some with what we might call double vision: one eye paying tribute, the other seeking flaws. What is it that makes us pay homage to superiority and greatness, and yet regard it with suspicion, resentment, and even jealousy?

Usually the assurance that Pastor was truly as he seemed to be—that "what you see is what you get," to quote one of our popular comedians, was met with relief. But people sometimes seem to be undone by a vision of someone close to perfection, for it somehow brings out the knowledge of our own imperfection and frailty.

The congregations of Ozzie's four churches in Connecticut, Pennsylvania and Ohio, would perhaps know the real O. H. Bertram as well almost as I, his wife. For somewhat the same courteously loving attentions were paid to the individuals in his parishes as were paid to me.

Letters and notes were continually written, personal phone calls and contacts were made every day by Ozzie to assure his "flock" he cared. He made it known by the sheer force of that magnetic personality that he was and always would be available to anyone. And as genuine love is usually a two-way street, love flowed continually from the grateful, the encouraged, the uplifted, the changed, the captivated, the spiritually needy, men, women, and children alike.

In summing up Ozzie's character analysis, I'd like to quote from a book belonging to my husband entitled, *God's Psychiatry* by Charles L. Allen. I found many lines in this book underlined, so I know Ozzie read and absorbed its ideas. I read a paragraph that to me seems to shout out, "O. H. Bertram." Mr. Allen states:

> "Study the lives of those we call saints, those who have attained unusual spiritual power, and you will find their secret right at this point. They sinned, but they never surrendered to sin. They never accepted failure as final. They never ceased to look forward with confidence. They kept saying, 'I can, in Him.' And to the utmost of their power was added His power.
>
> "The same power is available for any one of us. You may look into a past of shame, or defeat, or sorrow, but I tell you that you can look into a future of peace and victory. Only believe, only believe all things are possible. This is the Christian faith."

If this doesn't sum up my husband, his person, his life, his beliefs, I don't know what does. In my opinion, he *was* one of the special saints whose whole life was dedicated to his Christian principles, and who lived the abundant life Christ promised His followers in John 10:10; "I am come that they might have life, and that they might have it more abundantly" (King James Version).

Others recognized, felt, and appreciated this special "worker in the Kingdom" that was my husband. Here are some phrases that I read over and over again as I went over the hundreds of letters, notes, and cards of condolence that arrived from viewers and listeners of his programs after Ozzie's death.

"He was a great man."
"He expressed such love and hope for me."
"A true man of God."
"The program for shut-ins was so important in my life."
"I will miss him so."
"His sermons always had so much meaning for me."
"He was God's man for me."
"Your husband was one of God's beautiful people."
"You two were a testimony to commitment and love in marriage."
"Your marriage and love is a beautiful love story—is, because your love doesn't die; and you and Pastor's love for each other was God-centered."
"Sorrow isn't forever. Love is!"
"He took time to listen when I had problems."
"No words can express how I feel."
"He was a very special person to us."
"We loved him, and we love you."
"I was so aware of the joy you brought to Pastor."
"How lucky our dear friend was to find you."
"We are better people for having known Pastor."
"Pastor not only made a deep impression on our lives, but gave our sons a strong start in their Christian beliefs."
"He reached far and touched many with endless love."
"Those who knew him had a special blessing in this life."
"His devoted faith to our Lord and his concern for us will forever be remembered and treasured."
"May the Lord comfort you *and* us!"

"He was one in a million."

With such a worthy man to honor, I sometimes got very angry with myself when I thought of how long it took for me to complete this book.

Why do I procrastinate so? I'd wonder. Anger at myself for not being a more diligent writer only served to make me feel guilty about not working single-mindedly toward finishing the job I clearly felt was directed by God.

It seemed as though other less important things kept occurring for me to do, and I used each one as an escape from the task of writing. I thank God for a remark that Eve Rockwood (she of the "wading in the Dead Sea with me" fame) made to me one day when I was recriminating myself for not getting down to my writing for several months. She said, "Sally, did you ever stop to think that perhaps God is allowing you more healing time before you tackle the illness and dying chapters?" She "saved face" for me in my own eyes; for that seemed to me to be very plausible, and I suddenly was able to go ahead with the writing.

28
His Gifts

"I look around
In a world of gifted people
And wonder, a bit wistfully,
What is my gift?
What do I have to give the world?"
> Gordon and Gladys DePree
> "The Gift"

". . . but the gift of God is eternal life through Jesus Christ our Lord."
> Romans 6:23

Others express so well what O. H. Bertram's special contributions to his fellow humans were. The time and effort people expended to write or to tell me of Ozzie's special meaning to them, is to me indicative of the impact for the good that he had on so many people.

June Miller, one of Toledo's television personalities and Ozzie's co-worker at a TV station, said, "He reminded me of a pillar, or a great tree of strength. He stood tall, but could bend. He did not stagnate, but could and did grow each year. During the years after the death of his wife, he went through a stark and stern period, like a tree that has lost its leaves. Then, when happier circumstances occurred, he blossomed forth again, a tree with new leaves. He needed nurturing and love as a tree needs water and sun. His dynamic quality when he spoke made him stand out like a tall tree on a hillside."

Ozzie had what I call the "people touch." He could and did make everyone in our church, plus other acquaintances, feel appreciated, and important to his life. Many times I've been told of how people were amazed when they were informed they were "missed last Sunday," or heard a special favorite hymn of theirs added to the printed service when Pastor saw they were in church after an absence. What a memory he had! If anyone mentioned something they would like to hear, or sing, or had something to contribute to a class discussion such as a tape, he would always remember to include it, or ask for it in a future service or class. He knew the value of each member being made to feel important, and he had the adroitness, insight, and exceptional memory to be able to do this.

Violet Bugbee, another member, said she never knew a man who so consistently put the "best construction on everything." Rachel Harrold told of how she can never forget his instruction when she confided a problem to him. "A Christian always makes the first move. Let's pray about it, and God will guide you in what to do," he told her.

Tom McGarry, a long time member, said, "With Pastor Bertram there never was any scolding or recriminations—why didn't you do this or that—just his positive affirming of you, and his strong statement of faith." He recalled with grateful joy how Pastor had required his daughter's fiancé to come in to talk about his Christian beliefs before he agreed to marry them.

A young member was experiencing problems with a decision on which seminary to attend. Fritz Schmitt recalls Ozzie's vibrancy and enthusiasm, saying it was "effectual and contagious." Ozzie had the reputation of being down to earth in his advice. When Fritz's indecision reached an annoying peak in his own

217

mind, Pastor simply said, "Look, you were raised a Lutheran. Give the Fort Wayne Lutheran Seminary a try. If it's not to your liking, you can always change."

It is interesting to note the men who have gone on to be ordained ministers, or who are in seminary training now who have been connected with our church. They are Robert Bugbee, Fritz Schmitt, Mark Schreiber, Douglas Thompson, Scott McMahon, Mark Dressler, Dennis Liebich, Bryan King, Michael Osborne, Keith Less, and Tom Scher. This seems to me to be a high percentage of men Ozzie inspired to the ministry. I'm sure there must have been others in his former congregations.

As I have mentioned before, Ozzie was a natural to be put on a pedestal. He looked the part of the confident, mature clergyman; he was handsome in a distinguished way, and most important, he never expressed anything but a Christlike way of life, in behavior or speech. Marion Gust wrote to me, "Did you see the movie 'Jesus of Nazareth?' One scene reminded me of Pastor Bertram. Jesus was walking, teaching, and talking to his disciples. He had his arm around one of the chosen. Frequently, as Pastor walked and talked with someone, he had his arm around their shoulders. His was the human touch."

Douglas Thompson, now an ordained pastor, mentioned Pastor Bertram as the "father figure" he looked up to. While he served as our church's summer vicar in 1974, he remembered how the lavalier microphone he was using as liturgist one Sunday tangled and pulled off as he was moving and speaking at the altar. He was horrified at what he thought was an unforgivable interruption, when he glanced at Ozzie. Ozzie's lovingly sympathetic smile seemed to say, "think nothing of it" to the young vicar, and he was able to fix it easily then, and carry on. One of my Pastor Honey's extra pleasurable experiences was to preach Reverend Thompson's ordination sermon.

Pastor Thompson and another vicar, now the Reverend Mark Schreiber, both lovingly looked up to Ozzie as a true man of God. Both mentioned to me how they felt they saw Christ expressed through this man. What a tribute from the men who worked so closely with him! He never asked them to do anything he wouldn't or couldn't do. It was obvious they noted and valued that extra something he had. Both mentioned the invaluable experience with television.

I have often thought that Ozzie was so impressed with the pastor he assisted in his first position, the Reverend Bernard W. Janssen, of the Immanual Lutheran church in Danbury, Connecticut, that he patterned his own behavior after him. In his role as the guiding pastor to the many vicars he had in his career, Pastor Janssen was always remembered and spoken about in glowing terms by Ozzie. He especially mentioned Pastor Janssen's meticulous ways—how he always stressed neatness and organization.

The Reverend Mark Schreiber mentioned this about Ozzie when he wrote, "One thing that was a certain quality about Pastor was his neatness. You remember that when I arrived in Toledo in August of 1975, my birthday was shortly thereafter. Pastor had evidently noticed for a couple of Sundays that my appearance was not professional enough, i.e., my shoes weren't shined properly. Lo and behold, my first gift from Pastor was a portable shoe shine kit, which I still have to this day. The result of his getting his point across has been that the virtue of shining shoes has become a regular part of my preparation for church."

Ozzie was always a stickler for good manners on every occasion. Mark gave a wonderful characterization of my husband when he wrote, "His way was not always to speak a word directly; sometimes visual contact was all that was necessary. I remember standing around the Thanksgiving table at the Bertram home, waiting for the others to come to the table. For some reason, the vicar's table manners had been the topic of conversation just a few days before, so I was sensitized to a few flaws in my style. As we both stood there waiting for the rest to come, Pastor kept giving me the eye as to when we should be seated. I had made a move to sit down, but was visually rebuffed before my carcass settled in the chair. So with a few glances back and forth like a tennis match, I finally caught the cue, 'Now is the time.' Pastor, always pleasant and cordial in his dealings with people, again showed his tactful approach to my somewhat artless comportment at the dinner table."

This particular vicar was a favorite with me. I have mentioned that Mark stayed at our home for a while, until a suitable apartment could be found. One day I teasingly said to him, "Mark, I don't care what Pastor says, *I* think you are doing a good job as our vicar." He looked at me in horror, believing I was serious, until he caught the twinkle in my eye and realized I was joking.

At the end of his vicarage, I invited him for a farewell dinner at our home. He obviously enjoyed the meal, patted his lips with his napkin, looked at me seriously and said, "Mrs. B., I don't care what Pastor says, *I* think you are a good cook." Mark and I had a special friendship, and he always called me his "Toledo mom." The gift of making people comfortable around him was one of Ozzie's most endearing qualities. But of course, it was his gift of touching people's hearts in a personal way that lasts in their memories. In a letter to me after my husband's death, Zeb Vasher, Good Shepherd church member and possessor of a beautiful tenor voice that occasionally enhances our services, said,

> I can't refrain from writing about some feelings and impressions. It was on the occasion of one of my favorite aunt's passing away that I called Pastor Bertram to inquire as to how I might approach this event that was causing me considerable anxiety. He responded by saying, 'Death was to be looked upon as a joyous occasion—that it was in fact a time for rejoicing for those who die in God's grace; a time to rejoice because the dead in Christ are at His banquet table feasting with Jesus', and then Pastor ended our discussion with a prayer as he always did after a conversation that concerned some kind of personal problem. He somehow always instilled a kind of confidence . . . His prayers were always extemporaneous, and because of this, I felt strangely personalized in them. It was as though he had a special "hook-up" to the Lord, and never got a bad connection, because his prayers always included several solutions or answers to solving every problem.
>
> Although Pastor was noted for having his feet on the ground in spite of his many successes, his soul seemed to me somehow mystically connected up with heaven and all its saints for consultation in his pastoral work, when he prayed.
>
> I'd sneak a glance at him sometimes when he prayed in the church service—it was as though some part of him ascended up to heaven when he prayed, and it showed on his face.

Pastor never failed to mention, after a sermon that included mention of God's wrath, or the 'wages of sin', that Christ's love, mercy and forgiveness were there for everyone for the taking. I experienced an expression of this love from Christ after the service in the reception line via Pastor's vigorous handshake and that gigantic, radiant smile. It seemed to say, 'Nothing personal intended in my sermon; just feel Christ's love.' Pastor was always so consistent in showing love, and compassion, and understanding.

Sages and scholars could have learned something from O. H. Bertram, and who's to say that a few did not.

How I treasure this letter of tribute from this talented church member and friend. And how the reminder of how my beloved felt about death has helped me during the difficult days of coping with his demise.

Another letter received expresses what I was told and written to so repeatedly about Ozzie. It puts his gift of the "people touch" in such a beautiful way that I cannot help but include it. Mrs. Eileen Nupp wrote these beautifully expressed words:

When the Lord took Pastor Bertram home, he left a great void in many lives—his presence here was a heaven-sent gift to us all . . . As Pastor said in his Sunday morning prayer after a death, "God in His wise providence hath summoned from this world the soul of ——." After all, this world had Pastor almost twice as long as it had His own Son. I think of the good Christ and all the other "good who die young" could have done if they could have stayed. But perhaps we feel constrained now to work with extra effort to continue their work and even more is accomplished.

Pastor was not only my earthly shepherd, but a dear friend, father and Christian brother with whom I could share my physical and emotional burdens and pains, and my joys, too. . . I am a consummate bookworm and theology was one of my many subjects I thoroughly enjoyed studying . . . In the last few years, Pastor would ask me to read and review books for him, relate the important parts, and give my opinion as to whether it was worth his limited time to pursue it.

He made me feel a new value and importance in Sunday school teaching; and as the assistant organist, I shared many tasks with him: worship services, weddings, funerals, holidays, and TV appearances. It was the communication ministry through television and his newspaper articles that made him extra special also to the many who never even met him.

He taught me (by his example) small but meaningful ways to convey thoughtfulness or thanks through a phone call, a note, or simply a warm hand clasp . . . Besides all this, he was fun to be with. Indeed, he was on a pedestal as an example for all of us and our children, but never too high to not have a down-to-earth laugh with someone . . . I'm sure Jesus must have also had a sense of humor and would not have liked us to be somber all the time.

I'm thankful to God that my children were guided by Pastor Bertram through the ten most important years of their growth and development. Many things the kids say now, tell me the valuable impression he made upon them—much of which I never realized at the time he was here. I loved his firm German discipline that made the kids realize that the Bible, catechism, and faith were the most important and valuable things in their lives, and never to be taken lightly.

I never cease to be amazed at how nonchalantly many young people today regard the church and their spiritual welfare. The beautiful part with Pastor was that not only did the kids have a healthy respect (yes, a little fear, too) for doing their memory work right and paying attention in class, but they realized the two-way love that radiated whenever he taught them. I remember the older kids advising the neophytes in catechism class, "When you recite, never look at his face, or you will see that big smile and go blank!"

After confirmation services one year, one of the young confirmed came running up to my newly confirmed son. "Hurry up if you want to get a big hug from Pastor. He's going to leave!" How eagerly they ran to help him; and such joy and triumph they shared. He was their loving, caring, and very human coach, and they had won the game! He had made confirmation that important to them.

As a teacher myself, I had noticed my husband's gift for teaching. How could what many parents felt be expressed more graphically than through Eileen's poignant letter.

How I wish I could include all the examples of "the people touch" Ozzie had, that many have shared with me. Tolstoy wrote, ". . . Leave traces on the souls of other people and the spirit never dies." This was Ozzie's greatest talent, and the fact that people remembered his words in their exact phraseology gives credence to this.

Leila and Loren Stevens recall what Ozzie said to them on the special occasion of their renewing their wedding vows on their twenty-fifth anniversary. They told me he said, "You have weathered the storms of life; you know what real love is."

Cindy Addison, church secretary, was taking notes one day when Ozzie was dictating his sermon for the following Sunday. Our little granddaughter, Holly, was visiting the office at that moment, and was crying and fussing and needing attention from her "Boppa," as she called him. As Ozzie bent to pick her up, Cindy recalls him saying, "She's not spoiled, she's loved!"

Cindy also tells of the young Polish groom's reaction at his own wedding. He told her, "Pastor Bertram badly mispronounced my last name. Out of love and respect for him, and my own nervousness, when it came time for me to repeat my own name, I repeated it the way Pastor had pronounced it."

Dr. Earl Perrigo recalls how he was considering accepting a fine offer of a position in Milwaukee during the time after they had found their "church home" at Good Shepherd Lutheran Church, and with the Reverend O. H. Bertram. They decided against leaving Toledo. After Ozzie became ill, Dr. Perrigo became his physician. He told me that he cared for many dying patients, but never one who expressed "such optimism, warmth, and love of Christ. He felt the normal fear at times of leaving his family, but always counteracted it by expressing joy at what he had had in life. I had never before been asked to pray with anyone over the injections that I needed to administer. Pastor was honestly looking for strength and healing; not to do frivolous things, but to get back to his beloved church work."

I have felt strongly that this doctor was the chosen one to administer to my husband during his illness. His particular brand of expertise in medicine, plus his Christian principles, together with a joyous, loving, humorous approach, was just what Ozzie needed at this difficult time. We spoke many times of an unforgettable moment after Ozzie's initial surgery, when we wheeled my husband down to the hospital chapel for a prayer. My daughters were also there. After my husband's prayer, Dr. Perrigo began to softly sing, "I wonder as I wander out under the sky, how Jesus the Savior did come for to die." His voice grew louder and more beautiful as we listened entranced. Tears came into all our eyes, and we listened to this spontaneous expression of love toward God and my husband.

One of the most interesting stories concerning Ozzie's impact on people concerns "Brother Tom Scher," as he is known, and his wife Anne. They called Ozzie their "lighthouse," and considered his way of teaching and the thoughts he gave them in learning God's word to be in "spansule, not capsule" form.

I'd like to quote from an article that appeared in *The Lutheran Witness* of March, 1981, in order to tell their interesting story. The article was called, "Anne and Chester Thomas Scher, Old and New Testament People of God."

"It's a miracle that I've been born. It's a miracle that I've been reborn," says Chester Thomas Scher of Toledo, Ohio. Scher was born an orthodox Jew, sixty-five years ago and was confirmed a Christian just three years ago.

"We had many Christian friends as we grew up in New York City," says Scher about his and his wife's Anne's childhood. "And I spoke to Christ—He was in my heart."

Both Anne and Brother Tom, as he is known in their congregation, Good Shepherd Lutheran Church in Toledo, came from strict and pious Jewish families where tradition and the heritage of Old Testament teachings were unquestioned.

Scher, accustomed to the rough-and-tumble world of business and large speaking engagements, missed "the daily fire of work" after his retirement. He had commuted to Detroit from Toledo for seven years, and his inactivity depressed him.

At that time Rev. Oswald H. Bertram of Good Shepherd featured in a weekly thirty-minute program called 'A Worship for Shut-ins,' on twelve television stations across the country, on ten radio stations with "Moments of Comfort," and in a weekly column, "The Clergyman's Corner," in nine newspapers. Bertram, a respected scholar, had opened Congress several times with prayer and had been an invited guest at the National Prayer Breakfast in Washington, D.C. on three occasions. Anne suggested that Scher visit him.

He left an indelible stamp upon me," says Scher with tears in his eyes. (Bertram died of cancer in 1979.) "He led both of us to Christ through the Word and through his example."

Scher has had ten serious abdominal operations in the past few years, and after waking from one, he describes seeing the tall, long figure of Bertram with his flowing face above the hospital bed. "After that, I called him my lighthouse," says Scher.

Bertram brought back water from the Jordan River after a tour of the Holy Land and used that to baptize the Schers. Both were confirmed on Christmas Day 1977.

Both consider their baptism the most momentous occasion of their lives.

Scher was recently accepted into the colloquy program at Concordia Seminary, Fort Wayne, Indiana, and will begin his study for the ministry.

It was something I had thought about," he says. "But one day I was looking through some books I had inherited from Pastor Bertram and a note in his handwriting fell out of a book on the seminary: "Tom, look into this." Further, my Lord through His Holy Spirit has called me.

"I want to work in breadth and in depth," he says simply. "I'll continue to work for Him—His will be served first.

"We are happier than we've ever been or could imagine," he smiles. 'Now we're New Testament people as well as Old Testament people."

Ozzie's gift of writing for the masses—not just the strictly intellectually oriented theologist, is mentioned in detail in the chapter on the "Clergyman's Corner" newspaper articles. His way of delivering a sermon was possibly his most effective gift to those hearing him, either in person or over the airways.

Part of a beautiful tribute to Ozzie, written by a young school teacher and talented writer, Julie Niebaum, now Mrs. Paul Harris, says:

> At church, Pastor's sermons left a lasting impression on me. As he preached, it was as if God were really talking to me. He stirred countless parishoners to act according to their faith in Christ. He appealed directly to each person in the congregation. It was as if he knew what our needs, fears and hopes were.
>
> His God-given talent of preaching throbbed and breathed with life. He was a marvelous, effective speaker. He had a feeling for the meaning of the Bible and he related the Scriptures in a way we could relate to in our everyday living—in a way in which we could "chew, swallow and digest" his message. His sermons would linger in my heart from week to week.
>
> I used to try and sit in the first row because I'd love to hear Pastor's prolific voice sing his praises to the Lord. He demonstrated his faith in Christ by singing with such vigor.
>
> Pastor Bertram was a marvelous teacher. During my last year of Lutheran instruction, I noticed that each student held a great deal of respect for him.
>
> He was very serious about us learning the basic principles set forth by Martin Luther. We memorized countless verses that have come to my aid many times when I needed strength. One verse he often said was his favorite was Isaiah 41:10: Fear thou not; for I am with thee; yea, I will help thee; yea, I will uphold thee with the right hand of my righteousness."
>
> He did not hesitate to take an interest in each and every student. If we were troubled over the problems we were

confronting, he could sense this and would counsel us individually.

Some other gifts he possessed were his ability to impart knowledge of the Bible, his good judgment, tact, efficiency, flexibility, as well as his humor. He was devoted to help us successfully bridge the gap between childhood and adulthood in such a way as to prepare us for the adult Christian life ahead of us.

I end this chapter with a quote from Charles Walcott: "The quality of a man's life is measured by how deeply he has touched the lives of others."

29
Widow's Workables

"The sorrows of widowhood will be remembered no more, for your Creator will be your 'husband.' "
Isaiah 54:4-5 The Living Bible

"Blessed are they that mourn, for they shall be comforted."
Matthew 5:4

When you are a widow you will discover you can do all kinds of things you never would have thought you could do; for instance:

You learn how to fill your own car gas tank and get your own car license.

You find you can turn the bed mattress yourself. It's a struggle!

You discover you can budget, balance check books, make out census forms, do an income tax report, and drive and find places you need to be, by yourself.

These are some things you can do to help yourself get through the difficult months after the death of a spouse:

Plan to invite people over for lunch, Sunday brunch or dinner.

Make a list of friends who are widowed or alone, couples who have been especially kind, or even some young friends, and systematically plan to have them for a meal.

The planning, shopping, and preparing will be a wonderfully busy and giving type of activity. You will feel good in your productive activity, and they will love seeing you adjusting to your status.

If it was your habit to go out to a restaurant for dinner or lunch quite often with your mate, plan to continue doing this with a woman friend, or friends. God does not wish you to give up life's little joys; on the contrary, He has provided a world of pleasurable activities through which I'm sure He intends to allow you consolation of a sort.

Don't neglect good eating habits, and exercise every day! Plan an activity or project for each day. Writing them down ahead of time seems to give more meaning to life that first difficult year after the death of your beloved. It could be a housekeeping task to be accomplished or a committee meeting to attend, or a lunch with supportive friends, or an exercise class. One spring I took a dance-exercise class two evenings a week, as I discovered the evenings seem the hardest to get through alone. Other constructive activities might be working or "playing with" your hobby (mine is a lovely doll house, Ozzie's last Christmas gift to me), or reading, or sewing, or a knitting or crocheting project, a class you might be taking, or volunteer work, or letters to write, or babysitting. Whatever each day's plans, write them down on a calendar with spaces for each day. Just looking at the month filling up with worthwhile activities is consoling in some way.

Slowly you realize that life somehow goes on, even though you think at first that it cannot possibly do so. Through much prayer for God's guidance, you will find a goal in life. Doing for others really does seem to be the most satisfying kind of activity. This is so important if you, like I, enjoyed being a good wife and suddenly you are deprived of this goal. You will be utterly purposeless in getting through the rest of your life without a definite direction, aim in life, or goal. You may not know what it is right away. It took me eight prayerful months before my goal was slowly divulged to me. But life began to definitely assume a brighter hue.

If you are a career woman, or just like to work, go back to your job as soon as possible. It will fill your mind with things other than your own sorrow. Physical activities are so good for you. I've found that when I work hard, I sleep better. Sleep seems to be a real problem after the death of a mate. Your body even in sleep misses the reassurance, I think, of that other warm body near you, and your sleep time seems shorter, of a lesser quality, and that old mind of yours just won't seem to stop thinking about all the things you don't want it to.

If you must move to another residence, plunge into the physical work that it necessarily entails, reveling in the occupation of your mind with decisions and plans. The healing of your sorrow seems to need time, and occupying it with other ideas than dwelling on your sadness is therapeutic. Never just be "stuck in your grief." Be with loving family members and friends as often as you or they can plan or stand it. It helps during that transition time, if you live alone, to realize and be assured by others that you are *not* all alone. Even though we know God is always with us and loves and cares for us, we are human! The physical touch of loving family pats and hugs, and the sympathetic words of friends are how I feel God sometimes works to heal our sorrow and assure us He really cares.

When a dear neighbor, upon seeing me sitting out in the backyard a couple of months after Ozzie's death, asked how I was doing, I replied, "Oh, I miss him so. I long to feel his arms around me!"

She replied, "Oh, but if you *really* have the Lord in your heart, you will feel *His* loving arms around you." I said I was sorry, but I did not feel any sensation of arms holding me. I think she was a little shocked as I explained I was just human and still needed those human experiences of expressed love.

Only one who has lost a loved husband or wife will know what I mean. You know God is there helping you cope every step of the way, but you still are "of this world" enough to miss the touch of your beloved. I know she meant to be consoling, as she truly is a lovely Christian lady in every sense of the word, but quoting platitudes is a temptation that your friends will be unable to resist in their caring desire to lift your spirits. You will learn to receive them in the loving spirit they were intended, and go on meeting your sorrow in the way *you* have found best in order to get through each day.

This brings us to the most important of the widow's workable suggestions—the use of your conscious will to surmount your sorrow. Abraham Lincoln wrote, "I have found that most people are about as happy as they make up their minds to be." When you can learn to accept the things that life brings that cannot be changed, you are really on the way to overcoming burdening sorrow. To accept circumstances as they are takes a conscious "making up your mind" decision of how you are going to live and express the rest of your own life without your spouse.

Of course you must firmly believe in yourself as a person. Thank goodness God is not burdened by our world's value system. You need only to truly accept the idea that He sees us perfect through our acceptance and belief in Christ as our Redeemer and Savior. Remember David making this very clear to us in Psalm 4:1 where he says, "Oh God, You have declared me perfect in Your eyes. . ." Think about all the really gross sins and failures David experienced. He seems like one of the soap opera characters on television in one phase of his life. And yet, when he repents, we see a conscious show of making up his mind of what he *will* do from that time on. All through the Psalms we see: "I *will* trust. . . I *will* sing. . . I *will* cry unto the Lord . . . I *will* bless the Lord . . . Oh, Lord, I *will* praise you . . ."

Somewhere along the path of sorrow after your loss you must make a definite decision. You either go on in a questioning, self-pitying, aimless, unjoyful, limp, felled attitude toward life, or you talk to yourself firmly and say something like this:

"I, with the help of God, choose to accept this happening in my life. I choose to rise above it. I choose to express a different picture to my family, friends, and the world, than the poor widow or widower."

"Your ways, Father, are not the ways of this world. I believe completely that you have my good at heart. I can hardly wait for each day to see what you have planned for me, what lessons I can learn from this experience, and what I can express to the world as a Christ centered, man or woman. Let me *give*—love to others, time, understanding, and even comfort to those who come to comfort me.

"I choose to work through my grief in a positive way."

I really believe in the power of Infinite Mind, God, and that all-knowing, all-powerful Mind's ability to work in and through us. Remember Paul saying in 1 Corinthians 2:16 (The Living Bible),

"But strange as it seems, we Christians actually do have within us a portion of the very thoughts and mind in Christ."

When we can consciously take a stand for pushing away all negative "tearing down" feelings and adopt a new attitude of praise, joy, calm acceptance, and giving, then it is that we become "conquerors through Christ." Just think, you can have the "mind of Christ" within you!

It certainly and understandably will be a while before you are ready to "take yourself in hand," unless you are an unusually strong person or Christian. My "taking myself in hand" day came almost a year after my husband's death, when I realized that it had been a year ago that month that he was taken home, "falling asleep in Christ" as he liked to say about the death of a Christian. I heard the Reverend Robert Schuller say in his super positive way, "If it's going to be, it's up to me!" I had a talk with myself, decided my deep-down attitudes needed to be more positive and joyful and expressive of gratitude to God. I now wish I had made this conscious decision months before, but remember, I don't claim to be the most knowledgeable of Christians. Like the button I've seen teenagers wear that says, "PBPWM—GIFWMY" which means, "Please be patient with me, God isn't finished with me yet," I'm sure I'm not fully molded into God's plan for me as His child. And also remember the uniqueness of the man I lost; plus our lovely "love affair" type marriage. It has been difficult not to let Ozzie come between me and life, but I feel I am progressing well. About a year after Ozzie's death, I became active in a widowed persons support group called THEOS, an acronym for "They Help Each Other Spiritually." Participation in these worthwhile meetings led to my attendance at a nationwide conference of THEOS chapters in Philadelphia. Our word enthusiasm comes from the Greek word entheos, meaning in God or God with you. The God-given spirit I saw expressed at this conference gave me encouragement in my bout with the most excruciating grief known to humans—the loss of one's beloved mate. I highly recommend looking into and attending a support group of this nature. Much comfort, understanding, love, and new friends are to be found.

It is as though you become almost "blood sisters" with your fellow widows through shared grief, enlightening discussions, and

231

the actual physical hugs or pats on hands or arm. Someone touching you in sympathetic love seems almost like some ancient ceremony of shared pain and wound binding; and in the process you become part of each other.

Several have questioned me about the lack of the physical or sexual side of marriage that being a widow brings. I feel as Masters and Johnson do in their research reports. They found that real love is expressed in so many tender ways besides sex. They reported that the game of "sex politics" can in fact be detrimental in the enjoyment of consistently good communicative relationships. As a widow I have found that creativity is enhanced when one is celibate.

I feel that here is an appropriate place to include the "Message to Mourners" written by my husband. This very popular sermon of November 10, 1974, was put into tract form a few years before his death and proved to be most comforting to those going through a period of grief. No one seems to have said it more succinctly except God Himself of course, on whose Word Ozzie's messages were always based. I feel my Pastor Honey is speaking directly to me with assurances from God.

Message for Mourners

"Why do we grieve when someone we love goes through the changes called death? It may be that we reproach ourselves for the things we did not do, the things left unfinished, or the things that were said we cannot recall or take back. Or it may be that we feel that God has dealt cruelly with us by removing the one human gift which we held so dear.

"The comfort we need is not only knowing that the dear one is alive with God in heaven by faith in Jesus Christ, but we need to have some word of assurance that our life is not hopeless but worth living. We know our inner needs and desires, and we must recognize that there is no time in life in which there is a perfectly sublime circumstance. It is only when the Holy Spirit of God dwells in our hearts with a heavenly vision that there is happiness and contentment. Knowing this, we should not deprive a dear one who has gone before us of this complete happiness. We know that the answer lies outside ourselves, not with other persons, but with God.

"When a dear one has left our home permanently it causes us to feel that we cannot go on without him, and that we are unable to live our life without his love and kindness. It is not easy to face life on our own. We must realize that we are never alone, we are never on our own. We always have the assurance of God, "I will never leave you nor forsake you." The death of Christ atoned all who believed in Him as their Savior. His resurrection is the guarantee of eternal life in heaven. By authority He says, "In My Father's house are many mansions, I go to prepare a place for you" (John 14:2). Even though a dear one has entered these mansions, we still have the sense of being loved and cared for, we look forward to that day when we shall be living together in those mansions and be the guest of the living Christ.

"The absence of our loved ones has opened our eyes to a new trust, given us a larger vision, and has brought us to a new understanding. We see that love reaching new capacities that we had not suspected. We uncover new depths of courage and faith that we had not known were a part of our life. We do not mourn as those who have no comfort, but feel a natural absence of a dear one and a personal loneliness seeking the comfort only God can give. The Bible assures us, "Weeping may endure for a night, but joy cometh in the morning" (Psalms 30:5). After the night of grief, the light of a new day brings the joy that God has a purpose in life for us. It may be that He wishes to direct our eyes heavenward and to make us conscious of our spiritual relationship to Him, and to minimize our earthly and perishable issues of life. Supporting you are the everlasting arms of a loving God. He would have you believe, "That all things work together for good to those that love God."

O. H. Bertram

The reading of this tract has revived me many times during my sorrow. Also how privileged I am to actually hear my husband speaking, seemingly right to me, on the many tapes I have of

233

his Bible classes, sermons, and radio programs. WTVG, Toledo television station has treasured and kept for me the televised "Worship for Shut-ins" programs of Ozzie's last couple of years. They graciously used excerpts from some of them for a televised memorial program which was aired in 1982. The memory of this remarkable pastor is still fresh in the minds of all who knew him.

This fact has made it hard for me. A lesser man would have been more forgettable, and the task of carrying on my life without his presence and guidance has been made more difficult at times by people recognizing my last name and associating me with him. This is why I sometimes go by Sarah (or nickname, Sally) Bertram, instead of continuing always to be known as Mrs. O. H. Bertram.

Joy and comfort have come to me . . . but it has taken time. Some of the things I have done to fill my days are substitute teaching, working at the University of Toledo four times a year during registration periods, part-time work at a department store, and the fashion modeling at several stores—which I'm pleased to say, recognize the need for an experienced older model with a realistic figure—and speaking at various women's groups or seminars on the topic, "Woman Alone." I have found that in the process of preparing to instruct and console others, I am instructed and consoled.

Participation in the many activities connected with being on the executive board of the Toledo Opera Guild is a task I have enjoyed; I guess because it is sometimes involved with one of my favorite things, the eating of good food. I have been chairman of the Viennese torte table at this group's annual international buffet, assisted in the writing of the Opera Guild's Cook Book, and worked on dinner and luncheon committees. Involvement with an Association of University Women study group has been a worthwhile activity, as has been the attendance at the Educational Honorary Delta Kappa Gamma meetings. The latter serves to keep up my interest in the education of children. In 1990 I was invited to be on the board of the Auxilliary to the Ability Center (formerly the Handicapped Society). I also enjoy the work of serving on my condominium board.

The most satisfying, yes even therapeutic work, has without a doubt been the writing of this book to honor my Lord, and my Ozzie. If I had not had a real calling to make it my goal, I know

I could not have done it. The Holy Spirit, the Comforter, the Enabler has been with me every moment, and I know Christ's promise in John 14:26 is real. "But the Comforter which is the Holy Ghost, whom the Father will send in my name, he shall teach you all things, and bring all things to your remembrance. . ."

I know that I have always been plagued with a poor memory, and that the setting down the many facts in this book could not have been done solely relying on my own poor memory.

I thank God for allowing important memories to come back to me day by day. And I especially thank Him for His Word. These verses have been meaningful to me day after day in the healing process and recovery from the loss of a beloved mate, in a world that seems to go along "two by two."

John 14:18
"I will not leave you comfortless: I will come to you."

Isaiah 54:5
"For thy Maker is thine husband."

Isaiah 41:10
"Fear thou not, for I am with thee; be not dismayed; for I *am* thy God; I will strengthen thee; yea I will help thee. . ."

Isaiah 61:2-3
". . . to comfort all that mourn; . . . To give unto them beauty for ashes, the oil of joy for mourning. . ."

Jeremiah 31:13
". . . for I shall turn their mourning into joy. . ."

Psalm 30:5
". . . weeping may endure for a night, but joy cometh in the morning."

30
Husband Helpers

"What we obtain too cheap, we esteem too lightly;
It is dearness only that gives everything its value"
Thomas Paine
The American Crisis

Usually one thinks of Proverbs 31 as general directions for women, but they also apply to men. They can be the Bible's subtle helpful hints on how to make a *wife* happy. Look at each verse as the direct result of a husband's manner, conversation, or action toward his wife.

Verse 10)
"If you can find a truly good wife, she is worth more than precious gems!" My husband continually made me feel I was a good wife, thus encouraging me to even be a better one. Good psychology.

Verse 11)
"Her husband can trust her, and she will richly satisfy his needs." Ozzie could trust me because he knew I trusted him. He let me know that I satisfied his needs. Nothing I did was ever taken for granted as a wifely duty.

Verse 12)
"She will not hinder him, but help him, all her life." He made sure I knew the Lord came first, but he made second place so attractive, I *desired* to aid him in his work.

Verse 13)
"She finds wool and flax and busily spins it." He encouraged my activities in and out of the home—especially the satisfying creative ones.

Verse 14)
"She buys imported foods, brought by ships from distant ports." He appreciated the good things in life, and was a good provider.

Verse 15)
"She gets up before dawn to prepare breakfast for her household, and plans the day's work for her servant girls." He made his companionship so desirable that early rising was a pleasure.

He noticed and vocally commented with praise on every household accomplishment. He knew I knew his strategy, but oh, how it brought out the best in me.

Verse 16)

"She goes out to inspect a field, and buys it; with her own hands she plants a vineyard." He always made me aware that he valued my judgment. He was not a chauvinist.

Verse 17)

"She is energetic, a hard worker . . ." He loved my activities with other non-church-connected groups. "If you are with Christian gardeners all the time, where can you plant a new seed?" He'd say. I never refused a request he made of me because I knew where his source of direction was based.

Verse 18)

". . . and watches for bargains. She works far into the night!" You husbands will create willingness on the part of your mate to please by your positive and loving actions toward her. Ozzie was a master of this principle.

Verse 19, 20)

"She sews for the poor, and generously gives to the needy." He approved of my personal and pet charitable activities.

Verse 21)

"She has no fear of winter for her household, for she has made warm clothes for all of them." A generous husband giving monetarily *and* of himself seems to make for a generous wife. The more I was given, the more I wanted to give to others. I had no fear of hardship because I came to know it is God who provides every good thing. Ozzie derived joy from the fact that I could sew clothes for myself, and make gifts for our daughters.

Verse 22)

"She also upholsters with finest tapestry; her own clothing is beautifully made—a purple gown of pure linen." He was not ashamed of claiming the best God has to offer! He appreciated a beautiful, artistically arranged home, and he loved me to dress beautifully.

Verse 23)

"Her husband is well known, for he sits in the council chamber with the other civic leaders." Ozzie made his life such that I could be proud of him, a prime condition for a happy marriage. Wives want to honor a worthy husband.

Verse 24)

"She makes belted linen garments to sell to the merchants."

What qualities can you bring out in *your* wife that others would admire and emulate?

Verse 25)

"She is a woman of strength and dignity, and has no fear of old age." I was made to feel I *was* growing in strength as a Christian, simply by being listened to and praised. As to being dignified? Well, he tried to encourage this in me, but I'm sure I bubbled over a bit much in natural exuberance, a fact that usually delighted him. Old age held no threat for me. I *knew* he loved me for my inner being, not that fading physical exterior beauty. He made me sure of that fact by every interaction we ever had.

Verse 26)

"When she speaks, her words are wise, and kindness is the rule for everything she says." He spoke and lived kindness. Through this, I learned Christ's teachings and wanted to be this way, too. Just as simple as that. Monkey see, monkey do. You want love and kindness from your wives, men? Give it and you'll get it back.

Verse 27)

"She watches carefully all that goes on throughout her household and is never lazy." It was expected that I be a good housewife; but every feminine art was encouraged and appreciated. How could I resist striving even more.

Verse 28)

"Her children stand and bless her; so does her husband. He praises her with these words": Words, men, words! Women crave your verbalizing your thoughts."

Verse 29)

"There are many fine women in the world, but you are the best of them all." My daughters and sons-in-law and two granddaughters are a blessing to me; the students I taught were a blessing to me. Why? Because when you are truly happy, know who you are, and do God's will not your own, you *are* blessed with satisfying, loving, rewarding experiences with your own and with other's children. How grateful I am for my precious experiences with children, and how I have learned from them.

Verse 30)

"Charm can be deceptive, and beauty doesn't last, but a woman who fears and reverences God shall be greatly praised." Can you bring out the quality of revering God in your mate? If you reveal God and Christ, and show it in every facet of your life, your spouse will want to emulate you. Ozzie did; and I grew to revere God by his example of a Christ-like life.

The best, most concise book Ozzie and I ever read together—written by a man for men is, "Do Yourself a Favor: Love Your Wife," by H. Page Williams and published by Logos International in 1973.

In an age where most marital advice seems to be given to wives, and the Bible teaching of "Husbands, love your wives, even as Christ loved the church, and gave himself for it"; seems to be somewhat overlooked, this small, 131-page manual for men ruthlessly pursues the "nitty gritty" of what the husband's part is in a happy successful marriage.

How blessed among women I was to experience what real marriage can be. How simple it would be if all men would strive to avail themselves of this "foretaste of heaven" as Ozzie called a good marriage.

31
"Lessons Learned"

"Per crucem ad lucem"
Old motto meaning, "From sacrifice
flashes forth the light."

I do realize that the man, Jesus, and my husband had certain similarities that serve to make them sometimes combine themselves in my heart and mind. When I read a favorite poem, I think of Jesus as the "large sweet soul" Walt Whitman spoke about in "When Lilacs Last in the Door Yard Bloom'd." The physical body has gone from us—but I think also of Ozzie as "the sweetest, wisest soul of all my days," from the aforementioned poem. I experienced Him through Ozzie, a human being; living with, learning from, and reacting to, in a very human way.

I am sure God knows my heart means no irreverence when sometimes I find my prayers become confidential talks with my Triune God, the Father, Jesus Christ, the Holy Spirit—and Ozzie, too. With every iota of my being, with every fact I have learned from the Word, I believe this is what God's gift to us was all about. I have certain knowledge where Ozzie is because of his

239

utter unquestioning, unflinching belief that he would be with Christ after physical death. Because he lived and expressed God's teachings in a way that I saw revealed to me by his day-to-day living, I became a firmer believer in Christ's promises. I know that "my Redeemer liveth." And I also know that the "large sweet soul" of O. H. Bertram is with Christ. Is it any wonder that the talks with God are tinged with references to my past with Ozzie? Gratitudes are expressed which, besides including accolades to the greatness of God's goodness to me, include gratitude for spiritual lessons learned that seemingly could only be learned by the actualities of flesh and blood experience with the special human being that Ozzie was.

One day last week, while taking off my glasses, the tiny pin from one of the sides fell out and it, of course, came off. Without my glasses, I discovered I could not see well enough to replace the pin. What frustration! Then I discovered light was an important factor; the brighter the light, the more success I was having with getting in the pin. Finally, after holding the glasses under the brightest bulb in the house, I was successful in getting them together again so that I could see to continue my writing.

There are many references in God's Word to the "light" of the world. I almost feel like Paul, who, unlike the writers of the Gospel, (Matthew, Mark, Luke and John), seemed less concerned with the life and teachings of Jesus than with His death and resurrection, and *their* meaning for mankind. For Paul, the Light, the ultimate manifestation of God's power and love for undeserving mankind, was in the resurrection—Jesus' victory over sin and death.

With this Light to guide and inspire me, I seem to be "getting it together." Without the day-to-day guidance of divine light expressed through the Holy Spirit, how can *any* human get through living in the world we are experiencing today, let alone survive as a widowed person? I only know I have to live and work "in the Light."

In Georgio Vasari's *Lives of Italian Artists*, the author calls Leonardo da Vinci "divine," but then he tells us that the artist was known to leave important pictures or sculptures unfinished when he felt that to continue working on them would have diminished their expressive effect. Vasari wrote of Leonardo, "he felt

240

that his hand would be unable to realize the perfect creations of his imagination."

Where would we be if God had felt that way about His humans when He dreamed us up? He has given us everything we need in our strivings for a more perfect life. We have our hero, our Light, and we have our goal—heaven!

My husband pointed the way to this Light; and that is why he was respected, loved, and honored in this life, by many.

I have noticed that I feel close to my husband at times, and at other times far away in loneliness. When I go, as I did this past Christmas, to the mausoleum where my darling's earthly remains lie, I press my hand on the cold marble above his name. It warms shortly, and I fuse for a moment with it; with life, with earth, with the present and the hereafter. I suddenly realize that although I am of this world, I am not completely separated from inanimate things. Stone is not so different from me at this moment. It is made of molecules of substance, a part of creation, and so am I.

On occasion, I used to say to my six-year-old students, "Aren't you glad you weren't born a stone? (Giggles would ensue from the first grade listeners.) You can move around, see, feel, think, and love!"

Now my hand seems to melt into the warming marble, and I feel a real kinship with all creations—not just the living ones.

Somehow these times are consoling, not sad or depressing. As the years pass by, I find these rare visits are becoming a time for expressing gratitude for the life with my husband; for the joys that the knowledge and reliance on Jesus Christ as my Savior, have allowed in my life since Ozzie's human death.

Besides, in the eyes of the world, my flowers there at the mausoleum carry a message of the respect and honor I give to my husband's memory. A small tribute that shows people passing his space that I remember him with continued love and gratitude.

The lessons I've learned have not all been joyous. One learns that you don't get over grief for a long time. You learn to live with it, and by the varied experiences, reactions of others, and the pain and the joyous occasions that occur, you are edified.

My personal hurt from some I thought to be friends, but who seemingly deserted me when I most needed support, for reasons they never would clarify, even though I begged them to, has faded.

I trust God's will for me, and though it might appear to be rationalization, I now feel that God meant these particular people, so wrapped up in themselves and their self-righteousness, to be eliminated from my life. I feel my progress in my Christian growth has flourished because I took the steps Christ directed in Mark 11:25. If you have "ought against any," you must forgive them so the Father in heaven may forgive you. My human attempts to find out the "whys" were never satisfied, and I am content, yes even grateful, that these sources of unhappiness were removed from my life.

One who has lost a mate must prepare her or himself for small rejections from those who are bewildered, confused, afraid of, and repelled by anything that brings them up short against the realization that death has to be faced, and is a reality in this world.

I remember with sorrow, the person who confessed she walked down another aisle at the supermarket to avoid meeting me—so fearful was she of seeing and having empathy with my loss, that she felt she would not know what to say or do!

I re-experience humiliation when I remember the rejection I felt upon not being invited in when I called on a woman whose husband had recently died. I had a chapter of this book in hand to read to her—offering her hope, comfort, and what I felt to be a little insight into what we were both going through. I wanted so much to help, to console, to be "together" with her in shared sorrow. To be rejected on the doorstep helped me realize in a small way how Christ must have felt at his rejections. I know *all* things work together for good for those who love the Lord, and I choose to believe that the way is hard sometimes for our own good—to strengthen us for the future trials that we may have.

I used to think that to pray once for something was all that was necessary—that to continue to pray over one's desires would be expressing a lack of faith. I now realize that Christ taught perseverence in prayer. It is only through some of the setbacks, rejections, and sorrows I've had that I have been forced to my knees in repetitive prayers. It is only through my life's experiences and contrasts that I have come to learn from my lessons. "For whom the Lord loved he chasteneth, . . ." (Hebrews 12:6).

I used to wonder why God had allowed the demise of such a godly man as O. H. Bertram. I see his "falling sleep in Christ" as Ozzie called it, now, as a triumphant reward for a God pleasing life; achieved sooner than what we who are left behind would selfishly like, but thrilling to my husband who is at this moment reveling in the presence of his Lord.

Jonathan Swift said, "Life is a tragedy where we sit as spectators awhile, and then act our own part in it." For a while this seems to be all there is for us who mourn. But then all the promises in Isaiah about "beauty for ashes, joy for mourning" (Isaiah 61:3), and the promises our Lord Jesus Christ makes through the New Testament, especially John 14:18, "I will *not* leave you comfortless," and John 16:20, "Your sorrow *will* be turned into joy" can be claimed, holding God to His promises, as it were. I eventually felt and saw "the light."

Again there does seem to be a power beyond our comprehension in the positive attitude. As the Reverend Robert H. Schuller says, "If it's going to be, it's up to me." Of course he means with reliance on the enabling power of the Holy Spirit.

I have learned it is selfish to be sad. The man who loved me for seven wonderful years would not have liked me to wallow in unhappiness. There is an obligation to our families and friends not to revel in the feeling of nobleness that being "becomingly unhappy" brings to some. Robert Louis Stevenson wrote, "By being happy we sow anonymous benefits upon the world that remain unknown even to ourselves." Think about how many times the word "joy" is used in the Bible—usually telling us we should express it. What lovelier tribute can we pay to someone who has meant a great deal to us, than to resist the temptation to be forever sad; to sow anonymous benefits in his or her memory?

Cicero often wrote of death. He insisted that there is no sound reason that we should overly concern ourselves with mourning or death. He said, "Death should be held of no account for it brings but two alternatives: either it utterly annihilates the person and his soul, or it transports the spirit or soul to someplace where it will live forever. What then should a good man fear if death will bring only nothingness or eternal life?" As a Christian, I look forward to eternal life with Christ. What a joy, what a comfort I have!

On October 27, 1982, a huge stained glass window depicting Christ as the Good Shepherd was dedicated in the memory of the Reverend O. H. Bertram. It fills the whole space behind the altar and fulfills a dream that my husband had for years. The larger

243

than life figure of Christ with a compellingly strong expression seems to be stepping into the sanctuary. Clear glass surrounds the huge "Good Shepherd," so that sky, trees, and ground can be enjoyed in the different seasons of the year. All who donated toward this fine example of Christian art can be proud.

The renowned Norwegian artist, Robert Berg, executed the design and Steven Purdy, who studied art in England chose the vibrant colors that echo the crimson carpet and the natural wood tones of the church. Harold Hollman of City Glass in Fort Wayne, Indiana, personally chose some of the unusually marked pieces of glass in Germany, France, and England. It was all hand blown. The "glass capital of the world" as Toledo is known, can be proud of another fine example of the beauty of glass.

I was proud to have been asked to speak on the importance of Christian art at the dedication service.

As the last men left the sanctuary after the work of installing it was completed, I remember sitting alone weeping because my husband would not be walking out of the sacristy to admire his dream for our church come true. Suddenly an angel thought filled my mind to lift my spirits. "Why Ozzie doesn't need to see this depiction of Jesus! He's with the real thing!" Suddenly I could see my Ozzie actually talking with Christ; probably saying something like, "You know Lord, I've always wanted to ask you this. . . ."

The church was filled the evening of the dedication, and I was delighted that many from the community who had been admirers of my husband came. Among them was Toledo's mayor Douglas DeGood, who sat with me, several sisters from Lourdes College, pastors, and members of the business community.

How our church reacted to the death of their beloved Pastor would take up a complete chapter. Suffice it to say that shock, the inability to function wisely at first, was the initial reaction. People seemed dazed; their faith was challenged and some unwise decisions ensued. It seemed for a while that when Ozzie died the devil tried to walk in the front door.

Then the force for good rallied and eventually triumphed. The Reverends Otto Schultz and Timothy Krupki, interim pastors, were much beloved. Dennis Liebich, C.E.D. and the men of the council held most of us together with good leadership. After four and one half years of substitute pastors, refused calls, an experience with a man who resigned from the ministry of our church, and hundreds who left the church for one reason or another, we now have a wonderful man of God again.

The Reverend John V. Moyer, former vicar of Ozzie's in Philadelphia and most recently pastor of St. Peter's Lutheran Church in Brownstown, Indiana for fifteen years, has accepted the call to serve our church. He loved my husband, and my husband loved him. Ozzie had asked him a few days before his death if he would come and "take care of my sheep." I remember John scolding him for this suggestion, as Ozzie "would be back in his own pulpit." All things worked together for good, and we are now blessed with this exuberant Christian as our pastoral leader. How happy Ozzie would be at this outcome! He knew John as completely Bible based and a believer in Scripture. I cannot help but feel that this particular pastor will bring us all together with enthusiasm once again. God does seem to be working out His will.

32
Eyes Are Opened

"Ye fearful saints, fresh courage take!
The clouds ye so much dread
Are big with mercy, and shall break
In blessings on your head."
William Cowper
"Light Shining Out of Darkness"

"What next, Angel?" I seem to hear Ozzie's voice as I think of the many times on our travels he would ask me this. I then would read the day's travel itinerary to him.

As I ask myself this question, I answer myself. "Whatever!" I know that whatever does occur tomorrow, next week, six months from now, or ten years from now will be under the umbrella of God's protection and plan for me. It will be good and exciting, or calming and peaceful. God has the unique talent for making each of us feel "special" in His sight.

You know the old saying, "loving someone is just like riding a bicycle—you never forget how to do it." Well, who knows, I might just start pedaling again, if it be God's will. In a parody on the old cliché, I know it will be just as easy to fall in love with a Christian, as a rich man. Perhaps a new human love is around the corner waiting for me to experience it. Perhaps not. It is difficult for me in this particular time frame of life to conceive of, but I've learned never to say "never," as this is sometimes God's way of showing me more lessons to be learned; through having me experience the very thing I am sure I will never do. Besides, I've always loved men and enjoyed being in their company. I attribute this to having an older brother with his friends around a lot when I was growing up. And also, men have always given me extra attention, for one reason or another.

I know God gave me "the abundant life" which He promised in John 10:10. Why would He stop now with His surprises? I am content with this promise, "The sorrows of widowhood will be remembered no more, for your Creator will be your husband" (Isaiah 54:4-5). And I know nothing can separate me from this "Husband's" love. Neither my fears for today, nor my worries about tomorrow, neither distances, nor depths—nothing will ever be able to separate me from the love of God demonstrated by our Lord Jesus Christ when He died for me. (My own paraphrase from Romans 8:38, 39.)

By the sharing of my experiences with just one of God's many workers in the Kingdom, my husband, the Reverend O. H. Bertram, I hope I have conveyed the idea that it was not a life blessed because of the two personalities involved, but two lives blessed through God's grace alone. It can, it does, and it should happen to everyone. One just yields oneself to the Holy Spirit, and He will fill you with the power to live for Jesus Christ. And that is really what this book was meant to be all about.

The blessings I have experienced since Ozzie's physical death have been many. Spiritual growth has been enormous, I feel; I've made new uplifting friends to replace ones who tore down rather than built up. I've experienced a new closeness with my brother, sister-in-law, daughters and sons-in-law that I never knew could be improved upon. I've had beautiful experiences on trips with friends, and satisfying work in my community. The birth of two granddaughters has brought a special kind of joy. The return to the "speaker's circuit" has fulfilled me, as has my return to my special talent of working with young children as a substitute teacher. My modeling career is also continuing. I have clung to God's promises that "weeping may endure for a night, but joy cometh in the morning" (Psalm 30:5). Nights of despair do resolve into the dawn of a new kind of happiness. I experience and express joy. People notice and comment on my joyous attitude, now again part of my personality.

I have found it to be true:

> "He shall wipe away all tears from our eyes, and there shall be no more death, nor sorrow, nor crying, nor pain. All of that has gone forever."
>
> Romans 21:4

and

> "Everyone who conquers will inherit all these blessings."
>
> Romans 21:7

In times of discouragement in the work (and it *is* laborious physical work) of writing this book, I have thought, "Who am I to presume that my mind and hands can create the book of my imaginings—one that will not only be acceptable in literary value, be interesting and fun to read, but also one that will be encouraging to troubled, lonely people?"

As with the story of my glasses and their home repair job, I can only work "in the Light." Everyday starts with prayer to be under His guidance in finishing this project.

As for the loneliness for my mate, at times "I have been half in love with easeful Death . . ." as John Keats said in his "Ode to a Nightingale." But claiming Jesus' promise, "Blessed are they that mourn, they shall be comforted" (Matthew 5:4), as though He was directly speaking to me, became my special blueprint for living.

And so, as William Allen White wrote about his daughter, Mary, I feel O. H. Bertram's "body sank to its last sleep. But the soul of (him), the glowing, gorgeous, fervent soul of (him) surely *(is)* flaming in eager joy upon some other dawn. . . !" (Paraphrased.)

This I know. And you who come to understand who you are, and what you are, and why you are, will know it too. I promise! And better than that, God promises!

The raising of people's spirits in an unrehearsed and unexpected choreography of joy was one of O. H. Bertram's outstanding abilities. I end our special love story with a conversation that took place a few weeks before Ozzie's death.

"Angel."

"Yes, darling."

"If you ever do write about me, don't have it end with me dying—but with you going on!"

APPENDIX

TWO CONTRASTING POEMS
Sarah Breck Bertram

FALL
Almost bare twigs hold up my sky now—
For it is the November of my days.
Few drops of golden April fall through
Into the valley of my sorrow—
    But each is treasured more than spring's
    Cloying compliments were.
And yet grief hides its face
Behind spring memories.

WIDOWS
Pressed to our knees
Ourself brought low,
We tried to fathom it.

"Things work toward good"
Our minds would say,
To pain we must submit.

But our hearts felt grief.
And the work began to glorify His name.
Seemed over—and nothing was the same.

Then truth emerged
As a newborn bird
And we began to know.

That the pain, and the end
To an earthly work
Gave us a chance to show

That those who suffer
Are more effective proof than
Many in this world.

And joy within us mounts
As we realize through a trusting faith
We are the stage from which He shouts!

A Short Biographical Outline of Pastor O. H. Bertram

Born: Reinbeck, Iowa on August 18, 1917

Schools: Elementary— St. John's Lutheran School, Reinbeck, Iowa

Trinity Evangelical Lutheran School, Lowden, Iowa

Confirmation date—March 29, 1931 at age 13

High School— Concordia Preparatory School, Fort Wayne, Indiana

College— Concordia College, Fort Wayne, Indiana

Concordia Theological College and Seminary, Springfield, Illinois. Graduated in 1940.

Graduate Courses— Concordia Teachers College, River Forest, Illinois

Yale University Divinity School, New Haven, Conn.

LaSalle College, Philadelphia, Pennsylvania

The University of Toledo, Toledo, Ohio

250

The Toledo Bible College, Toledo,
Ohio Theology Masters Degree
earned
Awarded an honorary Doctor of Divinity degree in February 1970
from the Toledo Bible College

Churches served:
Immanuel Lutheran Church, Danbury, Connecticut, Assistant Pastor and instructor in the day school, 1940-1941
Zion Lutheran Church, Wallingford, Connecticut, Pastor 1941-1946
St. Paul's Lutheran Church, Naugatuck, Connecticut, Pastor 1942-1955
Established a mission church at Madison, Connecticut, Pastor 1949
Redeemer Lutheran Church, Philadelphia, Pennsylvania, Pastor 1955-1964
Good Shepherd Lutheran Church, Toledo, Ohio, Pastor 1964-1979

Founder of:
"Moments of Comfort" radio program; begun in 1941.
"Moments of Comfort" television program; began in 1952
"Worship for Shut-ins" television and radio until 1979
"Religion in the News" one-half hour television program each week for several years, WSPD, Toledo, Ohio.
"30 second spot Spiritual Commercials" and "sign-offs" until 1979
Once a week appearances on Gordon Ward's Noon Report and on the "Deadline" news team for WSPD-TV, Toledo, Ohio.

Other Activities:
Speaker at many group meetings, workshops, conferences, special occasions, and Circuit Counselor for the Lutheran Church-Missouri Synod for thirteen years.
Served on L.C.-M.S. National Boards.
Chaplain at the Middlesex County Prison and at Wethersfield, both in Connecticut.
Lutheran Chaplain at Connecticut State Prison and Veterans Hospital, Newington, Connecticut.

Chaplain and conducted services at the Lucas County Correctional Institute, Whitehouse, Ohio.
Conducted weekly services at Golden Haven Nursing Home, Toledo, Ohio.
Conducted services at the Army Reserve Headquarters, Toledo, Ohio.
Death: May 29, 1979, at Toledo, Ohio.

The following is a list of television and radio stations that have carried O. H. Bertram's programs:

Television
WSPD-TV (now WTVG), Channel 13, Toledo, Ohio
WJIM-TV Channel 6, Lansing, Michigan
WKJG-TV Channel 33, Fort Wayne, Indiana
WTNH-TV Channel 8, New Haven, Connecticut
WSBK-TV Channel 38, Boston, Massachusetts
WGGS-TV Channel 16, Greenville, South Carolina
WEZF-TV Channel 22, Burlington, Vermont
WHMB-TV Channel 40, Indianapolis, Indiana
WNDU-TV Channel 16, South Bend, Indiana (known as the Notre Dame station)
WCFC-TV Channel 38, Chicago, Illinois
WHCT-TV Channel 18, Hartford, Connecticut
WRIP-TV Channel 61, Chattanooga, Tennessee
KBSA-TV Channel 46, Anaheim, California
WBKB-TV Channel 11, Alpena, Michigan
WKID-TV Channel 51, Fort Lauderdale, Florida
WECA-TV Channel 27, Tallahassee, Florida
WRCV-TV, Philadelphia, Pennsylvania
WFIL-TV, Philadelphia, Pennsylvania
Thirty-second "Spirit-lifters" also heard in Washington, D.C.; St. Louis, Missouri, Knoxville, Tennessee

Radio
Voice of America, Radio—Munich
HCJB, Quito, Ecuador
WELI, New Haven, Connecticut
WSPD-AM, Toledo, Ohio
WCWA-AM, Toledo, Ohio

WGLM-AM, Toledo, Ohio
WMHE-FM, Toledo, Ohio
WNDH-FM, Napoleon, Ohio
WHFD-FM, Archbold, Ohio
WATR-AM, Waterbury, Connecticut
WOWW, Naugatuck, Connecticut
WBIS, Bristol, Connecticut
WNAB, Bridgeport, Connecticut
WTOR, Torrington, Connecticut
WONS, Hartford, Connecticut
WHAY, New Britain, Connecticut
WNHC, New Haven, Connecticut
WCHU, Daisy, Tennessee ·
KFUO-AM and FM, St. Louis, Missouri
WKDN, Camden, New Jersey
WMAY-AM, Springfield, Illinois
WRIP, Chattanooga, Tennessee
KNDR, Mandan, North Dakota
KLIT-AM, Pomona, California
WBNO-AM, Bryan, Ohio
WBNO-FM, Bryan, Ohio
WGLX-AM and WQLX-FM, Gallion, Ohio
WGOR-AM (now WVOI), Toledo, Ohio
WABS-AM, Arlington, Virginia
WAVA-AM, Arlington, Virginia (Washington D.C. area)

Cablevision Stations:
Augusta, Georgia
El Reno, Oklahoma
Tulsa, Oklahoma
Jacksonville, Arkansas
Stockton, California
Georgetown, Texas
New Kensington, Pennsylvania
Baton Rouge, Louisiana
Des Moines, Iowa
Kingsport, Tennessee
Tuscaloosa, Alabama
Bristol, Tennessee
Port Arthur, Texas

Little Rock, Arkansas
Camp Hill, Pennsylvania
Greensburg, Pennsylvania
Martin, Oklahoma
Huntington, West Virginia

The following is a list of newspapers which have carried "The Clergyman's Corner" as written by the Rev. O. H. Bertram:

The West Toledo Herald, Toledo, Ohio
The Rossford Record, Rossford, Ohio
The Naugatuck News, Naugatuck, Connecticut
The Bristol Press, Bristol, Connecticut
The Messenger, Perrysburg, Ohio
Leader Newspaper, Pemberville, Ohio
The Reinbeck Courier, Reinbeck, Iowa
Henry County Review, Holgate, Ohio
The Wauseon Republic, Wauseon, Ohio
Greenfield Recorder, Greenfield, Massachusetts
Berkshire Eagle, Pittsfield, Massachusetts
Bennington Banner, Bennington, Vermont
The Free Press, Burlington, Vermont
The Concord Monitor, Concord, New Hampshire

Honors

1. Honorary member of the National Exchange Club.
2. Recipient of the "Honorary Dignitary" Bible at the Gideon International Society's annual banquet in 1971.
3. The Gold Medal Freedoms Foundation Award, Valley Forge, Pennsylvania, in 1969, given to WSPD, Toledo and O. H. Bertram, producer, for an outstanding television program that referred to some aspect of the American way of life. It was entitled, "Lest We Forget."
4. Honorary Doctor of Divinity Degree from the Toledo Bible College in 1970.
5. Appointed to the National Board for Lutheran Television Productions by the Board of Directors of the Lutheran Church, Missouri Synod in 1974.

6. Appointed to the National Board for Evangelism for the L.C. M.S.
7. Appointed to the National Board for Communications for the L.C. M.S.
8. Invited to be a guest speaker for the world acclaimed "International Lutheran Hour," broadcast July 31, 1977.
9. Received the Servus Ecclestae Christi Award in recognition of effective ministry among God's people in today's world—presented by Concordia Theological Seminary, Fort Wayne, Indiana in May, 1979.
10. Received a special posthumous award from the National Religious Broadcasters Association for recognition of leadership, and thirty-seven years of continuous outstanding religious broadcasting; and in tribute to his pioneering efforts in the utilization of the split-screen method of signing for the deaf. Awarded in January of 1980.

The following is a small sampling of the various activities enjoyed by The Reverend and Mrs. O. H. Bertram.

April 18, 1972	Sarah spoke to Sunday school teachers of Good Shepherd Lutheran Church on "New Methods of Teaching."
April 25, 1972	Two months before marriage, announced our engagement when he addressed the Portage Valley Federation of Lutheran Men in Woodville, Ohio.
October, 1975	Invited to speak at Concordia Senior College in Ft. Wayne, Indiana, on "Mass Media and the Presentation of the Gospel."
July, 1975	Addressed Rotary Club in Naugatuck, Connecticut.
January, 1976	Many 3-½ minute interviews with Christian Senators and Congressmen to be incorporated into the television and radio program, "A Worship for Shut-ins."
January 1974–79	National Religious Broadcasters' Conference held at the Washington Hilton in Washington, D.C. for around 3,000 religious broadcasters worldwide.

Various times	Trips to the TV stations at Lansing, Michigan, Milwaukee, Wisconsin, Ft. Wayne, Indiana, Chicago, Illinois, New Haven, Connecticut, Burlington, Vermont, Boston, Massachusetts, for public relations.
May 16, 1961	Prayer for opening of the U.S. Senate.
January 30, 1973	Prayer for House of Representatives in Washington, D.C.
January 24, 1978	Prayer for House of Representatives in Washington, D.C.
June 2, 1974	Preached as guest in brother-in-law's church, St. Paul's in Napoleon, Ohio. Also preached for St. Paul's 125th Anniversary in 1976.
April 2, 1974	Spoke to Catholic nuns at Madonna Home in Toledo, Ohio.
October 27, 1974	Spoke for Reformation Service at Concordia Jr. College, Ann Arbor, Michigan.
May 5–10, 1975	Attended the Institute in Basic Youth Conflicts, with Bill Gothard, instructor in Detroit, Michigan.
January 1975	Spoke at Ottawa County Grangers, Oak Harbor, Michigan.
November 1975	Spoke on, "Parable of the Mustard Seed" for Women's Community Service Group in Toledo.
October 1974	Main Speaker at Business and Professional Women's Club luncheon.
December 1975	Speaker at Crestview Nursing Home (also luncheon) where Pastor and Sarah sang, "Stille Nacht."
May 1976	Speaker for the Golden Age Club, Wauseon, Ohio.
May 1976	Speaker at Compass Club meeting in Toledo, Ohio.
1976	Speaker at Christian Singles Club, Toledo, Ohio.
1976	Speaker at Trinity Lutheran Ladies' Group, Toledo, Ohio.
April 1976	Speaker at United Brethren Church of Walbridge, Ohio.

March 1976	Speaker at Concordia Seminary, St. Louis, Missouri.
August 1976	Speaker at Bethel Lutheran Mission Festival, Defiance, Ohio.
September 1976	Speaker at McClure, Ohio Church Institute.
July 1976	Flat Rock Lutheran Church, 125th Anniversary speaker.
March 1978	Traveled to Irvine, California for Board of Evangelism.
1972 and each year thereafter	Dined at the U.S. House of Representatives Dining Room.
August 1977	Interviewed as a guest on "Chicago," televised live on Channel 38, Chicago, Ill. Interviewed by Dan Wilson and Thurman Faison.
September 1977	Visited Mr. and Mrs. Dick Beach in Boston, Mass. Mr. Beach with WSBK-TV, Boston.
July 1977	Guest preacher at Zion Lutheran Church, Ft. Worth, Texas.
August 1977	Dinner with Mr. and Mrs. Cal D. Mahlock in Ft. Wayne, Ind. Mr. Mahlock with WKJG-TV, Ft. Wayne.
July 1977	Discussion leader at Lutheran Church-Missouri Synod Evangelism Conference in Dallas, Texas.
	Participated in the installation of four new pastors.
December 1973	National Management Association, Toledo Chapter, Guest Speaker.
1973	Opening prayer at Wood County Fair.
June 15, 1973	Guest speaker at Zoar Lutheran Church, Perrysburg, Ohio.
1975	"World Day" Speaker, Luckey, Ohio.
1972	A Unity Service, Port Clinton, Ohio, speaker.
May 1977	Women United, Sandusky, Ohio, speaker.
May 1978	Guest speaker for Memorial Day Services in Holgate, Ohio.
June 1978	A Confirmation Reunion Service at Peace Lutheran Church in Deshler, Ohio.

1975–76	Sarah gave lectures in many denominational churches on Christian womanhood.
February 1972	Invited and attended National Prayer Breakfast in Washington, D.C.
February 1974	Opening prayer for City Council, Toledo, Ohio.
February 1974	Benediction for Lincoln's Day Banquet of the Fifth Congressional District with Governor John Connally of Texas.
October 21, 1973	Guest speaker for a "Key 73" Reformation Rally in Monroe , Michigan.

Prayer for the Opening of the United States Senate on Tuesday, May 16, 1961, given by the Rev. O. H. Bertram of Redeemer Lutheran Church, Philadelphia, PA.

Humbly we praise Thee for the countless blessings that are ours in this country as in no other land on earth, and contritely we beseech Thy pardon for our repeated ingratitude and our thankless neglect of Thy mercy. For the sake of Thy Son, our only Savior, who laid down His life in payment for our sins, and then rose from the grave to seal our eternal salvation, forgive us these sins of selfishness, and fill us with a new fervor of faith! Make us a repentent people! Take away from us all pride and bring us down on our knees in repentence and true supplication! Send Thy Holy Spirit into our lives and hearts to break our pride and hold our hands in humble petition to Thy grace.

Reject and restrain all who seek to overthrow Thy Church and destroy the blessings of our free government. In Thee do we place our trust, not in our own might or power. To this end, help us walk more closely with Thee, in greater love to our fellow man and in deeper devotion to Christ's Golden Rule. Teach us to exercise godly fear above personal favor, policies and principles above politics. May Thy guiding hand rest upon this body of our government that all they do may serve to Your glory and the welfare of our nation.

In Thine everlasting compassion, comfort all the sick, the sorrowing, the destitute and dying, with that love and comfort which only Thou art able to give. Graciously provide for the homeless and hungry throughout the world, and lead us to share our bounties with them in their need.

Above all, loving Father, draw us closer to Thee, to seek that counsel which was offered to us through Thy Son, "Ask and it shall be given unto you, seek and ye shall find, knock and it shall be opened unto you." For these heavenly blessings we humbly implore Thee through Jesus Christ, Thy Son, our Lord.

Amen.

Prayer for the opening of the United States House of Representatives on Tuesday, January 30, 1973, given by the Rev. O. H. Bertram of Good Shepherd Lutheran Church, Toledo, Ohio.

Gracious Lord, Heavenly Father, there are times in our lives when we are not able to match the challenge and the problems that confront us with our own strength and mentality. In moments such as these, we come to You, seeking guidance and assurance of Your counsel. We ask that You might grant to the Members of Congress direction for the great responsibilities in guiding our national affairs. There is always the danger that we may speak without thinking, and make decisions without Your Guidance. May all the discussions and decisions made in these hallowed halls reflect Your will.

We thank You for the peace which has been established. We are grateful for having guided our President, his representatives, and the Members of Congress in this longed-for achievement. May we ever seek to please You in order that we might be spared further conflict, not incurring Your wrath, but Your favor. We ask this through Jesus Christ, our Savior. Amen.

Prayer for the opening of the United States House of Representatives on Tuesday, January 24, 1978, given by the Rev. O. H. Bertram, Pastor, Good Shepherd Lutheran Church, Toledo, Ohio.

Let us bow our heads and pray.

Gracious Lord, our Heavenly Father, let our prayers not be a mere form, but a heartfelt need by all of us. Let our motto, "In God We Trust," not be a mere phrase, but a confession. Let our declaration, "This Nation, under God," not have a hollow ring, but be a hallowed proclamation. We thank You for the blessings of the many freedoms offered to us in our Nation. Let us use them wisely, and use them as a gift from You.

On behalf of our Congress, representing millions of people, we implore that You might direct their deliberations and endow them with wisdom to make God-pleasing and beneficial decisions. May our Nation be a better place because of their leadership. May corruption be uprooted and honesty be exalted.

We stand humbly before Your throne, asking for undeserved blessings through Jesus Christ, our Lord. Amen.

Prayer for the 40th Annual Conference of Ohio Association of Chief of Police, Thursday, August 26, 1971.

Gracious Lord, our Heavenly Father: In these turbulent days of national unrest, we would ask that you might endorse the people of our nation with a respect for law and order according to the precepts of your Ten Commandments. We see on all hands the turbulence of restless spirits who do not seek Your guidance, nor the welfare of our nation, but those who would destroy the land that we have learned to love, and for which many stout hearts have died. It is only through the indwelling power of Your Holy Spirit, changing the heart of the individual, that we might anticipate better days.

We are grateful for the law enforcement agencies that would seek to uphold and defend our Constitution and the laws of our country. While evil forces are trying to disrupt them from fulfilling their obligation, give them the needed courage and bravery to stand the ground for righteousness' sake.

We reflect with gratitude and sadness on the memory of law enforcement officers who have given their lives in the line of duty. Comfort their dear ones who mourn their loss. Have mercy on those who have snuffed out their lives in a spirit of rebellion and vengeance.

Bless the President of our United States, the Governor of our Commonwealth, the mayors of our cities, and all those who are in authority, granting them the power of righteous leadership and God-fearing principles so that we may lead a quiet and peaceful life. In all matters pertaining to our national, local and personal lives, we seek Your counsel and guidance.

Through Jesus Christ, our Lord. Amen.

Samples of special occasion prayers:
Prayer for Lincoln Day Banquet of Fifth Congressional District,
Ohio February 22, 1974.

Gracious Lord, our Heavenly Father, we are reminded this day
of paying tribute to those who faithfully have served and still
serve our nation. Human as they are, they need to have Your
guidance and directive in life if they are to be effective leaders in
our nation. Without You by their sides, they fail and we fail with
them. In this fifth Congressional District we express gratitude
for a dedicated servant of our nation, Delbert Latta, who places
principle above party, and who places right above applause.
Grant him continued good health and judgment to help lead our
nation in the paths that are pleasing to you, dear Lord, and that
seeks the welfare of the American citizens.

We also must pause to give thanks that you spared the life of
your servant, John Connally, on that tragic day, November 22,
1963, when a president was assassinated and he seriously
wounded. For his continued dedication of service to our nation,
for his leadership and guidance, we express our thanks. As he
brings the message in this evening hour, may it inspire us to
be more loyal citizens, more dedicated Americans, and zealous
individuals to right the wrongs that exist and to further moral
principles.

On this occasion of observing Lincoln's birthday, we are reminded of one upon whose shoulders in troubled times fell the
mantle of great responsibilities, in whose heart there lived that
passion for union, that sense of brotherhood that neither war's
alarms, nor the tides of politics, nor the hatred of his foes could
change or diminsh. We are grateful that Abraham Lincoln resolved in all things to be on the side of God.

We humbly explore that the same spirit that was in Lincoln
may dwell in our leaders now, that they may see as clearly as he
saw that only right makes right, and that only if we are on the
side of God can we hope that our affairs will prosper.

Send the Holy Spirit into the hearts of all men and women in
government who will seek the right, even though they stand
alone, knowing that the individual with God always makes the
majority. Do not let the pressure of groups, the attacks of opposing
parties, or the hatred of individuals cause them to be deterred

from doing that which is right, but may they seek the common good and the will of God. We ask all this in the name of Jesus Christ, man's only Savior and Redeemer. Amen.

Following is a typical newspaper article taken from the *Waterbury American*, Connecticut, dated April 13, 1953.

Borough Cleric to Talk on Voice of America

Naugatuck, April 13—A thirty-minute sermon, typical of Pentecost Day in free America, by Rev. O. H. Bertram, pastor of St. Paul's Lutheran Church, will be beamed via the Voice of America to nations behind the "iron curtain" in Europe and the Far East, it was learned today.

Mr. Bertram, whose radio and television programs have gained wide popularity in Southern New England and New York, will broadcast on the Voice's "A Nation at Worship" program beamed abroad weekly. Arrangements for the May 24 Pentecost broadcast were completed in New York Friday by Mr. Bertram and Voice officials.

Because of the response to his weekly radio and television "Moments of Comfort" programs, Mr. Bertram recently informed Rep. James T. Patterson that he would be willing to prepare special programs for the Voice of America. Rep. Patterson immediately contacted officials of the Voice in Washington and arrangements were made to have Mr. Bertram broadcast.

Theme of Mr. Bertram's initial broadcast will be "Pentecost Power for You." A recording of the broadcast will be made this week at Waterbury and sent to Voice broadcast headquarters, New York, for transmission via shortwave May 24.

Mr. Bertram expects to be called upon for other Voice broadcasts in the future. All of the "Nation at Worship" programs beamed to "iron curtain" nations are designed to give people of captive nations a true picture of the freedom of worship enjoyed in this country.

An Article Appearing in *Christian Life Magazine* of August, 1954 Concerning the Origin of the First "Split Screen" Use.

Gospel TV For The Deaf

"Moments of Comfort," a nondenominational television program, is the first in the country to use a split-screen technique to extend the Gospel to the deaf.

Every other week on the once-a-week telecast over WNHC-TV, New Haven, Conn., the Rev. Oswald H. Bertram and his staff are seen speaking and singing on one half of the screen while the image of the Rev. George R. Kraus of New York City interprets the words simultaneously into sign language on the other half.

As the principals stand before one camera, the interpreter picks up their words from a loudspeaker in another room and "speaks" them to the deaf through another camera. On the viewer's screen, the images are merged so that speakers and translator appear side by side. The reason for the two camera technique is to allow the Rev. Kraus to stand continually before one camera, as he must, when the other is switched smoothly and quickly to the various speakers and singers.

"Moments of Comfort," which started as a radio program over station WATR, Waterbury, Conn., in 1946, is now carried over six radio stations and two TV stations in Connecticut to an audience of 750,000, according to the Hooper Rating.

It has been accepted for transmission in German, which the Rev. Bertram speaks fluently, over the Voice of America's regular foreign broadcast, "A Nation at Worship," and HCJB, the Voice of the Andes, Quito, Ecuador, has begun broadcasts of the German translation to all Latin America and Europe.

The program operates on a budget of $200 to $250 per month, most of which goes for giveaways like New Testaments, wall mottoes, and portions of Gospels. The money comes from the audience with amazing regularity, although operating capital once dipped to eight dollars.

Dedicated to shut-ins, "Moments of Comfort" has the material and spiritual support of the 220 members of St. Paul's Lutheran Church in Naugatuck, Conn. At Pastor Bertram's direction, they pray for the success of every extension of the program.

The fifteen-minute format follows a similar pattern on television and radio, opening with the ringing of church bells, followed by announcement of the day's program, a hymn by soloist William Boyd accompanied by the Rev. Bernard W. Janssen at the organ and six minutes of meditation by the Rev. Bertram on a Bible-centered theme.

Script for the radio program "The Lutheran Hour" of July 31, 1977, by O. H. Bertram:

Topical Sentence, Prayer And Meditation

A well known theologian has written a book entitled, "The Gospel of Suffering." In other words, "The Good News of Suffering." What kind of presumption is this? Seen through the Christian faith, it makes sense.

Prayer:

As we turn to God in prayer, let us remember the discouraged and lonely, the sick and bereaved:

Gracious Lord, our Heavenly Father, take away from us our fears and worries, and teach us how to pray for ourselves and our loved ones. Take away all bitterness and rebellion over the illness we are suffering and the bereavement we endure. Bring us closer to you through a trusting faith in Christ, Who says, "I will never leave you nor forsake you." Touch those who are ill with your healing power according to Your will. Make our weak spirit strong, so that we may pass through the trials and tribulations of life with a calm faith, trusting in Your goodness, and to firmly believe "that all things work together for good to those who love You." We pray because we know that when we reach out to You, You are reaching down to us with mercy and grace in time of need. In Jesus' Precious name, we ask this, Who intercedes for us before Your heavenly throne. Amen.

Conquering All

Dear Friends in Christ:

The well-known theologian, Kierkegaard, wrote a book entitled, "The Gospel of Suffering." In other words, "The Good News of Suffering." What kind of presumption is this? Seen through Christian faith, it makes sense. The Lord says, "For my thoughts are not your thoughts, neither are your ways my ways, saith the Lord, for as the heavens are higher than the earth, so are my ways higher than your ways and my thoughts than your

264

thoughts" (Isaiah 55:8, 9). This gives us the courage to conquer all of our trials and troubles, our sufferings and our sorrows.

Courage is an essential part of our life. It is not only during these turbulent days that we need it, but in every moment of life when reverses and afflictions seem to swirl in upon us. It is only through a courageous faith in God that we can resist the whirlpools of depression and defeat. Through such a faith and trust in God, we can conquer all.

The thought of spending lonely hours alone strikes fear into some hearts. Here is the widow or widower who has spent twenty-five or fifty years with a loving spouse suddenly thrown into the dark life of loneliness. Where will he or she find the courage to face the future? Here is the healthy person suddenly stricken with a sickness that destroys all hope for a future normal life of work and pleasure—the doctor described it as a "terminal illness." How shall he or she face the future? Here is the young lady, engaged to a young man, making plans for a happy wedding day, when suddenly she is jilted. How shall she face her embarrassment? Where will these individuals find courage to face the future?

Psychologists say, "Talk it out and then forget about it!" It is not so easily done. The Lord offers a solution. He says, "Be strong and of good courage: be not afraid, neither be thou dismayed: for the Lord thy God is with thee whithersoever thou goest" (Joshua 1:9). The Lord is aware of our plights and problems, and also of our cowardliness. Jesus put his finger on our problems when He began His earthly ministry with the words, "God sent me to proclaim relief to the captives." This is the very heart of the Gospel of Jesus Christ, for it spells freedom from fear and causes our fears to be allayed. In order to emphasize His great concern for us and to show that He is concerned about our every need, He became man, and says to us, "I know what you are enduring, for I have endured it also."

He has given us the message of redemption and adoption; we are told, "He that spared not His own Son, but delivered Him up for us all, how shall He not with Him also freely give us all things? (Romans 8:32.)

By a trusting faith in Jesus Christ as your Lord and Saviour, as the Lover of your soul, you can be set free from the fears which beset you, and experience His love and adoption whereby He says,

"I have redeemed you, I have called you by name, you are mine" (Isaiah 43:1). You, the spirit captive, have been set free.

Frequently, during World War II I would listen to Axis Sally reading the list of American prisoners held by the Nazis. Can't you see the parents of dear ones listening patiently to hear a specific name as she read the names in alphabetical order: Abbot, Abramson, and so forth? It reminds us of another list on which, I trust, your name and mine will appear, those whom God has called out of captivity of sin and despair to the new life of courage and confidence in Him. We are the people whom God has called friends, and promises us courage and comfort through Christ.

You are an important person to God. In this vast universe you are not just another person, you are an individual. When Apollo 9 was circling the moon, the astronauts said they could block out the earth with a nickel, so small did it appear from outer space. Yet, how important are two specks, you and me, to the God Who loves us beyond human comprehension.

Basically, not many people really care what you and I are or what we do, but God does. Through the Sacrament of Holy Baptism, He has called us to become His own dear children and promises to take care of us. The hymn writer, Joseph Scriven, says,

> "Can we find a friend so faithful
> Who will all our sorrows share?
> Jesus knows our every weakness:
> Take it to the Lord in prayer.

We understand more clearly what it means that Christ bore His cross for us when we must bear our crosses in life. Our suffering serves as an end for the refining of our faith, for it is through the affliction of the body and mind that we are purified in our souls.

Several years ago, my family and I were traveling north on Route 7 from Burlington, Vermont, we approached a beautiful New England valley. In the middle of the cornfield was a billboard with a passage, "I can do all things through Christ, Who strengthens me." That evening as we stayed at a nearby motel, I learned that the owner had erected the billboard. He and his wife had lost a fourteen-year-old son by drowning several years before. Their confidence was in Christ and His salvation and assurance

266

of love. Through the billboard, they were hopeful of giving strength to those who suffer bereavement and sorrow.

Does your courage conquer all? Are the perils of life getting you down? Are you being beaten down by trials, worry, and fearsome thoughts? Your constant question is, "How can I overcome these defeatist thoughts?" Start where everything must start—in your thoughts and in your heart.

The word "courage" is derived from the French word, the heart. For example, the surname of Richard the Lionhearted, "Coeur de Lion", meant that he was a man with the courage of a lion. It is the condition of your inner thoughts, which are affected by thinking courageously. We become what we think. We are really today what we thought we would be like ten years ago, and you will be ten years from now what you are thinking today what you would like to be. The Bible says, "As a man thinketh in his heart, so is he." If you think that God is with you and that you could do all things through Christ who strengthens you, you can confidently and courageously say, "If God be for us, who can be against us?"

Whatever your responsibility is, take the challenge. Don't be afraid if it will serve to the glory of God and the welfare of your fellowman. If God had not thought you capable of doing it, He would not have assigned it to you.

Do you have some great objective that you want to achieve, but are afraid that you are unable to attain the goal? Stop being afraid, and ask your closest friend, Jesus Christ, to give you the necessary courage and help: You and He can achieve the goal successfully.

In Christ we can also conquer some of our tragic domestic problems. The marital strife, the household unhappiness, the friction between parents and children, could all be resolved if Christ were welcomed into our family circles. Dying love could be revived, broken hearts mended, and unfaithfulness prevented, if Jesus Christ would be a member of our family. Our daily prayer should be, "Come, Lord Jesus, be our Guest." This is done through Bible reading and family worship. It is achieved as we take the steps of doing things together in worship and play, in work and recreation. It takes a courageous parent to stipulate what the objectives of family life must be. A father should heed well the command of the Lord, "Bring up your children in the nurture and admonition of the Lord."

Parents will be called "blessed" by their children only when they lead the children to Christ. Many heartaches and much disgrace could be avoided if parents would be as exacting with their children's religious instructions as they are about their music and dancing lessons and social activities. The eternal success of a child depends on his knowledge and respect for God.

It is reported that in 1976 fifty percent of our crimes were committed by juveniles. Does not this reflect the lack of training on the part of the parents or the bad influences set by the father and mother. Vice and immorality, crime and corruption, will not disappear from the nation to any degree until it is erased from the home scene. Parents should set the example for their children of selecting for their future life's mates husbands and wives who have Christian principles and convictions. Only in Christ can we conquer all!

Too often individual parishes and church bodies seem to be fighting a losing battle in the winning of souls and influencing the community and our nation. We hear of clergymen and laymen throwing up their hands in despair and saying, "What is the use?" If the message of the Holy Scripture is loud and clear, and Christ is affirmed as man's Saviour and Redeemer, then, "the gates of hell shall not prevail against it."

A newspaper story out of Iowa a few years ago told about a thunderstorm that shook up the community in more than one way. A particularly loud rumble apparently activated the chimes in a church steeple, and for the next several minutes, while the lightning flashed and the thunder boomed, a famous hymn rang through the town: it's title: "How Great Thou Art."

Our church life must be activated by the Holy Spirit and through the study of the Holy Bible. It is in knowing Christ, the Head of the church, that we can sing out with confidence, "How Great Thou Art!" Christ must be exalted as the head of the church, and it must be "built upon the foundation of the apostles and prophets, Jesus Christ Himself being the chief cornerstone." It is then that we pray, "Thy Kingdom Come," not, "My kingdom come." There can be no room in the church for man-made teachings and neo-orthodoxy. When the church is aware that it is dealing with preciously bought souls, redeemed through the priceless blood of Christ, then we must adhere to the entire truth of Holy

Scriptures, or as Jesus says, "Teaching them to observe all things whatsoever I have commanded you."

We as individuals must remember that we are more than conquerors through Christ Who loves us, as we acknowledge our sin, repent of our transgressions, and accept the pardon of Jesus Christ, obtained for us on the Cross of Calvary.

Sin, repentence, and pardon are like to the three vernal months of the year, March, April, and May. Sin comes in like March, blustering, stormy, and full of violence. Repentance proceeds like April, showering, weeping, and full of tears. Pardon follows like May, springing, singing, full of joy and flowers. Our eyes must be full of April, with the sorrow of repentance; and then our hearts shall be full of May, with the true joy of forgiveness.

We are truly conquerors through Christ, even in the midst of our suffering and trials. When we have embraced Jesus Christ as our Lord and Saviour, and have been born into Him anew, it is then that we understand the purpose of suffering in our lives.

Author Robert E. Luccock states, "In God's suffering we encounter something more than misery-loving company; there is real soul therapy, great spiritual healing in the companionship of a God who shares our deepest grief, our sharpest pain, our darkest despair. For one thing, it assures us that in the vast scheme of life we have not been forgotten in the vale of trouble. For another, it encourages us to discover that God does not willingly afflict us or complacently stand by as a spectator. Whatever we suffer, He suffers with us."

St. Paul indicates that through suffering we become partners with God. As the Apostle asked the Lord to remove his affliction, he was assured by God, "My grace is sufficient for you, for my strength is made perfect in weakness." With resolute faith, the Apostle answers, "Therefore I take pleasure in my infirmities, in reproaches, in necessities, in persecution, in distresses for Christ's sake: for when I am weak, then am I strong." We gather holiness from woe and affliction; we gather strength in weakness as we place our hand into the Hand of God, who will never leave us nor forsake us. With Him by our side, we can conquer all!

Because God is our friend, we can overcome every fear, all lonesomeness, every thought of insecurity and doubt. Believe with confidence His promise, "Be strong and of good courage; be not afraid, neither be thou dismayed: for the Lord thy God is with thee whithersoever thou goest."

God give you the faith to conquer all through Christ.

There follows a partial list of books that O. H. Bertram found inspiring for sermon material and his own edification. (They are much underlined, as was his habit when he especially agreed with something, or wished to learn from it. I get messages and a continual source of being in touch with my husband's thoughts through the reading of these underlined passages.)

All of Walter A. Meir's writings
Graham R. Hodge's *Fifty Children's Sermons,* a Congregation-
    alist Pastor
Robert Schuller's *Power Ideas for a Happy Family*
Larry Richards' *Born to Grow*
Norman Vincent Peale's writings
Billy Graham's writings
Charles L. Allen's *God's Psychiatry*
Robert V. Ozment's . . . *But God Can*
(Note: These last two books are published in one volume.)
Maxwell Maltz's *Psycho-Cybernetics*
Peter Marshall's *Mr. Jones, Meet The Master*
Francis A. Schaeffer's *How Should We Then Live*
Catherine Marshall's *Beyond Our Selves*
Warren W. Wiersbe's *Be Joyful*
Paul Tournier's *To Understand Each Other*

Favorite Hymns*
  1. "A Mighty Fortress"
  2. "How Great Thou Art"
  3. "Beneath the Cross of Jesus"
  4. "Oh, For a Thousand Tongues"
  5. "In the Cross of Christ"
  6. "My Faith Looks Up to Thee"
  7. "The Church's One Foundation"
  8. "Blest Be the Tie That Binds"
  9. "Jerusalem the Golden"

*Thanks to John Vance and Karl Klenk for helping me recall these.

10. "Abide with Me"
11. "Take My Life and Let It Be"
12. "Crown Him with Many Crowns"
13. "On Christ the Solid Rock I Stand"
14. "Bless This House"
15. "Amazing Grace"
16. "I Know That My Redeemer Lives"

Pastor Bertram's Favorite and Most Often Used Bible Passages

Isaiah 55:8,9	"My thoughts are not your thoughts, neither are your ways my ways, saith the Lord. For as the heavens are higher than the earth, so are my ways higher than your ways, and my thoughts than your thoughts."
Heb. 13:5	"I will never leave you nor forsake you."
Rom. 8:28	"All things work together for good to them that love God, to them that are called according to His purpose."
Joshua 1:9	"Be strong and of good courage; be not afraid, neither be thou dismayed; for the Lord thy God is with thee whithersoever thou goest."
Romans 8:32	"He that spared not His own Son, but delivered Him up for us all, how shall He not with Him also freely give us all things?"
Isaiah 43:1	"I have redeemed you, I have called you by name, you are mine."
Phil. 4:13	"I can do all things through Christ, Who strengtheneth me."
Rom. 8:31	"If God be for us, who can be against us."
Eph. 6:4	"Bring up your children in the nurture and admonition of the Lord."
Matt. 28:20	"Teaching them to observe all things whatsoever I have commanded you."
II Cor. 12:9	"My grace is sufficient for you, my strength is made perfect in weakness."
Isaiah 41:10	"Fear not, for I am with you. Do not be dismayed. I am your God. I will strengthen you; I

271

	will help you; I will uphold you with my victorious right hand."
James 1:22	"But be ye doers of the word, and not hearers only."
Rom. 10:17	"Faith cometh by hearing, and hearing by the word of God."
John 13:35	"By this shall all men know that you are my disciples, if you love one another."
Acts 24:16	"Herein do I exercise myself to have always a conscience void of offense toward God and toward man."
Eph. 5:1	"Be imitators of God as beloved children. And walk in love, as Christ loved us and gave Himself up for us."

A Sermon Outline Delivered by O. H. Bertram
("Do You Know The Good Shepherd?")

"I am the door: by if any man enter in, he shall be saved, and shall go in and out, and find pasture. The thief cometh not, but for to steal, and to kill, and to destroy: I am come that they might have life, and that they might have it more abundantly" (John 10:9, 10).

Many people in life are defeated. We see all too many people who give up the struggle in life because they feel it is impossible to face and to overcome it. It has been said that people in trouble consult four types of persons: taxi drivers, athletic coaches, bartenders, and ministers. It was not specified in which order. However, recent studies indicate that at least fifty percent of the population turned to a minister, priest, or rabbi when discontented, uptight, or confused. This is very natural since God alone has the answer to man's problems and difficulties. It is the clergyman who can direct the individual to the source of strength and encouragement. Note the words of our Text.

It is important that we ask the question:

Do You Know the Good Shepherd?
1. He knows the individual sheep.

2. Do you trust him as the shepherd to find the answer to your problems?

The parable in our Text, of the sheepfold, a roofless enclosure that has walls about it with a single door at which the shepherd stands as guard and protector. Anyone not coming through that door is a thief. The true shepherd not only stands at that door but knows the sheep by name, and they recognize his voice.

I.

A. Jesus directs our attention to a spiritual fold.

   1. Note the phrase, "I am *the door.*" He is the only entrance into the church on earth and into heaven.

   2. We are received into the place of safety from the world of sin and spiritual deception.

      a. *The thieves and robbers are those who proselytize members from the church and then teach them false doctrine, misdirecting their faith or taking from them the joy of the Good News of Jesus Christ.*

      b. It makes a great deal of difference to which church you belong. You cannot be taught half-truths or distorted truths and still obtain salvation.

   3. The Church of Jesus Christ must warn the sinner of his condemnation and of the signs of our time prior to Christ's return.

   4. *We are living in the latter days.* Note the predication of events that will take place before Christ's return.

      a. *Disturbances in the social world.* Clashes among men and nations. Racial strife. Class warfare. Hate campaigns. Scandals. *Moral degeneracy.* Cold war. Cold peace. *The insidious evil of atheistic communism.*

      b. *Disturbances in the realm of nature.* Forest fires. Floods. Tornadoes. Hurricanes. Landslides. Waterspouts. Earthquakes. Tidal waves. Unseasonable frost. Viruses. Cancer. Mental illness.

      c. *Disturbances in the church.* Downgrading of Holy Scripture. Accent on human learning. Lack of conviction. False doctrine. Confusion. Conflict. Name calling. Legalism. Materialism Commercialism. Apathy.

      d. All of these developments point unmistakably to the impending Day of Judgment when all men living

273

shall be called to final account and they and all the dead shall receive their eternal due with the Lord in heaven or be separated from the Lord in hell.

B. *Jesus has been sent by the Father to redeem us* to make certain of our adoption as His children and sheep of His fold.
    1. "The Word has made flesh and dwelt among us . . . truth."
    2. "Neither is there salvation in any other."
    3. To belong to Christ requires a new heart and a new life. He says, *"A new heart I will give you."* That is what the defeated person needs, because the old one has given way. He adds, "and a new spirit I will put within you."
    4. In the name of Jesus Christ, our Saviour and Divine Lord we can in any defeating situation say with validity, *"I positively refuse to be defeated, by my own sinful self, because I have a new heart and a new spirit given to me by my Saviour."*

C. There are certain principles that apply here: *first, is the perceptual principle; second, persistence principle*; and *third is the power principle.*
    1. We must know the inner truth of our defeat, see the situation and have the insight to understand it. We cannot be our own worst enemy. We must know ourselves. Many try to analyze and help others but they do not know their own failing. We need self-examination. Much less do we want any one to correct us and this sermon is of no help to you unless you apply it.
        a. You must ask the Holy Spirit's help to become effective in your life. As a result you will receive the ability to cope with your problems, unite with God and have divine power in your life.
    2. *Persistence principle means to have perseverance.* You cannot give up if you have a worthwhile cause. You fight the defeat and become a victor through Jesus Christ. *Shakespeare said, "Much rain wears the marble."* Marble is hard, but rain can wear it.
        a. Never give up, Jesus is by your side if you let Him control your life. *"I can do all things through Christ, who strengthens me."*
    3. *Power principle* is the strength and vigor given to you by Jesus Christ. He puts a new rugged heart and a new

indomitable spirit within you that says, "I positively refuse to be defeated, in the name of the Lord, Jesus Christ, who gives me the power."

II.

A. The sheep know the identity of the shepherd since he knows them John 10:14.

  1. If you enter the *Jesus door*, you are received into the place of safety from the attacks of Satan.
  2. Eternal life is your assurance, John 10:10.
  3. *Already in this life you find peace of mind and the assurance of help which He grants especially on the rough road to life.*
  4. The "abundant life" is the assurance that on earth your ways are not unwatched by God and that your undertakings are blessed by Him that "all things work together for good to those who love God."

Illustration: Two little teardrops were floating down the river of life; one teardrop said to the other, "Who are you?" "I am a teardrop from a girl who loved a man and lost him. Who are you?" "Well, I am a teardrop of the girl who got him." Life is like that. *We cry over the things we can't have, but if we only knew it, we would probably cry twice as much if we had received them.* Paul had the right idea when he said, "I have learned, in whatsoever state I am, therewith to be content."

  5. The Good Shepherd removes our fears, takes away our sins and gives us a new perspective of life. He says, "Behold I make all things new."
  6. He helps us forget our past failures, weaknesses, and disappointments and permits us to look to a bright and better future.

B. Christ knows us. "I am the good shepherd, and know my sheep."

  1. He assures us that He hears our voices and answers our prayers.
    a. *We must always pray, "Lord, increase my faith."*
  2. In order to have a *healthy mind*, you must have a healthy *relationship with God*, who says, "Without me, you can do nothing." With Him by our side we can do all things.

275

Illustration: We often feel like the lamb, which is portrayed in the arms of Jesus in so many pictures, *helpless, cuddled in His arms, and held tight to His breast.*

    3. There is true contentment and security in His arms.
       a.   It is so well expressed in Psalm 23, read it with me (Hymnal: page 128).

The following article appeared in *The Naugatuck Daily News*, Connecticut on Thursday, May 31, 1979 and contained "The Clergyman's Corner" article received by this paper that week.

It was a distant shock yesterday morning, just about ten minutes before deadline, to learn of the death of the Rev. O. H. Bertram in Toledo, Ohio.

Rev. Mr. Bertram was a very vital part of the religious life of Naugatuck for many years before going to Ohio, and he kept in touch with his many friends and acquaintances in the borough through his weekly column, "The Clergyman's Corner" in *The News*.

In the mail yesterday morning, we received the copy for yet another column by Pastor Bertram and, after we had recovered from the shock of his death, we turned to read the copy.

It struck us as somehow especially significant, in the view of his unexpected and untimely demise. For it was full of hope and looking toward the future.

Without further comment, we offer the words of Pastor Bertram.

"If God would appear to you in person and say, 'What do you want most in life?' some of us might answer, 'Give me the assurance of tomorrow.' Perhaps you would say, 'Give me health, happiness, strength, and vitality.' We all admit that our lives rest in God's hands. He has the power to give and to take away, and every new day is a gift from God.

"The apostle Paul realized that he had not achieved perfection in his life and offers this high goal: 'Not as though I had already attained either were already perfect: But I follow after, if that I may apprehend that for which also I am apprehended of Christ Jesus. Brethren, I count not myself to have apprehended: But this one thing I do, forgetting those things which are behind, and reaching forth unto those things which are before, I press toward the mark for the prize of the high calling of God in Christ Jesus.' (Philippians 3:12-14). The apostle did not dwell on his past mistakes, but looked ahead for the attainment of a more perfect life.

"What do you do with your reverses or troubles? So often well-meaning friends say, 'I feel sorry for you. I know how you feel.' This is not really true unless we have experienced a similar reverse or trouble in life and can place ourselves in the position of our friend.

"Too often we are inclined to dwell on the hardships and heart-aches of life. We become despondent when we are overwhelmed with difficulties and problems, and resort to harsh methods to deal with them. At least thirty percent of all illness coming to the attention of the family doctor is primarily mental, and another twenty percent is secondarily so. At least one in a hundred of any population is suffering permanently from a severe mental disorder, and at least ten in a hundred will be so affected at some time in their lives. One death in every hundred is by suicide.

"The wonderful thing about life is that yesterday need not determine what we are today or will be tomorrow.

"In His infinite goodness and wisdom, God has given us the solution, 'Therefore, if any man be in Christ, he is a new creature: Old things are passed away; behold, all things are become new' (2 Cor. 5:17).

"Jesus gives that new life, a spiritually new life, which brings about a vibrant physical and mental life. When the Almighty God reaches down to an individual and lifts him to Himself through regeneration and rebirth, it is the greatest of all miracles.

"We can then say, 'All of my burdens went rolling away, down at the Saviour's cross.' "

Taken from the *Naugatuck News* (Conn.) Saturday, June 30, 1979, "The Clergyman's Corner."

Editors Note: This is the final column received from the Rev. O. H. Bertram who died May 29, 1979, in Toledo, Ohio. Pastor Bertram endeared himself to his flock at St. Paul's Lutheran Church here before heeding the call elsewhere. We find it fitting that his last message was one of faith and love.

God's Hands

To speak of God's hands is not uncommon, for the Bible refers to them figuratively many times. One of the most impressive statements regarding God's physical hands is the encounter that the disciple Thomas had with Christ. After Jesus' resurrection, He appeared to the disciples, but Thomas was absent. Perhaps he was alone somewhere, with his hopes and dreams shattered and his faith weakened. Upon his return, the disciples said, "We have seen the Lord." Thomas replied, "Except I shall see in his hands the print of the nails, and put my finger into the print of the nails, and thrust my hand into his side, I will not believe." Eight days later, Christ appeared to the disciples again, Thomas being with them, and said, "Thomas, reach hither thy finger, and behold my hands; and reach hither thy hand, and thrust it into my side; and be not faithless, but believing" (John 20:27). He was convinced that it was the physical body of his Redeemer and said "My Lord and My God!"

Architecturally, the hand is a marvelous instrument. There are the loving hands of a mother, warm and soft, always loving and caring. There are the hands of a surgeon, strong, skillful, deft, yet tender; the hands of a musician, long and tapering; the hands of the farmer and the laborer, strong and rough, yet holding a kindness that beauty never knew. There are the hands of expression: scorn, accusation, clenched fist, upraised to strike, begging hands, blessing hands, hands clasped in prayer.

The most beautiful hands of all are the hands of Jesus of Nazareth. They were filled with love and compassion, taking the children into His arms, touching the outcast leper, healing the blind, deaf, and dumb, raising over the turbulent seas to calm them.

But the wounded hands of Christ crucified are the ones that say, "I love you with a love beyond human understanding." These are the hands that say, "Come unto me all ye that labor and are heavy laden, and I will give you rest." "Him that cometh unto me, I shall in no wise cast out." The wounds in His open hands are like mouths to tell us of the love of God. Jesus holds out His hands to you today and says to you as He did to Thomas, "Because thou has seen me, thou has believed; but blessed are they that have not seen and yet have believed."

An outline for a lecture to seminary students at Concordia College, Ft. Wayne, Indiana.

Utilizing the Media in Church Work
A. Radio
    1. Determine if management wants denominational programs or general religious programs.
    2. It should always be of a professional caliber with proper format (timing, sound, etc.).

3. A variety of programs should be offered for radio and television.
   a) Special events (e.g., church year, Christian Education Week, etc.)
   b) Program for Shut-ins
   c) Year-around program for general devotions
   d) Minute thoughts or prayers (Blueprints for Living)
   e) Panel programs
4. A network can be established because of the amount of free time granted by stations.

B. Television is the best medium today.
   1. Professional format must be written.
   2. Selection of speakers according to ability and appearance.
   3. Regular programs:
      a) Religion in the News (news and interviews)
      b) Daily meditations (Moments of Comfort)
      c) A Worship for Shut-ins (liturgist and preacher)
      d) Special events (e.g., Memorial Day, Good Friday, etc.)
      e) Vacation Bible School
   4. Special features:
      a) Sign language for deaf audience
      b) Choirs and soloists from various areas increase the audience

C. Newspapers
   1. Dignified style of writing
   2. Weekly meditations
   3. Ads with attractive design:
        Utilizing the Media in Church Work

D. How are contacts made?
   1. Don't stop at the bus boy, go to the chief.
   2. Do business on a businesslike basis:
      a) Know your subject or suggestion well before you approach management.
      b) Perhaps a luncheon or dinner will help buy time for you.
   3. References from former contacts for new contacts are good.

E. Let Christ be glorified in all undertakings and presentations:
1. The communications media looks for the clergyman to live up to his profession and message.
2. Approve all formats and releases before they are submitted. One error may close the door.

Sample of "Blueprint for Living" (a thirty-Second Spot)
Each year nearly 16,000 people in the United States come to the conclusion that life isn't worth living. Some take poison, others jump from bridges or apartment houses, while others resort to firearms. Are these people right? Is life really worth living? Life is not worth living if you live it only for self, fortune, fame, power, or sinful pleasure. It is worth living when you come to the conclusion that God loves you and that He has a purpose for your existence. This Loving God can transform your life and make you say, "Life is worth living."

Questions sent by Rev. O. H. Bertram to those in politics before being interviewed for television programs.

1. How do you apply your Christian principles in government?
2. What is the reaction of others to these principles?
3. Give an illustration how prayer has sustained you as a congressman (senator) in helping you reach a decision.
4. Do you ever have to violate your Christian principles in voting on issues?
5. What part does God play in the U.S. Congress today?
6. Do any members of Congress ever publicly speak of their Christian convictions and urge decisions of law to be made in conformity to God's Will?
7. If you could speak to the American people as a whole, what would be your advice to them along spiritual lines?
8. Why do we so seldom hear our congressmen (senators) make a strong personal testimony of their trust in God and in Christ?

A Typical Television Taping Format

Taping Date: December 11, 1976   Christmas Special
Playing Date: December 19, 1976   "A Worship for Shut-ins" Sundays
                                                           11:00-11:30 a.m.

Itemized Time	Sight	Sound	Total Time
	Film	(Bells) ANNOUNCER: "The bells ring out an invitation to	
	Video	all, but especially to our shut-in friends in a special Christmas service.	
		HYMN: Adeste Fidelis—ET (Up & Under)	
	Super	ANNOUNCER: "The joy of Christmas is in the air. We	
	over:	invite you to adore the Christ child in "A Worship for	
	Worship	Shut-ins." The altar service is conducted by the	
	For	Rev. Earl Key, pastor of Zion Lutheran Church, Luckey,	
	Shut-ins	Ohio. The sermon will be preached by the Rev. O. H. Bertram,	
	Key	pastor of Good Shepherd Lutheran Church,	
		Toledo, Ohio. The anthems will be sung by Miss Rose Bruno	
1:00	Bertram		1:00
	Key	CALL TO WORSHIP: "In the name of the Father and of the Son and of the Holy Ghost. Amen." "For God so loved the world that He gave His only begotten Son, that whosoever believeth in Him should not perish, but have everlasting life."	
	Key	PRAYER	
	Slide	AMEN (cartridge)	
5:00	Key	Scripture Readings	6:00
3:00	Bruno	"Away in a Manger"	9:00
11:00	Bertram	SERMON	21:15
3:00	Bruno	HYMN: "Virgin Slumber Song"	22:30
2:30	Key	Prayer, Lord's Prayer, Blessing	25:00
2:30	The Bertrams singing	HYMN: "Silent Night"—ET	27:30
	Film	ANNOUNCER: "The joy of Christmas has been brought	
	Key	to you in "A Worship for Shut-ins." The altar service was conducted by the Rev. Earl Key, pastor of Zion	

Bertram	Lutheran Church, Luckey, Ohio. The sermon was preached by the Rev. O. H. Bertram, pastor of Good Shepherd Lutheran Church, Toledo, Ohio. The anthems
Rose Bruno	were sung by Rose Bruno, accompanied by Dorothy
Gift	Diller Sidewell. As a remembrance of the Christmas Worship for Shut-ins, we would like to send you free and postage paid, a daily devotional booklet entitled, "Portals of Prayer." For your gift of the "Portals
Address	of Prayer" devotional booklet, send your request to "A Worship for Shut-ins," 3934 Laskey Road, Toledo, Ohio 43623. (Repeat address). Your producer has been _____. This is _____
1:30	wishing you the best Christmas you ever had." (up on music) 28:45

The following pages contain typical "Thirty Second Spots" for TV and Radio.

Thought for the Day
March 25, 1979
Endurance

When we know that the Lord is by
our side, we can suffer and endure
many trials.

We must remember that we belong
to Him and He belongs to us.

In our world of trouble, we ask,
God to take us by the hand and
lead us until we stand on higher
ground.

We must pray for God's assurance
and our endurance.

283

Thought for the Day
April 1, 1979
Encouragement

Everyone thirsts for
encouragement—for some
outward assurance that
he is on the right track.
A few well-chosen words
and a bit of encouragement
could help these
people.

One of the greatest
kindnesses we can bestow
upon our fellow man is
to help him think well
of himself, and direct
him to God who is our
source of strength.

Thought for the Day
August 13, 1978

Life is often trying and
disappointing. Sometimes
we must suffer affliction
in order that God can
cross the ego of the
pronoun, "I," and make
us say, "Thy will be
done."
True joy is the result
of a full reliance upon
God's promise that "All
things work together for
good to those who love
God." This brings
victory after defeat
and joy after sorrow.

284

We must not ask for
a life of ease and
complacency, but a life
of trial and victory.

Thought for the Day
May 28, 1979

Just because we live in a scientific
age does not mean we can solve our
problems with computers. We cannot
analyze our difficulties with slide
rules, nor distill our views in
chemical laboratories. A computer
does not bring solace, nor does a
slide rule mend a broken marriage.
Only God can mend the broken heart
and bring peace to the disturbed.
God says, "Be anxious about nothing,
but in everything by prayer let your
request be made known unto Me."

Thought for the Day
April 23, 1978

Learn these Principles of
life:
Think clearly without
hurry, thus avoiding
confusion.
Love everyone sincerely,
even though not everyone
will love you.
Act with the highest
motives, and do not
react to those who try
to tear you down.
Trust in God completely
and not in yourself.

Have faith in God that
He will answer your
prayers, knowing that
"All things are
possible to those
that believe."

Thought for the Day
April 9, 1978
Are You True to Yourself?

Many people are searching
for identification and
follow the crowd,
regardless of the crowd's
purpose. Do you dare to
be different? Do you
stand alone?
Living a double standard
of life and compromising
the truth violates one's
conscience and convictions.
God says, "As a man
thinketh in his heart,
so is he."
Get your thinking in
line with God and be a
person of conviction.
Then you can say, "God
and I always make a
majority."

Thought for the Day
March 26, 1978

True love never knows a plateau,
but soars to new heights daily.

Love, like bread, should be made
fresh daily. It overlooks the
shortcomings of the other and
forgives the wrong-doings.

Genuine love is permeated by
God, who says, "Love one another
as I have loved you."

The music of romance is the
beating of a loving heart. Show
love and it will return to you
many-fold.

The Bible says, "Be kindly
affectioned one to another."

Thought for the Day
April 2, 1978

Weak men are slaves of situations;
Strong men are the masters of the
situation.
Weak men are the victims of their
environment; Strong men are
conquerors of any environment.
Strong men may not change
circumstances, but they will
use them to serve their purpose.
Strong men will somehow coerce
the winds to fill their sails
while they keep a progressive
course in life.
Confident men are resolute in
their will, unselfish in their
purpose, endeavoring in all things
to serve God and man.

Thought for the Day
A "Spot" Public Service Announcement on TV

Toledo is a city of churches and synagogues. They invite you and your family to attend their worship services. A welcoming hand is extended to you as you enter the portals of the churches and synagogues of our community. The help you need for your personal life, for your domestic problems, and for your everyday needs can often be found through the message presented in these places of worship. Has God had the opportunity of speaking to you lately? He wants to help you and bring you inner peace and joy. The houses of worship in Toledo welcome you!

Thought for the Day
Memorial Day

The freedom of our nation was purchased
with the blood of patriots. The coward
who refuses to defend his nation, the
subversive who tries to destroy it, has
no sense of sacrifice. May the cross-
marked graves of Americans throughout
the world remind us that men have given
their lives, and that dear ones mourn
their loss because they placed their
country and freedom above themselves.

May God bless America with loyal and
patriotic citizens who say, "Long may
our land be bright with freedom's holy
light; protect us by thy might, great
God, our King!"